Brain of Britain

ULTIMATE QUIZ BOOK

Published by Collins

An imprint of HarperCollins Publishers
Westerhill Road
Bishopbriggs
Glasgow G64 2QT
www.harpercollins.co.uk

First edition 2017

ISBN 978-0-00-825330-1

10 9 8 7 6 5 4 3 2 1

By arrangement with the BBC.
The BBC logo and Radio 4 logo are registered trademarks of the British Broadcasting Corporation and
are used under licence.
BBC logo © 2005. BBC Radio 4 logo © 2011
Questions and Answers © 2017 BBC
Introduction and Appendix © 2017 Russell Davies

A catalogue record for this book is available from the British Library.

If you would like to comment on any aspect of this book, please contact us at the given address or
online.
E-mail: puzzles@harpercollins.co.uk

 facebook.com/collinsref    @collins_ref

Printed and bound by CPI Group (UK) Ltd, Croydon, CR0 4YY

MIX
Paper from
responsible sources
FSC™ C007454

This book is produced from independently certified
FSC™ paper to ensure responsible forest management.

For more information visit: www.harpercollins.co.uk/green

CONTENTS

INTRODUCTION

As I write, the BBC radio show *Brain of Britain* is approaching its 65th season, which makes it the most venerable of general knowledge quizzes anywhere. It's beautifully simple: one mark for each correct answer, and a bonus mark for five correct answers in a row. The contestants come from all over the United Kingdom, and many of them seem to feel honoured to take part. An information sheet used to be sent out to them, with the times and places of the recordings, and a little note saying that there would be a small broadcast fee of £50. The producer of the time used to get letters back asking, "Where do we send the money?". Our quizzers believed they had to pay to take part – and they were happy to do it.

What kind of knowledge is being tested? What does "general" mean? Well, the debate about that goes on from decade to decade, with the answer changing, not quite visibly, all the time. In the old days, for instance, you could get away with knowing almost nothing about science at all: in fact, the subject was more or less avoided. But now, since it's clearly one of the bases of civilisation, science must be properly covered – but preferably without baffling us all with jargon. It's a difficult balance to strike, but ideally there should always be that moment of delight when we learn something new. A good quiz question, I think, is the one that makes the listener say, "Really? Well I never knew that", in a pleased sort of way. A while ago on the show, I found myself reading out a question which seemed to sum up the quiz experience as we see it. "Which character in a Dickens novel," I asked, "often used the saying 'When found, make a note of?'" What interested me most was not the answer (Captain Cuttle in *Dombey and Son*) but the idea that a certain class of information is interesting enough *in itself* to merit jotting down. It won't normally be useful information, vital to the task of living, but there's some element of surprise in it that makes it pleasurable to learn, and keep in memory.

There will never be a better moment than this to tell the programme's story, so I'm going to do it, if only to pay due tribute to its originators: the pioneering producer Joan Clark, and John P. Wynn the inventor and first question-setter of the show, which originally went by the name of *What Do You Know?* Wynn in particular is a slightly mysterious figure, though he was a familiar name in the *Radio Times* of a lifetime ago, whether as author, scriptwriter, or what BBC memos liked to call the "devisor" of programmes. (Here, the quiz-master's passion for correctness kicks in, causing me to protest that "devisor" is a legal term meaning testator, one who bequeaths things: one who shapes and plans things is their "deviser".) But I imagine that few listeners at the time knew how the life story of "John Peter Wynn" had developed up to that point. How many were aware that he had been Hans Wolfgang Priwin, a Jewish immigrant from Germany – indeed, a member of the Executive Committee of the Association of German National Jews? To me, Wynn's turbulent pre-quiz history is fascinating, but its complexities (which even involve Ian Fleming at a certain point) would hold up the story if I told it here. Readers with an interest in bumptious mavericks will find the whole tale in the Appendix at the back of this book.

We can join that tale in 1947, the year when, with a decade's worth of sponsors to back him up, Hans W. Priwin became a naturalised British citizen. For a brief period, he was known as John Peter Priwin, until in 1948 he changed his name by deed poll to John Peter Wynn – a nonchalant variation on the original syllables. He had used J. P. Wynn before the war, as a nom-de-plume, and now he was busily writing for the BBC again, while his future producer, Joan Clark, was beginning her career as "Quiz-Queen of Radio" by getting *Top of the Form* off the ground. That general knowledge quiz for secondary schools ran for 38 years, starting in 1948, and Joan Clark remained in charge of it until her retirement. The lack of a parallel series for adult contestants must have been noted quite soon, but it wasn't remedied until Wynn produced a plan for the "experimental 45-60-minute programme" that became, in 1953, *What Do You Know?* Embedded in this feature was to be a quiz called *Ask Me Another*. (Apparently not even the term "quiz" itself was securely planted in the BBC mind at this stage, for when the Assistant Head of the Midland Region informed London that he'd been working up a programme with the same title, which he agreed to relinquish, he referred to his production as a "Quizz" throughout.)

But the title-within-a-title has caused confusion ever since. When Wynn's Clark-produced quiz eventually escaped from its housing within the bigger programme and went solo, it became *What Do You Know? Ask Me Another* reappeared later as the title of the televised adaptation of the same quiz. It was only in 1967 that *Brain of Britain* was announced as the new title, though that form of words appeared in Joan Clark's internal BBC communications as early as 8th January 1954, when she wrote:

> Throughout the run of this programme we have arranged the quiz session *Ask Me Another* with a definite purpose in view – namely to find a Brain of Britain.

That wasn't completely true. At the beginning of the story, competitors drawn from the general public were token presences only. Celebrities of the day took three places out of four on the panel, and the first professional trio were Lionel Hale (a radio question-master in his own right), Anona Winn (actress, and a regular panellist on *Twenty Questions* and, later, *Petticoat Line*), and Bernard Palmer, introduced as "a very brave young man who challenged these well-known broadcasters, a twenty-three-year-old university student from King's College". Ten years later, when a recreation of that inaugural panel was attempted for commemorative purposes, this particular Bernard Palmer could not be located (though there were others in the broadcasting sphere). The celebrities gradually dropped out over the following two seasons, one reason being that they had to be paid according to professional standards, while "civilians" cost only a small standard broadcast-fee, plus their expenses.

But Joan Clark had always taken a more democratic view of panellism anyway, so that once her scheme (another Wynn invention) for auditioning amateur contestants on a regional basis had been accepted, she was able to write a triumphant memo to BBC Radio's Head of Variety: "The Quiz has really reached the dimensions of the 'Brain of Britain', as I have auditioned hundreds of people throughout the British Isles…" this was actually an arduous process. If suitable contestants for the microphone were to be assembled, reliable auditioners had to be nominated, briefed and pressed for results all over the country, and a large amount of the programme's paperwork was taken up with this preparatory rigmarole. Eventually, the telephone proved a workable, and of course much cheaper, option. Today's system involves testing every hopeful with a sequence of twenty-five questions, which they answer without being told whether their answer is correct or not. When all the responses are in, and arranged in order of merit, the top 48 are offered the chance to participate.

Hardly had the first series got going in 1953 when a couple of problems emerged. While rare in their subsequent occurrence, they would always have to be borne in mind as possible dangers to the normal running of *What Do You Know?* and later, *Brain of Britain*. The first was simple error in the question-setting, which as early as August 1953 required the Light Programme continuity announcer to add, at the end of one broadcast:

> Before leaving *What Do You Know?*, we would like to thank all those who wrote in pointing out that in last week's quiz, we made the common mistake of confusing Isinglass with Waterglass. Isinglass is not, as we said, used for preserving eggs. It is principally used for the clarification of fermented liquors such as beers, wines, etc. Sorry for our mistake!

The attempts to soften the blow here – objectors are thanked for their help, it's a "common mistake", and so on – don't quite set aside the embarrassment of the moment. Another point that producers and presenters make in self-defence is that "nobody protested about it at the time", which is very often true. People tend to be polite and accepting, preferring to grumble afterwards at most. That's why contestants today, and for some time past, have been encouraged to speak out forcefully as soon as they suspect a real mistake has been made, because waiting to lodge an objection, even just till the end of a round of questions, can distort the rightful shape of a contest in ways that are impossible to remedy.

Downright errors don't appear often, and disappointing behaviour from a contestant is even rarer – but it can happen, as Joan Clark found on one of her earliest outings. The incident required a detailed report to the Radio Variety Manager:

> During the rehearsal for the quiz session of the above programme yesterday, Miss C. A. Lejeune, the film critic, had a fit of temperament because she couldn't answer any of the questions put to her, and flatly refused to take part in the recording. I was faced, then, with the task of finding a replacement exactly one hour before the recording. Phillip Slessor was the Announcer on duty, and I accordingly asked him to take part, which he did, and incidentally won the contest! This means he will have to take part again in the Semi-final match to be recorded next Wednesday…

Miss Lejeune's fee was cancelled. We've rarely seen such a tantrum in recent times, though there was one mid-recording walkout in living memory, leaving three willing contestants still fighting it out to the end. Robert Robinson, the question-master of the day, was all for continuing as if nothing had happened, but Richard Edis, producing, foresaw a likely deluge of baffled phone-calls and letters, so the matter was delicately explained on-air. From time to time, we do see candidates so frantically nervous that they insist their performance is being subverted – the usual culprit, in their eyes, being the button-press system that activates the light (other quizzes use a buzzer) showing that they want to hazard an answer. "Mine's not working!" they cry, and no amount of technical demonstration will convince them that their light didn't come on because somebody else pressed their own button first.

Franklin Engelmann, the first question-master, is remembered as one of the BBC's great all-rounders. Equipped with a military moustache and a brisk manner, but also a sense of humour, he already had a decade's experience in front of the microphone. Alert listeners in 1944 might have heard him, as Captain Engelmann of the Royal

Engineers, introducing one of Glenn Miller's concerts from the famous aircraft hangar near Bedford. With Engelmann in charge, the national response to the new show was extremely heartening. Radio reviews in newspapers and magazines enjoyed generous space in those days, and perhaps the most influential to arrive in Joan Clark's office came from Bernard Hollowood, doubling as a writer and cartoonist at *Punch*, where he took over as the magazine's Editor in 1957. The virtues he identified on 5th May 1954 were very much the ones we still prize in the programme today:

> The final of the Light Programme's *Ask Me Another* competition, which resulted in a convincing victory for D. Martin Dakin, was vastly entertaining. This is a quiz of extreme simplicity: there is no "signing in" or "celebrity spot", no tintinnabular guillotining, no facetious humour, no frippery or calculated rudeness. The questions are posed briskly and neatly and the competitors trot out their answers with commendable conviction.

It was perhaps unfair of Hollowood to praise the radio quiz by bashing the familiar features of television's *What's My Line?* (where Gilbert Harding was synonymous with "calculated rudeness"), especially since the TV show was in no way a quiz. And if there was no "tintinnabular guillotining" in 1954, *Brain of Britain* certainly does include it now, in the sense that a bell rings to signal the end of a contestant's ten permitted seconds of thinking-time. But Hollowood's piece was more interesting on the perennial subject of what kind of knowledge was being, or should be, tested. To him, the term "general knowledge" seemed to denote something desirable, but fairly banal:

> My one criticism of this programme is that too many of the questions call for information from the by-ways of learning, and that not enough questions test the competitors' general knowledge. Mr Dakin might reasonably have been asked for the finalists in the F.A. Cup Competition, the Bank Rate, the price of butter, Bradman's Test average, the cost of a dog licence and so on. No doubt he would have produced pat and accurate

answers in every case, but in doing so he would have won the hearts as well as the admiration of his "Light" audience.

Surprisingly perhaps, Joan Clark's internal reply to her departmental bosses recorded her entire agreement with Hollowood's points, and admitted that questions had perhaps got a bit too tough:

> Towards the end, as the dead contestants were weeded out, we did indeed stiffen them deliberately. Would you please inform Mr Adam [Kenneth Adam, Head of Light Entertainment] that we will watch this point and also always provide a certain number of topical and general observation questions.

"General observation" seems roughly to mean "to do with the day-to-day life around us", and questions of that kind do still occur. One of the semi-finals this year (2017) began with the question: "In February 2017, who was named the first ever female Commissioner of the Metropolitan Police, succeeding Sir Bernard Hogan-Howe?" That appointment had only just been made, so the question came as a kind of check that contestants had been reading the news, as well as the histories and reference books. In the event, the right answer, Cressida Dick, came at once. But to my mind, if the quiz were littered with questions taken straight out of the flow of current events and circumstances, as Bernard Hollowood seemed to wish, both the listening public and the competitors would soon tire of it. Part of the pleasure of quizzing is that the contestant impresses and the listenership is impressed, and dog-licence questions are not going to maintain that effect for long. Don Bradman's Test average, on the other hand, being a famous and memorable statistic, seems a reasonable thing to ask for today, now that it has dropped into the long-ago of cricket history.

Those were matters for John P. Wynn to consider. The question-setter's name enters rarely into the collected memos of Joan Clark's office during this period, but that isn't to be wondered at, since the two collaborators had been married since 1953, and were living in Dorset Street, W.1. It's comical to see the two of them solemnly answering enquiries from the outside world with a formula like "I will refer this to our producer, Joan Clark", or likewise the other way round, when such "referrals" must often have been a matter of pillow-talk. Today's BBC rules supposedly ban cooperation between married partners, on the grounds that they may "put work each other's way", award each other inflated fees, and so forth. Certain senior figures still manage to find ways round this restriction, but in the mid-fifties, nobody seemed to care.

As interest in the show continued to spread, Wynn was contracted to prepare a *What Do You Know?* quiz-book of one thousand questions and answers. It was published in 1955 with a dedication to "Joan, for her unfailing support, helpful encouragement and realistic criticism". Wynn's introduction called upon his German background to explain the appeal of the programme to "between five and six million persons":

> We all like to accumulate odd fragments of knowledge and, such is human nature, we all enjoy a certain degree of what the Germans call "*Schadenfreude*" while we are watching others undergoing an examination. If they know the answer and we don't – well, we say that they are supposed to be experts and we cannot attempt to emulate their brilliance. If they don't know the answer, does that not prove that they are not better than we are? But frequently there is that sweet occasion when the expert proves his ignorance while we – we, the unbrilliant, anonymous listeners – beat him in his own field, and are rewarded with the admiring exclamations of our wives, husbands, children and parents.

Wynn's remarks about his chosen range of questions (and the book includes the controversial "What is Isinglass, and what is it used for?") indicate how influential Bernard Hollowood's strictures had been:

> Experience has shown that it is not the specialised expert who is particularly good at this kind of contest. Therefore, complicated, technical and scientific questions have been omitted altogether and greater attention has been paid to more ordinary and popular matters. Here we often fail to find

the right answers: it is astonishing to see how little we know consciously of the little things in life – the colour of a three-halfpenny stamp, the cost of a telephone call, the number of lace holes in a man's shoe – in short, the things we take for granted, and on which we hardly ever waste a second thought.

Men of fashion today will be astonished in their turn to see that in 1955, the number of lace holes in a shoe was assumed to be standardised and invariable. In setting his questions, Wynn had his little ways, one of which was to ask two questions at once, as in the isinglass example, or more typically: "What is the difference between a cineraria and a cinerarium?", where you need to know both terms to answer satisfactorily. He was even capable of splitting a question explicitly into two ("What is a. a Hydrangea and b. Hydraemia?") or calling for three definitions at once: "What is the difference between a philologist, philogynist and a philodendron?" – where probably "What is a philogynist?" (a lover of women) would have sufficed to test most competitors.

Never slow to exploit a success, even in its days of broadcasting monopoly, the Television Service of the BBC brought *What Do You Know?* into the picture in 1954. A technical failure spoilt the chances of the sample programme shown to the Controller, Programmes, Television, though Cecil McGivern found other grounds for disdain. "It was more than a pity," said his memo, "that the producer lost one camera in Studio H before this programme started. Shooting it on two cameras ruined it, for me, anyway… I felt in its present form it was not strong enough for television, and that we have better ideas we are not using yet." A lucky escape for the show, perhaps, but not a permanent one.

Safely back in radio, Joan Clark turned to the cosy task of choosing a trophy for the winner of her next series, and getting the object paid for. A nine-and-a-half-inch high sterling silver cup on a long stem, she discovered, would cost £20, with engraving something under £1 extra. A diploma printed on parchment with capital letters in gold at 8 guineas, with 2 guineas extra for framing, proved more acceptable to the managers. Yet on the programme side, costly expansionism was not discouraged. Going into Europe with a set of *What Do You Know: Continental Exchange* quizzes, Miss Clark passionately requested travel-permission on her husband's behalf, enabling Wynn to assist the compère at the European end of the wire. "He is fluent in Danish, German and French," she assured the Assistant Head of Variety. The couple were prospering, as could be seen in the early days of 1957, when the producer Alfred Dunning took temporary charge of *What Do You Know?* Its usual proprietors were absent, but would be contactable, they said, at the Bird of Paradise Inn, Tobago, and thereafter at the Sunny Caribbean Hotel, Bequia, via St Vincent, both in the British West Indies.

A moment of relaxed celebration was perhaps in order, since further expansion of their quiz empire lay ahead. BBC Television had not gone away. Even though the doubting Cecil McGivern was now its Deputy Director, the service had decided that *What Do You Know?* would suit the screen after all, with a revised format, and lightly disguised under a title rescued from its earlier habitation, *Ask Me Another*. With Franklin Engelmann again in the chair, the show came on air in June 1958, presenting what strikes us now as an Egghead-like scheme: a trio of regulars against a team of challengers. In time, a classic trio of *What Do You Know?* veterans formed itself, with Dr Reginald Webster (Brain of Britain 1959), Olive Stephens, a rector's wife from Wales, and Farmer Ted Moult, as he was usually billed in those days.

Moult wasn't a champion at all. He was knowledgeable, but hadn't got beyond the first round of *What Do You Know?* – causing him to confess disarmingly forever afterwards that his entire career had been based on failure. Yet the radio audience had recognised him at once as a potential national treasure, in the ripe-eccentric category, and he soon became a popular guest in many odd corners of broadcasting. *Ask Me Another* thrived on TV: its very first edition, Joan Clark wrote in a delighted memo, "had an Appreciation [Index] of 78, which I have been told is the highest this year in BBC Light Entertainment, with the exception of the appearance of A. E. Matthews in *This Is Your Life*". (Almost ninety at the time, the hilariously unpredictable actor A. E. Matthews took over the show, during which, according to the autobiography of its host, Eamonn Andrews, Matty "snorted, contradicted, interrupted, laughed, and at one stage even stretched out on the couch and said he was going to have a snooze".)

The success of its television cousin had no traceable effect on the reputation of the radio original – though it's true that by now, quizzes in general were beginning to come under fire from academic specialists. In 1958, the *Brain* office took note of a report in *The Times*:

> In an article entitled "BBC Quiz Shows Misguided", Professor Cannon from Manchester University gave a talk to 500 schoolboys which espoused the view: "Do not follow the lead of the BBC in their accursed quiz programmes and think that mere knowledge of facts is education. ... The whole idea is utter nonsense and is definitely against the ideas of education which the teachers are trying to instil in you."

Nobody at the BBC had actually equated education with "facts". Professor Cannon (who must have been the zoologist Herbert Graham Cannon, FRS FRSE FLS FRMS) would have been on surer ground if he'd attacked the notion that a command of facts makes you " brainy", in the popular sense. Many Brains of Britain have been hailed by journalists as "the cleverest man in the country", but not many have made any such claim on their own account. In fact, plenty of excellent contestants in my own time have said, "I'm not hugely intelligent, but I organise information quite well, and I've always had a very good memory," or words to that effect.

If anyone besides Professor Cannon thought *What Do You Know?* needed refreshment, they certainly felt some uplift in 1961, with the popular series win by Irene Thomas, a former singer and chorus-girl. The tournament had not been a relentless pleasure for Mrs Thomas. She revealed, for example, that after her first appearance on the show, the rest of the competitors had shoved off to the men-only Garrick Club without her. What's more, Mrs Thomas had kept a file of letters from BBC producers, recording the various reasons given, over several years, for turning down her applications to appear in radio programmes.

It's hard to imagine that Joan Clark was one of the guilty respondents, at least judging by the schedule of engagements she drew up for Mrs Thomas in the immediate aftermath of her win:

> I have arranged with Geoffrey Edwards of Publicity the following coverage:
>
> 1) A 10-15 minute recording for *Today* on Friday
> 2) A piece in *South-East News* on Friday evening
> 3) A press conference – to which a number of newspaper and radio columnists have been invited – on Thursday afternoon.

Irene Thomas went on to win the *Brain of Brains* title, in which the three most recent winners competed. But she failed to carry off the *Top Brain* accolade, which comes round on a nine-year cycle, bringing the three most recent Brains of Brains into contention. That prize was taken by the 1956 Brain of Britain, Antony Carr from Menai Bridge, who had been only 18 at the time, and was now 24. Carr had just left school in 1956, and was delivering newspapers for something to do. He recalled "Paperboy Wins Brain Of Britain!" as one of the choice headlines of the time. Carr took home one of the famous diplomas, and a £5 record token. Later he became a Professor of Welsh Medieval History, and is still an Honorary Research Fellow in the Department of History and Welsh History at Bangor University.

The BBC, eccentric in so many things, felt it worthwhile to preserve a small list of the questions young Carr didn't get right during his climactic Top Brain triumph. One of them shows John P. Wynn manfully trying to keep up-to-date as the sixties got into gear:

> Q: "Ya Ya" seems to be the latest expression to come to this country from America. What does it mean?
>
> A: It means, so we are told, a "steady date".

In neither the question nor the answer did Wynn sound fully confident of that information.

Generally, when he faltered in setting a question, it was over low-level trivia, the sort of day-to-day stuff that Bernard Hollowood had recommended he specialise in. Wynn should have known better, for example, than to ask "Which football club is known as 'The Blues'?", and to insist on the answer "Birmingham City", when half a dozen clubs are known to their most faithful fans by that name. Ruling "Chelsea" to be a wrong answer, as he did (Wynn appeared on stage as a silent adjudicator) was sure to incense large numbers of Londoners. The BBC Radio sports producer Bert Kingdon, later Head of Outside Broadcasts, was one of those who registered an objection in writing, and the personal reply Wynn sent him, intended to defeat his argument, only demonstrated that Wynn himself didn't quite grasp the nature of his error:

> I have to be very careful when setting question[s] for this programme. Had Franklin Engelmann accepted the answer "Chelsea", as you suggest, we would have got thousands of letters from Birmingham City fans accusing us of malpractice and tearing my pants off. So, I have made it a rule to stick very closely to authoritative reference books and information given by the official bodies concerned.

Evidently Wynn hadn't realised that the authority of a reference book is a lifeless thing when set against the raucous passions of traditional football supportership. His mollifying tactic on this occasion was to undertake to consult Bert Kingdon over any niceties lurking in future sports questions. And a P.S. from Kingdon's follow-up letter ("I was pleased to be able to help you on some of your questions this week") suggested that the belly-tickling had worked.

Of course, many of the questions Wynn posed couldn't be answered in the same way now. In asking which of the bridges over the Thames was nearest to the mouth of that river, he was looking for the answer "Tower Bridge". There was no elevated Dartford Crossing (Queen Elizabeth II Bridge) till 1991. But more telling are the questions that would be answered differently now because of changes in the social, rather than material, landscape. In the summer of 1964, there came the question: "How many Cathedrals has London?" The desired reply was three: "St Paul's Cathedral, Southwark Cathedral and the Roman Catholic Westminster Cathedral." But calls came in immediately from licence-payers who already lived, mentally, in a multicultural Britain. "Listeners point out that there are, in fact, two more – St Sophia's (Greek Orthodox) and the Cathedral of the Holy Assumption of Our Lady (Russian Orthodox)." Joan Clark, whose assistant Sylvia Kirby signed this internal memo, was not inclined to accept the point. "However, we were obviously referring to the famous London Cathedrals, and did not expect our contestants to have any knowledge of the Russian or Greek churches." Well, it is no longer "obvious" that only the "famous" cathedrals should be counted, so those expectations have irrevocably changed.

With retirement just a few years away now, Miss Clark was in commemorative mood. She suggested a ten-year Anniversary show, to be coupled with a 300th Programme celebration. But in the event, the unfindable Bernard Palmer was not needed, because George Campey, Head of Publicity, judged that nothing would be gained from such an exercise. Similarly in 1966, Miss Clark announced that the Final of *What Do You Know?* would also celebrate the 1000th Programme made for the BBC by John P. Wynn. She threw the matter open to all comers. "If you need any further information about Mr Wynn, perhaps you would ring him direct: FINchley 2333." But seemingly all that came of the plan was the usual "small cocktail party" generally hosted by the Wynns after a Final, if necessary at their own expense.

Without their knowing it, the future of the Wynns' programme had been in their midst since 1964, when Ian Gillies became Brain of Britain. He was destined also to win the *Brain of Brains* and the nine-year *Top Brain* titles, but even at the start of his career as a champion, he was giving evidence of a lively character. It leaps out of the 1964 press release drawn up by the BBC to celebrate his first win, which offers a fine anecdotal insight into the mind of a pure quizzer:

He attributed a bonus mark he earned to the fact that he was listening to the Home Service 'Today' programme on the morning of the Final when people in the street were being quizzed [sic] on the Bible. This, he said, set up a train of thought, and asking himself the same afternoon what he knew of the books of the Old Testament – which was the last, for instance? – Mr Gillies visited a reference library to find out. When the very same question turned up a few hours later in *What Do You Know?*, and Mrs Key failed to give the right answer, Mr Gillies knew.

The difference between Ian Gillies and the rest of us, in 1964 at least, was that the gap in his knowledge bothered him so much that he *went to a reference library to find out*. That kind of driven curiosity is much harder to spot nowadays, when most of us have the world encyclopaedia of the internet plugged into a handy socket at home. The press release, by the way, annoyingly fails to give us the name of the last book of the Old Testament, as correctly supplied by Mr Gillies. The answer is Malachi.

It was on 11th July 1967 – a year of much change in BBC Radio broadcasting – that the Controller, Light Programme, a name which itself was about to lapse, announced that *What Do You Know?* was no more:

To H[ead] L[ight] E[ntertainment] copy Miss J. Clark, Ch. Asst. L[ight] P[rogramme].

This is to confirm that I should like the next series to be titled "Brain of Britain 1968".

Robin Scott.

And so the programme at last shared the name of the title it had been awarding for years. "It seems more indicative of the contest," Joan Clark explained. With the Light and Home Services gone, and the new numbered networks bedding in, not always comfortably at first, *Brain of Britain* spent a couple of seasons on Radio Two, but moved over in 1970 to its obvious natural home, Radio Four. In doing so, it joined a company of familiar programmes that represented the BBC's continuity: *Desert Island Discs*, *The Archers*, *Woman's Hour*, *From Our Own Correspondent*, and the other show that occupied much of Franklin Engelmann's time, *Down Your Way*.

It was a good moment for the Brain of Britain 1968, Ralph Raby, to attract some publicity by committing himself to a provokingly jocular article called "How To Be A Brain of Britain":

> The first essential is – don't be too intelligent. Some of my friends at school had such penetrating minds that they were soon buried deep in one subject and lost sight of all others.
>
> Do not waste time seeing a new play or film, or reading a new book – just read a good review to learn the theme and characters.
>
> Thirdly, listen to BBC Radio, which pours out a torrent of information, much of it true. With a transistor set, all your waking hours can be filled with talks on everything from Racine to Racing, until your wife gets tired.

Unfortunately, the readers most likely to take this seriously – especially the part about reading reviews instead of experiencing the work itself – will have been those critics already inclined to believe that the "quiz-world" (which was beginning to emerge as a thing in itself) was the haunt of philistines who knew *about* things, but never engaged with the deeper truths within.

In February 1970, the 500th edition of the quiz was noted by Joan Clark in a routine memo. It was estimated that her husband had set 30,000 questions since 1953. And then, suddenly, the lady was gone, with one last request, dated 13th May that year:

Thank you for sending me the photographs taken after the Final of *Brain of Britain 1970*. I return them herewith duly captioned.

As I am retiring from the BBC in two weeks' time, would you be kind enough to let me have a copy of the group (No. 10A) for my personal retention?

J.C.

She left not only *Brain* still running, but also *Top of the Form*, which continued until 1986 – a 38-year career, in which her work as the scorekeeper had incidentally made her voice familiar on the air. John P. Wynn did not retire, but continued to set the questions for *Brain*, and indeed compiled and copyrighted the 1972 quiz-book *Brain of Britain*, which appeared under the BBC's own imprint. The format Wynn chose was strange. The book was divided into nine quizzes, each one with its questions further divided into subject categories – history, geography, people, literature, sport and so on. So, you get a pageful of questions on sport, followed by a pageful on history, and the glorious sense of miscellany and assortment on which the broadcast quiz relies is lost. Even more curiously, one of the nominated sub-categories was "General Knowledge", as if that were a topic separable from the rest.

A brief introduction was supplied by Joan Clark's successor in the producer's chair, John Fawcett Wilson, the most melancholy part of whose task was to pay tribute to Franklin Engelmann. The popular question-master had died suddenly on 2nd March, just one day before he was due to record the 1000th edition of another of his favourites, *Gardeners' Question Time*, and a couple of days before his 64th birthday. "His obvious enjoyment of the competition communicated itself to listener and contestant alike," Wilson wrote.

Since *Brain* was in mid-run, a replacement for Engelmann was required instantly, and was found in the man who knew most about the quiz, apart from its begetters – the multiple champion Ian Gillies, who chaired the ten or so remaining programmes in the series. Did he feel that he had done enough to take over the job permanently? Some

22

signs emerged later that it was so. Meantime, a letter from Martin Fisher, a future Head of Light Entertainment (Radio), explained the position:

Dear Mr Gillies

I am taking over the Production of *Brain of Britain* from 1973 from John Fawcett Wilson and I understand from John that you have very kindly agreed to act as an official referee/umpire for the series to whom we can refer on doubtful questions and answers in the programme.

I am sure you will be interested to know that Robert Robinson is taking over the job of Chairman this year.

"Interested" was one way of putting it. But Ian Gillies did indeed go ahead with the adjudicating role, which Fisher himself had previously essayed and found daunting. The series thus took its course, but at the end of it, Gillies in a letter showed signs of lingering disappointment:

Despite my earlier misgivings, I very much enjoyed working on the programme, even with my light hidden under Bob's bushel, and I am glad if I contributed to the smooth running of the show and helped ease your burden as producer. If the need and opportunity is there for the next series, I shall be pleased to consider playing the same role.

Before 1973 came to an end, there was one definite complaint to be fielded, and unusually, it came from the reigning Brain, A. W. G. (Glyn) Court. Addressing himself to the Controller of Radio Four, with a copy to Martin Fisher, Dr Court noted that six months had gone by since the Finals, leaving him "rather disappointed with the lack of further opportunities arising from them. I had, after all, been led to expect that something of the sort would be provided…" How those expectations were aroused can't now be established, but it has never been the habit of *Brain* producers to raise hopes of further employment. Only once, in Richard Edis's memory, did something happen which might have contented Dr Court, and that was when Geoffrey Colton, Brain of Britain 1993, was flown to the United States to be interviewed on David Letterman's celebrated TV talk-show – purely because Letterman himself was such a fan of the programme.

Mr and Mrs John P. Wynn, by now, had retired to Skibbereen, in County Cork. Since 1969, the government of the Republic of Ireland had offered various tax exemptions to resident artists, and it appears that through his career in various media, Wynn had successfully established his credentials in that category. It was in Skibbereen that he died, anyway, in 1978 – which could have marked the end of the Wynns' involvement in the show they had devised and nurtured. But the tenacity of Joan Clark was considerable, and at such a moment, her desire to maintain the connection by taking over John P.'s question-setting role was hard to resist. It turned out not to be her forte. Here we can switch to eye-witness mode, with the arrival of Richard Edis as a producer in the Radio Light Entertainment department (alias the "Comedy Corridor" at 16, Langham Street, W.1). Richard, an old friend and my first producer on *Brain*, recently told me:

> By the time I arrived for the 1979 season, taking over from the double-act of Martin Fisher and Griff Rhys Jones, Ian Gillies was a very unhappy bunny. He was being paid for providing half the questions, but was having to spend inordinate amounts of time re-writing and re-writing Joan's not-very-good material before compiling the programmes.

It fell to David Hatch, one of the most constructive of all heads of department, to disentangle the situation:

> David Hatch persuaded Joan to retire completely from the show and let Ian do the whole lot, while she could just sit back and take the (tax-free) format fees. So, from 1980, Ian was in sole charge, until his final illness in 2002.

By the time that regime-change was sorted out, Ian Gillies and Robert Robinson, however guarded their initial relations, had become

24

the best of friends. In his role as on-stage adjudicator, Gillies had taken the name of "Mycroft" – a one-word solution to the light-under-bushel problem, because of course it signalled that Robinson deferred to his colleague: Mycroft was the name of Sherlock Holmes's *even more gifted* elder brother. That latter detail was perfect too, since Gillies was indeed older than Robinson – by ten days. Sherlock once said of Mycroft: "All men are specialists. His specialism is omniscience", which fitted Gillies well. His voice-of-adjudication was never heard on air, but wasn't needed. "Mycroft is shaking his head," Robinson would intone mournfully, and the phrase became famous.

Gillies was very proud of *Brain*, and regarded his onstage participation in it as a reward for months of slogging over the questions. He used to say that it was one of the very few radio programmes that met Lord Reith's prescription for BBC Radio: "inform, educate and entertain". Gillies took an amused view of John P. Wynn's decades of question-setting, claiming that the pioneer had been obsessed with diseases and other medical calamities. (The quiz, I must say, continues to find ailments a fruitful field of enquiry.) To please his colleagues, Gillies would very occasionally tweak a question to suit their preferences: for example, knowing Richard Edis to be a fanatical supporter of Arsenal F.C., he would insert into every Final a question with some connection, often outrageously distant, to the Gunners. Naturally nobody in the outside world ever noticed.

Edis recalls from that period one particularly remarkable contestant, called Peter Barlow:

Mr Barlow was stunning – well up to the standards of Ian or Kevin [Ashman]. He described himself as a "former diplomat". (Ian ascertained from him later that he was involved in the Rhodesia independence negotiations.) Unlike a lot of present day "semi-pro" contestants who appear on all the broadcast quiz shows and who just eat encyclopaedias, Peter Barlow was extremely widely read and genuinely knowledgeable about huge amounts of stuff. For the only time in living memory – or mine, at any rate – he remains the only contestant who scored five-in-a-row in each of his first three rounds. So, at the end of round three, along with a couple of bonuses, he'd scored 20-odd, and the others were on two or three. He would have done it again in the next round, but for the fact that he'd never heard of Elton John. Music question – "What is the connection between this piece of music and Watford Football Club?" I can't now remember which classic we played, but he'd no idea. Which was just as well as Ian was beginning to panic that we'd run out of questions!

Incidentally, that can happen – it did once while I was deputising for Robert Robinson, but fortunately a cache of spares was being carried that day in the programme-box.

When Ian Gillies died, the succession passed naturally to the latest specialist in omniscience, the multi-title winner Kevin Ashman. Bob Robinson was keen to see the "Mycroft" tradition continued with the new question-setter. But after considering the matter – and probably knowing, since he knows so much else, that Bob was a keen reader of Dickens – Ashman suddenly said, one evening at the Paris Theatre in Lower Regent Street, "You know, Bob, our relationship isn't really Sherlock and Mycroft – it's much more Spenlow and Jorkins." In *David Copperfield*, Spenlow and Jorkins are business partners, but the absent Jorkins's role is to be referred to by Spenlow as a stickler and nay-sayer. When David asks to be released from an apprenticeship, for example, Spenlow says *he* wouldn't object, but that Jorkins would be dead against it. When Robinson had stopped laughing, he agreed that Kevin should be Jorkins ever afterward – and he was, until the day when his celebrity as a contestant/performer took away all his time.

Since then, the overlord of the question-setting process has been the programme's producer himself, Paul Bajoria. Questions are gathered in from a handful of setters, and it's a "floating population", changing from year to year to keep the style fresh. The roster includes writers who provide questions to the other major quizzes of the day, from

University Challenge to *Round Britain Quiz*. Paul says it's noticeable that among these experts, "great minds think alike" to the extent that the same question will often emerge from two or more of the contracted contributors – which suggests that the setters do respond to the atmospheres of the world around us, even if they seldom produce the kind of dog-licence question Bernard Hollowood once requested. Sadly the well-known BBC economies have meant that nobody now appears on-stage as a consultant and referee in cases where an answer is half-right – the question-setter David Kenrick was the last to do the job – but now, Paul Bajoria and I have to decide such matters between ourselves, in brief and gnomic conversations down the wire between the podium and the technical booth.

Everything seems to continue smoothly, though there are occasional controversies over other matters. The last one to provoke journalistic outrage was the triumph of Barry Simmons in 2012. Some observers felt that since Barry had been a television Egghead (the sixth) since 2008, he was no longer the kind of "civilian" that *Brain of Britain* should be featuring. Paul Bajoria was called upon to defend the programme's position, and did so eloquently in a BBC blog: "When we saw that Barry Simmons had applied for *Brain of Britain 2013*," he wrote,

> we discussed whether he should be allowed to compete, and we realised almost immediately that there's no sensible reason why not. Barry's an experienced quiz player who reached the Final of *Brain of Britain* in 2008 – though, as it happens, he came last. Since then, he has built up his quiz CV to the point where he was invited to apply for, and won, a place on the resident team on BBC2's *Eggheads* quiz. Many of his fellow Eggheads are former *Brain of Britain* or *Mastermind* champions, or both. Small wonder that, after the requisite five-year gap, Barry was determined to go for the prize! When we offered him a place, we had a conversation to ensure that he realised a poor performance in the programme might harm his reputation. Barry was happy to take the risk, which is a mark of the man.

Brain of Britain is no walkover: you get, on average, about twelve utterly unpredictable questions of your own, plus a chance to score bonuses on other people's if your trigger finger is quick enough. As soon as you get one wrong, your turn ends. Many an accomplished quizzer has crashed and burned.

Barry is still a welcome visitor – in fact he was present for the wine and nibbles after this year's Final, at the BBC Radio Theatre in April 2017. The Theatre is certainly our most elegant home, but we have others – at BBC Maida Vale, in the studio where Bing Crosby made his last recording, and in Salford, where the programme team is now headquartered.

So how do you become a Brain of Britain? Can it be done simply by memorising things, list by list, from works of reference – I don't think so. Yes, there are certainly things everyone mugs up on: Kings and Queens of England (and elsewhere), the Periodic Table perhaps, the night sky, the works of some obviously great writers. But there is also a quizzing temperament, and my theory is that it has less to do with remembering things than with being unable to forget anything. It's almost more like an affliction than a talent – anything that presents itself as a FACT is grabbed by the brain and not allowed to escape. If you're a sufferer from a cranial overcrowding of that kind, you should probably be having a go at this quiz lark. Remember, there is no more majestic title to aim for than Brain of Britain, and you receive it engraved, as it should be, on a silver salver.

Brain of Britain: A Note on the Questions

Most of the questions in this book are drawn from *Brain of Britain* contests broadcast during the last ten years. There are always questions left over from every contest, and although most of those are recycled, it may be that a few here were never actually broadcast. A few more have been added for topicality's sake, or because, having popped up, they seemed too good to leave out.

Clearly whole classes of question which we can use in the radio programme don't suit the printed page at all – "How do you spell eczema?", for example, falls a bit flat. We have also had to say goodbye to music questions where the sound of the music itself is vital to the search for an answer, and to questions which follow on deliberately from the answer to the previous question (thus giving it away).

From the remaining huge pile of possibilities, it's actually not hard for a question-master (as we used to be called) to choose the good stuff. By its very nature *Brain of Britain* tends to eschew the kind of question which can easily be answered by that breed of quiz player (and there are such people) who spends large amounts of leisure time rote-learning reference books. We've never been very interested in robotic answers about capital cities, the colours on a particular country's flag, or the world champion in a particular sport in a particular year. One actually looks forward to asking a good question, for the pleasure either of hearing the correct answer given, or of revealing the answer because it is useful, surprising, entertaining, or downright odd. Some of the answers here, you'll quickly notice, are a lot longer than the questions – which is as it should be. There would be nothing more frustrating than giving an answer which merely left the reader (or listener) thinking, "I wonder what the story behind *that* is...?"

RD

MILD

The first ten quizzes are entry-level and are designed to warm up your grey cells before you tackle the steeper slopes!

Quiz 1

1. Pesto, a staple sauce of Italian cooking, combines pine-kernels parmesan cheese and olive oil with which herb?

2. In the Caribbean, what is a 'duppy'?

3. Barbara Millicent Roberts is the full name of which iconic figure o the 20th century, first introduced to the public by Ruth Handler in 1959 at the New York Toy Fair?

4. On the label of a bottle of wine, the letters 'DOCG' are ar indication that it has been granted a stamp of particular quality In which country will it have been produced?

5. In the world of antiques, the names of William Cookworthy Samuel Gilbody and Benjamin Lund are associated with high-quality 18th century examples in what field of craftsmanship?

6. 'Lackland' and 'Softsword' are among the nicknames given to which English King, the father of Henry III?

7. In the so-called 'Easter Rising' of 1916, which building in Dublin's Sackville Street was occupied and used as a headquarters by Irish nationalists, until they abandoned it when it caught fire as a result of being shelled by the British?

8. Which of the territories of Canada has the city of Yellowknife as its capital?

9. Ada, Countess of Lovelace, best known for having written the first description of Charles Babbage's mechanical computer, was the daughter of which English poet?

10. *Sabrina*, *The Apartment* and *Some Like It Hot* are among the films of which multiple-Oscar winning director who died in 2002?

11. Which type of wheat, with a name derived from the Latin for 'hard', is cultivated mainly to make pasta, couscous and macaroni?

12. Which fictional detective made his final appearance in a novel called *Curtain*, published in 1975 – and was the first fictional character ever to be honoured with an obituary on the front page of the *New York Times*?

13. Which Swiss sculptor, born in 1901, is best known for his works in bronze depicting rough-textured free-standing human figures with extremely thin and elongated limbs?

14. Which island group in the Indian Ocean, a popular tourist destination, has the city of Victoria as its capital?

15. Now considered a classic of cookery writing, the 1984 book *An Omelette and a Glass of Wine* is a collection of articles by which food writer?

16. Which British rock group, formed in the late 1960s, was named after an agriculturalist of the 18th century whose principal work was entitled *Horse-Hoeing Husbandry*?

17. Which Dublin-born actor played the role of Philip E. Marlow in Dennis Potter's television serial *The Singing Detective*?

18. Which organisation had its origins in Pulaski, Tennessee, founded there by Confederate Army veterans in the late 1860s?

19. Vanessa and Jesse, the children of Lorna Luft, are the grandchildren of which singer and actress who died in 1969?

20. In 1911, the American politician, explorer and archaeologist Hiram Bingham discovered which lost Inca city, on a mountain ridge above the Urubamba Valley in Peru?

Answers on page 36

21. Which spice is derived from the plant whose Latin name is *Crocus sativus*?

22. According to the prison warder Mr Mackay in the classic TV comedy series *Porridge*, 'In this prison there are only two rules. One is, you do not write on the walls.' What is the other?

23. *Justine, Balthazar, Mountolive* and *Clea* are four novels written by Lawrence Durrell in the 1950s, which are known by what collective title?

24. Ultra-violet radiation in sunlight helps convert ergosterol, a substance present in the skin, into a form of which vitamin?

25. Which of the American 'Ivy League' universities has its campus in the city of New Haven, Connecticut?

26. What name is given to the gold-coloured alloy of copper, zinc and sometimes tin, which is used to decorate furniture and ornaments?

27. By what name do we know the undesirable condition known medically as *Pityriasis capitis*?

28. Can you name the music-hall star born Matilda Alice Victoria Wood in 1870, who first appeared as Bella Delmere before taking the stage name by which she is best known?

29. Having formulated a law for the polarisation of light, which is named after him, the 19th century Scottish physicist David Brewster also invented a scientific instrument that became popular as a child's toy. What was it?

30. The 1930s children's books *Peter Duck* and *Pigeon Post* are sequels, featuring the same characters, to which highly successful novel?

31. In chemistry, what name is given to different forms of the same substance which may have different properties – such as carbon in the forms of diamond and graphite?

32. Which much-recorded country song, composed by Kris Kristofferson, has a refrain which begins with the words 'Freedom's just another word for nothin' left to lose'?

33. Which highly respected broadcaster, born in 1933, came to prominence as one of the regulars on television's *Late Night Line-Up* in the 1960s, and later presented the ethical investigative series *Heart of the Matter* for many years?

34. In which Hindu text, part of the Mahabharata, does Lord Krishna instruct Prince Arjuna on the importance of absolute devotion?

35. The novel sequence entitled *Gargantua and Pantagruel*, famously long and rambling and bawdy, is the work of which French Renaissance medic and satirist?

36. Which Scottish Premier League football club plays its home games at Tynecastle?

37. In the animal kingdom, the family *Leporidae* consists of which common British mammals?

38. What word is used in physics to describe an ionised gas produced at extremely high temperatures and, in biology, to the liquid component of the blood?

39. A psychopathic killer named Michael Myers is the central villain of a celebrated horror movie of 1978, and its series of sequels. Can you name that original movie?

40. Famously celebrated in music, Fingal's Cave is a rock formation to be found on which uninhabited Hebridean island?

Answers on page 36

Answers to Quiz 1

1. Basil
2. A spirit or ghost
3. Barbie
4. Italy. It stands for *Denominazione di Origine Controllata e Garantita.*
5. (English Blue) Porcelain
6. King John
7. The General Post Office
8. The Northwest Territories. In 1999 more than half of the Northwest Territories were carved off to create a new territory, the Inuit homeland of Nunavut.
9. Lord Byron
10. Billy Wilder
11. Durum wheat
12. Hercule Poirot – created by Agatha Christie
13. Alberto Giacometti
14. The Seychelles
15. Elizabeth David
16. Jethro Tull
17. (Sir) Michael Gambon
18. The Ku Klux Klan
19. Judy Garland
20. Machu Picchu
21. Saffron
22. You obey all the rules
23. The Alexandria Quartet
24. Vitamin D (specifically D2)
25. Yale
26. Ormolu
27. Dandruff
28. Marie Lloyd
29. The kaleidoscope

30. *Swallows and Amazons* – by Arthur Ransome
31. Allotropes
32. 'Me and Bobby McGee'
33. (Dame) Joan Bakewell
34. The *Bhagavad-gita*
35. Francois Rabelais
36. Heart of Midlothian/Hearts
37. Rabbits and hares (but either will do)
38. Plasma
39. *Hallowe'en*
40. Staffa

Quiz 2

1. Which building, one of the holiest places of Islam, stands on the top of Mount Moriah in Jerusalem and is traditionally the site of the prophet Mohammad's ascent to heaven?

2. What kind of strutting dance, especially popular at the height of the Ragtime era in early-20th century America, was named after the prize that was traditionally awarded to the best dancers?

3. The volt is an SI unit measuring the electrical energy converted by the electric charge moving between two points in a circuit. Although it's commonly referred to as the 'voltage', what two-word term is properly given to this quantity?

4. Which French mathematician and philosopher proved, in the late 1640s, that air pressure decreased with altitude, by taking a barometer to the summit of the Puy de Dôme in the Auvergne?

5. Edmund, son of Ethelred the Unready, who briefly succeeded his father as king in 1016, is usually known by a nickname reflecting his courage. What was the nickname?

6. *Stars and Stripes Forever*, directed by Henry Koster and starring Clifton Webb, is a 'biopic' of which American composer?

7. What is the highest mountain in the world outside Asia?

8. The origin of which snack is generally attributed to the aristocrat John Montague, who is said to have eaten food in this form in order to avoid having to leave the gaming table?

9. Which daily newspaper began life in 1754 as the *Leeds Intelligencer*?

10. The English poet William Langland, who lived from about 1330 to 1400, is known for one long alliterative poem which exists in several different versions. What is it called?

11. Which British no.1 rock album of the 1970s features the cover image of an inflatable pig flying above Battersea power station?

12. Which inventor, born in the USA and later a naturalised Briton, developed the first fully-automatic machine gun, manufactured by Vickers and adopted by the British Army?

13. Gibbon's *History of the Decline and Fall of the Roman Empire* and the plays of Shakespeare were all edited in expurgated form by which Somerset-born physician and writer?

14. In the name of the actor and former American football player O. J. Simpson, who was acquitted of murder in 1995, what do the initials O. J. stand for?

15. The Sargasso Sea, surrounded by and effectively created by the enclosing effects of the Gulf Stream, the Canary Current and the Equatorial Current, takes its name from the abundance of Sargassum in its waters. What is Sargassum?

16. Who was in overall command of the English fleet that defeated the Spanish Armada in 1588?

17. Whose music, though originally popular in the composer's lifetime, gained a resurgence in 1973 when his piece 'The Entertainer' was featured in the film *The Sting*?

18. What are the Aventine, the Caelian, the Capitoline, the Esquiline, the Quirinal, the Viminal and the Palatine?

19. *The Practical Handbook of Bee Culture, with some Observations on the Segregation of the Queen* is the full title of a scholarly work written by which fictional character, created in 1887?

20. What kind of soup has a name that means 'pepper-water' in the Tamil language?

Answers on page 42

21. The game called Noughts and Crosses in British English is more commonly known in the US by what three-word alliterative name?

22. The Minerals and Land Pavilion, the Power and Production Pavilion, the Sea and Ships Pavilion and the Lion and Unicorn Pavilion were all built for which major event of 1951?

23. Shakespeare's character Autolycus is described as 'a snapper-up of unconsidered trifles'. In which play does he appear?

24. Which 1979 film was advertised with the tag-line 'In space, no one can hear you scream'?

25. Born Karoline Blamauer in Austria at the turn of the twentieth century, the future wife of the composer Kurt Weill became known by what stage name?

26. Which European city was the birthplace of the sculptor Eduardo Paolozzi?

27. Which measurement of length, in the UK, can be defined as a tenth of a nautical mile?

28. Who was the author of the 1750s work *The Gentleman and Cabinet-Maker's Director*?

29. What's the popular name for the furcula, a forked bony structure in the bodies of birds, to which the muscles of flight are attached?

30. In the musical *West Side Story*, what are the names of the two rival gangs, equivalent to the Montagues and the Capulets in the source story *Romeo and Juliet*?

31. The Battles of the Boyne in 1690, Gettysburg in 1863, and The Somme in 1916, all began on which date of the calendar?

32. The first chapter of which novel, first published in 1954, is called 'The Sound of the Shell'?

33. Which English jeweller lends his name to the alloy of copper and zinc which he invented in the early 18th century?

34. Although her achievements in the Crimean War had for many years been eclipsed by those of Florence Nightingale, which Jamaica-born nursing pioneer was voted top of a 21st century poll to find the one hundred greatest black Britons?

35. To which famous couple was *Variety* magazine referring, with its June 1956 headline 'Egghead Weds Hourglass'?

36. What is the standard unit of luminous flux, used to measure the light that passes through an area in a second?

37. Which English king was defeated and captured at the Battle of Lincoln, in 1141?

38. Martin Cooper, a Chicago engineer employed by the Motorola company, is credited with being the first person ever to do what, on the 3rd April 1973?

39. What is the simplest proper fraction that expresses the decimal value 0.85?

40. Which aromatic herb gives its distinct flavour to Earl Grey tea?

Answers on page 42

Answers to Quiz 2

1. The Dome of the Rock
2. The cake-walk, because the couple who won the contest would win a cake
3. Potential difference
4. Blaise Pascal. The international unit of pressure is named after him.
5. Ironside. (Not to be confused with the television detective played by Raymond Burr.)
6. John Philip Sousa
7. Aconcagua. At 6,961 metres, or 22,838 feet. In the Andes between Argentina and Chile, it is an extinct volcano.
8. The sandwich. John Montague was the 4th Earl of Sandwich.
9. *The Yorkshire Post*
10. *Piers Plowman* (or more fully – *The vision of William concerning Piers the Plowman*)
11. *Animals* by Pink Floyd
12. (Sir) Hiram Stevens Maxim
13. Thomas Bowdler
14. Orenthal James
15. (Brown) seaweed. Scientific name *Sargassum natans.*
16. Effingham. Charles, second Baron Howard of Effingham and First Earl of Nottingham.
17. Scott Joplin. The revival of his music led to the first-ever performance of his ragtime opera *Treemonisha.*
18. The seven hills of Rome
19. Sherlock Holmes. The title is read aloud to Holmes in *The Last Bow.*
20. Mulligatawny (from *milagu*, pepper, and *tan-nir*, cool water)
21. Tic-tac-toe
22. The Festival of Britain
23. *The Winter's Tale*
24. *Alien.* Not to be confused with *Aliens* (1986), *Alien 3* (1992), *Alien Resurrection* (1997), *Prometheus* (2012) or *Alien: Covenant* (2017).
25. Lotte Lenya

26. Edinburgh

27. The cable. A nautical mile is 6,076 feet, or ten cable lengths.

28. Thomas Chippendale

29. Wishbone

30. The Jets and The Sharks

31. The first of July

32. *Lord of The Flies* by William Golding

33. (Christopher) Pinchbeck

34. Mary Seacole – also known as Mary Jane Grant

35. Arthur Miller and Marilyn Monroe

36. The lumen

37. Stephen

38. Make a call on a mobile phone. The phone on which he made the call weighed about a kilogram.

39. 17/20

40. Bergamot

1. Exhibited in 1849, Dante Gabriel Rossetti's first major canvas *The Girlhood of Mary, Virgin* bore his signature, the date, and the letters P.R.B. What did P.R.B. stand for?

2. Which prolific female novelist who died in the year 2000 was married twice, both times to men with the surname McCorquodale?

3. What's the name of the gorge, descending to more than 36,000 feet below sea level, that marks the lowest point of the Mariana Trench in the north-western Pacific, and is thus the deepest point anywhere on the Earth's surface?

4. *The Seven Lamps of Architecture* and *The Stones of Venice* are among the works of art criticism by which writer, who died in 1900?

5. Which writer, himself a noted theatre critic, defined a critic as 'a man who knows the way but can't drive the car'?

6. Obtained from the tree of the species *Quercus suber*, what material forms the centre of the best-quality cricket balls?

7. 'Night-writing' – a letter code devised in 1819 by the French army captain Charles Barbier for passing secret messages silently in the dark – gave rise to which form of communication still in use today?

8. The words 'Mistah Kurtz – he dead', used by T. S. Eliot as an epigraph for his poem 'The Hollow Men', are taken from which novel first published in 1899?

9. The same novel in turn inspired a movie of 1979, in which a character played by Dennis Hopper refers back to the final words of Eliot's 'The Hollow Men'. Which film is that?

10. The Hungarian ballerina Romola de Pulszky married a dancer and choreographer in Buenos Aires in 1913, and published a biography in 1952 chronicling the latter years of her husband's life. Who was he?

11. Which Greek sculptor, active in the 5th century BC, created the huge Statue of Zeus at Olympia which was named one of the Seven Wonders of the Ancient World, and also supervised the friezes for the Parthenon which are now preserved as the 'Elgin Marbles'?

12. Which two seas are connected by the Suez Canal?

13. Which American broadcaster, who died in 2009, used to sign off his news programmes with the phrase 'And that's the way it is'?

14. In *Alice's Adventures in Wonderland*, which character does Alice encounter sitting on a mushroom and smoking a hookah?

15. In seventeenth and eighteenth-century London, Garraways, Jonathan's and Lloyd's were all famous what?

16. How many oxygen atoms are there in a single molecule of sulphuric acid?

17. Ansel Adams is a renowned name in which of the arts?

18. Having written many of their biggest hit songs, including 'Easy', 'Still' and 'Three Times A Lady', the soul singer Lionel Richie left which group to pursue a solo career in the 1980s?

19. What's the common English name for the species of small bird whose taxonomic name is *Troglodytes troglodytes*?

20. Which Arabic word meaning benefits or a source of improvement, has come to be widely used in Indian cookery to mean a mixture of spices – and can be preceded in familiar phrases by the words *garam* or *tikka*?

Answers on page 48

21. In Mary Shelley's novel, what forename did she give to Dr Frankenstein, the 'Modern Prometheus'?

22. How is the artist born in Crete in 1541, and named Domenikos Theotokopoulos, better known?

23. Which term, originally a nonsense word invented by Edward Lear, is now used for a three-pronged pickle fork, shaped like a spoon and with one sharp edge?

24. A 22-storey triangular-shaped tower on the corner of Broadway and 23rd Street in Manhattan, built by the architect Daniel H. Burnham in 1902, is Manhattan's oldest remaining skyscraper, and was added to the US National Register of Historic Places in 1979. By what name is it commonly known?

25. The last recorded words of a certain British monarch were 'My dear boy, this is death'. Who made this astute utterance, and then died, on 26th June 1830?

26. The 19th century Edinburgh anatomist Robert Knox is said to have been the principal client of which notorious pair of Irishmen?

27. Which two sports are named in the full title of the All-England Club at Wimbledon?

28. CITES is an acronym for the agreement between nations sometimes referred to as the Washington Convention, regulating international trade in plant and animal species considered to be rare or at risk. What do the letters CITES stand for?

29. The first ten amendments to the constitution of the United States, passed in 1791, are collectively known by what name?

30. Which former child actor, whose best-known roles included Richie Cunningham in the teen comedy series *Happy Days*, became one of Hollywood's top directors with successes such as *Frost/Nixon*, *The DaVinci Code* and *Apollo 13* among his credits?

31. What would or could result from a *'casus belli'*?

32. Which three-word name is most commonly used in the UK for the game sometimes known as 'Rochambeau' in the United States, and as 'Jan Ken Pon' in Japan?

33. What's the equivalent decimal value of eight shillings and sixpence?

34. In Charles Dickens' *Nicholas Nickleby*, what's the full name of the wicked headmaster at the grim Yorkshire school Dotheboys Hall, at which Nicholas is employed as a schoolteacher?

35. In which continent would you find Wilkes Land, Queen Maud Land, and Marie Byrd Land?

36. Which famous sports team, founded in the late 1920s, originally featured members from a semi-professional team known as the Savoy Big Five?

37. What name is given to the peninsula that forms the detached former northern portion of Lancashire, preserved in the name of a borough in what is now Cumbria?

38. Which word is used to mean both a pidgin language which has become the native speech of a particular people, and a style of cuisine typical of New Orleans and the Mississippi delta?

39. In a film of 2015, the actor Alex Jennings played two aspects of the personality of which writer, in a device which allowed the character to be portrayed having arguments with himself?

40. The more common name for calcium magnesium carbonate is also the name of a range of Alps in north-eastern Italy. What is it?

Answers on page 48

Answers to Quiz 3

1. Pre-Raphaelite Brotherhood
2. Barbara Cartland. She married Alexander McCorquodale in 1927, and his cousin Hugh in 1936.
3. Challenger Deep
4. John Ruskin
5. Kenneth Tynan
6. Cork
7. Braille. 15-year-old Louis Braille adapted and simplified its use of raised dot patterns to represent letters.
8. *Heart of Darkness* by Joseph Conrad
9. *Apocalypse Now*, directed by Francis Ford Coppola. The words of Eliot's paraphrased in the film are: 'This is the way the world ends / Not with a bang but a whimper'.
10. (Vaslav) Nijinsky
11. Phidias
12. Mediterranean and Red Sea
13. Walter Cronkite
14. The caterpillar
15. Coffee houses
16. Four (H_2SO_4)
17. Photography. Known especially for his grand landscapes of Yosemite National Park, among other subjects.
18. The Commodores
19. The Wren. There are more than sixty wren species, all but one of which are found only in North America.
20. Masala/Mosalla
21. Victor
22. El Greco ('The Greek')
23. Runcible spoon. Lear wrote of a 'runcible cat' and a 'runcible hat' as well, and his own drawings give no hint of what he meant.
24. The Flatiron Building – because of its distinctive shape
25. George IV

26. (William) Burke and (William) Hare. Knox was never charged with any offence.

27. Lawn Tennis and Croquet

28. Convention on International Trade in Endangered Species

29. The Bill of Rights

30. Ron Howard

31. A war. A casus belli is an act justifying, or used as an excuse for, waging war.

32. Paper, scissors, stone (or whichever order you prefer)

33. Forty-two and a half pence

34. Wackford Squeers

35. Antarctica

36. The Harlem Globetrotters

37. Furness – as in Barrow-in-Furness

38. Creole

39. Alan Bennett. The film was *The Lady in the Van.*

40. Dolomite – after the 18th century French geologist Dolomieu

Quiz 4

1. The surname Fletcher specifically refers to a person who makes and sells what?

2. Mons Meg, a siege gun presented to King James the Second of Scotland in 1457, is now housed in which castle?

3. Which American poet, who died in 1886, was known as the 'nun of Amherst'?

4. Known as the master endocrine gland, which gland situated at the base of the brain secretes hormones that regulate a number of bodily processes, including growth, reproduction and other metabolic activities?

5. In literature, theatre and film, who is hounded throughout his life by Inspector Javert?

6. The song 'Here in My Heart', as sung by Al Martino, holds what particular distinction in the history of the British pop charts?

7. Wood-spack, hood-awl, eccle and yaffle are all local names for which bird?

8. The jazz musician Erroll Garner is most closely associated with which instrument?

9. The National Library of Wales is to be found in which coastal town?

10. Can you name either of the two other Patricians who, along with Julius Caesar, formed what's often called the 'First Triumvirate', to rule the Roman Empire in 60 BC?

11. Which American cartoonist born in 1954, whose first success was the syndicated strip-cartoon *Life In Hell*, is also the creator of The Simpsons?

12. The job of publishing a verbatim record of the proceedings of parliament was taken over by Her Majesty's Stationery Office from which family, whose established job it had been for much of the 19th century?

13. Which civil engineer born in 1832 became known as the 'Magician of Iron'?

14. The Eiffel Tower was built to celebrate the centenary of which event?

15. The use of which chemical, at the time being used to treat sewage in Carlisle, was pioneered from 1866 by Joseph Lister as an antiseptic, in solution, at Glasgow Royal Infirmary?

16. Jenkins Hill in Washington DC is now better known by a name referring to a building, begun in the 1790s, which stands upon it. What name is that?

17. The conspiracy to murder all the members of the cabinet in 1820 is known by the name of a street in the Marylebone area of west London: what's it called?

18. Which is the only English city whose name begins with T?

19. In geometry, what name is given to any angle that is greater than 180 degrees (but smaller than 360 degrees)?

20. The Austrian monk Gregor Mendel derived his genetic theories from his experiments during the 1860s with what kind of plants?

21. What type of star, the smallest and densest known, is produced when a massive star explodes as a supernova, exceeding what's called the Chandrasekhar Limit, and then collapses into itself?

Answers on page 54

22. Which fictional reporter made his debut appearance in a story called *Land of the Soviets* in 1929?

23. The Land of Green Ginger is the name of a street in which Northern British city?

24. *Ginger You're Barmy!* is a comic novel based on the author's own experience of National Service in the 1950s, by a writer and academic best known for novels set on university campuses. Who is he?

25. Which isotope of hydrogen is the principal component of heavy water?

26. 'Gimme a viskey, ginger ale on the side – and don't be stingy, baby' – was the first line ever spoken on film by which star?

27. In which decade was Switzerland admitted to membership of the United Nations?

28. What two-word term describes the temperature at which air becomes saturated and unable to hold any more water vapour?

29. What forename was shared by Jane Austen's mother and older sister?

30. Which English logician gave his name to diagrams of mathematical sets, in which intersecting areas denote elements that are common to the sets represented?

31. Who wrote the much-anthologised English poem that opens with the lines: 'So, we'll go no more a-roving / So late into the night / Though the heart be still as loving / And the moon be still as bright'?

32. The winner of the Nobel Prize for Literature in 1978, and the inventor of the domestic sewing machine in the 19th century, share the same forename and surname: what are they?

33. Which inland sea is bounded by Iran, Russia, Kazakhstan, Turkmenistan and Azerbaijan?

34. Although unrelated, the pop singers Joe Cocker and Jarvis Cocker both came from which British city?

35. The name of which artistic movement is thought to have originated in a less-than-complimentary comment by the critic Louis Vauxcelles, reviewing an exhibition of the work of Georges Braque, in 1908?

36. The man who was Surveyor of the King's, and later the Queen's, Pictures between 1945 and 1972, and Director of the Courtauld Institute of Art from 1947 to 1974, later became known to the general public for other reasons entirely. Who was he?

37. Which branch of mechanics is concerned with the motion of objects under the actions of forces?

38. First published in 1982, the anthology *The Rattle Bag* is a collection of the favourite poems of the two poets who edited it. They were Ted Hughes and – who else?

39. The rock 'n' roll song 'Blue Suede Shoes', recorded most famously by Elvis Presley, was written by which performer, another Sun Records recording artist?

40. In the familiar formula $E=mc^2$, what is the constant represented by c?

Answers on page 54

Answers to Quiz 4

1. Arrows – from the French *flèche,* an arrow
2. Edinburgh
3. Emily Dickinson – after the reclusive life she led in the college town of that name in Massachusetts
4. The pituitary gland (accept hypophysis)
5. Jean Valjean in *Les Misérables*
6. It was the first officially recorded no.1 hit – holding that position in what's regarded as the first reliable sales chart, published on 14th November 1952.
7. The (Green) Woodpecker
8. Piano
9. Aberystwyth
10. Pompey (Gnaeus Pompeius Magnus) and Crassus (Marcus Licinius Crassus)
11. Matt Groening
12. The Hansard Family – hence the name the publication still retains today
13. Alexandre-Gustave Eiffel
14. The French Revolution – of 1789. It was built for the Paris Exhibition in 1889.
15. Carbolic acid/phenol
16. Capitol Hill
17. The Cato Street conspiracy, led by Arthur Thistlewood
18. Truro
19. A reflex angle
20. Pea plants – *Pisum sativum*
21. A neutron star
22. Tintin
23. (Kingston Upon) Hull
24. David Lodge
25. Deuterium
26. Greta Garbo – in her first 'talkie', *Anna Christie*, in 1930.
27. The 2000s (in 2002 to be precise)

28. Dew point

29. Cassandra

30. (John) Venn – the 'Venn diagram'

31. Lord Byron

32. Isaac and Singer. They are Isaac Bashevis Singer (the writer) and Isaac Merritt Singer (the inventor).

33. The Caspian Sea – officially the world's largest lake

34. Sheffield

35. Cubism. The critic wrote of the painter's *bizarreries cubiques* or 'strange cubes'.

36. Anthony Blunt. He was unmasked as a Soviet Spy, and stripped of his Knighthood, in 1979.

37. Dynamics

38. Seamus Heaney

39. Carl Perkins

40. The speed of light (in a vacuum)

Quiz 5

1. First donated in 1892 by the Governor General of Canada, which ice hockey trophy is awarded each year to the National Hockey League play-off champions?

2. Which large building in London, opened in 1998, was described unflatteringly by Prince Charles as looking like 'an academy for secret policemen'?

3. A small fish found in the seas off southern Asia, the Bummalo, is generally known by what name when it's salted and dried and served as a foodstuff?

4. Which British locomotive, designed by Sir Nigel Gresley, set a world speed record for a steam-powered train of 126 miles per hour in 1938?

5. Mel Blanc, the actor who provided the voices for many of the best-loved Warner Brothers cartoon characters including Bugs Bunny and Daffy Duck, chose what valedictory three-word phrase for his tombstone?

6. In 2009 Dorothy Hughes and Winifred Phillips, both in their 80s, joined the ranks of which previously all-male institution?

7. What was the name of the Australian Prime Minister who disappeared while swimming at Cheviot Beach in Victoria in 1967, and was presumed to have drowned?

8. Which woodland north of Perth in Scotland is the setting for the climax of Shakespeare's *Macbeth* – in which the witches' prophecy is fulfilled, that the trees should march upon the castle of Dunsinane?

9. Acknowledged as one of the world's pre-eminent members of her profession, what position did Pauline Kael hold on the *New Yorker* magazine from 1968 until 1991?

10. *No Way Home* is the title of the 2007 rags-to-riches autobiography of which ballet dancer, who began life as one of eight children living in poverty in the back streets of Havana?

11. The capital cities of the two distinct states of the Republic of the Congo and the Democratic Republic of the Congo face one another across the Congo river: can you name them both?

12. The name of which household fixture is derived from an old French word meaning a pony or small horse?

13. Teenager Holden Caulfield is the hero of which American novel of the mid 20th century?

14. Now largely discredited, ECT was a common technique of psychiatric treatment in the 20th century. What do the letters ECT stand for?

15. Which word, sometimes used poetically to refer to the female sex, was given to a cleft stick measuring about three feet long, around which flax was wound, in the days before mechanised spinning?

16. The provocative New York-born singer Stefani Joanne Angelina Germanotta became one of the world's bestselling recording stars in 2009, thanks to hits such as 'Poker Face' and 'Paparazzi'. By what stage name is she better known?

17. In 1984 Alec Jeffreys of the University of Leicester discovered which now-common technique, of particular importance in forensic science?

18. Of the eight Kings of England called Henry, which one had the longest reign?

19. Which Premiership football club was, until 1900, known as Thames Ironworks FC?

Answers on page 60

20. While she was First Lady of the United States, Jackie Kennedy's stylish wardrobe was much-admired and imitated. Which French-born American designer and celebrity couturier was credited with inventing the 'Jackie Look'?

21. The standard unit of magnetic flux density is named after which American physicist, who invented the AC induction motor?

22. A cartoon character created by Max Fleischer, said to have been inspired by the singer and flapper Helen Kane, had to be drawn with longer skirts and fuller bodices to comply with the strictures of the Hayes Code of 1934. Which character?

23. Which ascetic sub-order of Cistercian monks was founded in Normandy in 1664 by the Abbott de Rancé?

24. The towns of Widnes and Runcorn stand facing one another across which major river?

25. In 1635, who founded the *Académie française*, the body charged with preserving French cultural heritage, and whose membership is limited to forty so-called 'Immortals'?

26. In which city would you find the cricket test match venue called Basin Reserve, often known locally as just 'the Basin'?

27. The slang word 'droog', amongst many others, was first coined in which novel first published in 1962, and filmed nine years later?

28. In which type of chemical reaction does a molecule of a compound split by reacting with water?

29. Which British statesman published a book entitled *Painting as a Pastime*?

30. In Christian tradition, if plain old Angels are the lowest rank of the nine-fold celestial hierarchy, which group of beings are the highest?

31. Along with the malleus and the incus, which tiny stirrup-shaped bone in the middle ear helps transmit vibrations to the organs of the inner ear?

32. What's the correct term for the pastoral staff carried by a bishop as part of the official vestments, fashioned in the form of a shepherd's crook?

33. Which building was the subject of a real-time film by Andy Warhol lasting over eight hours, the only action in the picture being the lights of the building going on and off?

34. In physics, which elementary particle has a name derived from the Greek word for light, which was first used by the physical chemist Gilbert Lewis in 1926?

35. 'One O'Clock Jump' and 'Jumpin' at the Woodside' are compositions by which jazz pianist and bandleader, whose live appearances continued until the 1980s?

36. Where in the solar system will you find the Cassini Division and the Encke Division?

37. 'Elk Cloner', created in 1982 by a fifteen-year-old schoolboy in Pittsburgh, Pennsylvania, named Richard Skrenta, was the first identified example of what?

38. What do you get if you multiply the square root of four by the square of four?

39. In the *Shrek* films, what is the name of the princess that Shrek woos and marries?

40. What type of creature is a boomslang?

Answers on page 60

Answers to Quiz 5

1. The Stanley Cup
2. The British Library
3. Bombay Duck
4. Mallard
5. 'That's all, folks!'
6. The Chelsea Pensioners. Miss Phillips was quoted as saying: 'It's just like the Army all over again, except you don't have so much to do.'
7. Harold Holt. Conspiracy theories abounded, including the suggestion that he had faked his own death and been picked up offshore by a Chinese spy vessel. His body was never found, alive or dead.
8. Birnam Wood
9. Film critic
10. Carlos Acosta
11. Brazzaville and Kinshasa. Nowhere in the world are there two geographically-closer capital cities.
12. Bidet
13. *The Catcher in the Rye* – by J. D. Salinger
14. Electro-convulsive therapy
15. Distaff
16. Lady Gaga
17. 'Genetic Fingerprinting'/DNA profiling
18. Henry III – some 56 years, from 1216-72
19. West Ham United
20. Oleg Cassini
21. Nikola Tesla
22. Betty Boop
23. Trappists. They were founded at La Trappe, hence their name.
24. The Mersey
25. Cardinal Richelieu
26. Wellington, New Zealand
27. *A Clockwork Orange* – by Anthony Burgess

28. Hydrolysis

29. Sir Winston Churchill – in 1948

30. Seraphim. It goes: Angels, Archangels, Principalities, Powers, Virtues, Dominions, Thrones, Cherubim, Seraphim.

31. Stapes

32. Crosier

33. The Empire State Building. Simply called *Empire*, the film shows the building from a single static angle, continuously between 8pm and 4am.

34. Photon

35. Count Basie

36. In the rings of Saturn

37. Computer virus – the first in the sense that it was the first to spread 'into the wild', beyond the confines of the system in which it was created.

38. 32

39. Princess Fiona

40. A snake – a highly venomous southern African tree snake

1. In August 2009, the founders of the internet messaging service Twitter failed in their bid to have which English word officially registered in the United States as a trademark of their own?

2. In 1709 Abraham Darby first successfully smelted iron with coke, at his furnace in which Shropshire valley, off what is now called the Ironbridge Gorge?

3. What, when originally discovered in 1781 by Sir William Herschel, was given the name *Georgium Sidus* in honour of King George the Third?

4. Relapsing fever, trench fever and typhus are diseases transmitted by the parasitic insect *Pediculus humanus corporis*, which is more commonly known by what name?

5. Which city in the United States was devastated by a fire started on the 8th October 1871, supposedly by a cow kicking over a lantern and setting light to its barn?

6. The author of novels such as *Cranford* and *North and South* was often just known as Mrs Gaskell. What was her first name?

7. The species of which long-armed member of the ape family include the Siamang, the Black Crested and the Hoolock?

8. Which of the noble gases takes its name from the Greek for 'something strange'?

9. What title, used by the hereditary spiritual leader of the Nizari sect of Ismaili Muslims, was first conferred on Hasan Ali Shah by the Shah of Persia?

10. The 56 pits known as the Aubrey holes are a feature of which English ancient monument?

11. Which best-selling children's book, first published in 1960 and written using a vocabulary of no more than fifty words, features the persistently enthusiastic Sam-I-am?

12. After Everest and K2, which is the third highest mountain in the world?

13. How are Jean de Dinteville and Georges de Selve referred to in the title of a 1533 canvas by Hans Holbein the Younger?

14. With its origins in the southern states of the USA, zydeco is a traditional style of which art form?

15. Which Greek goddess, the daughter of night, was the goddess of divine retribution?

16. Which British Prime Minister spent his last years in a house called Arundells in Salisbury Cathedral Close?

17. The purplish-red fruits of which plant take their name from the American judge and horticulturist who first grew it in 1881?

18. Mensa was founded in 1946 as the society for people with high IQs. What does Mensa mean in Latin?

19. What name is given in art to a brown discolouring effect, caused by dampness, that causes a mottled, spotted appearance on prints and the pages of books?

20. Coming to prominence in the 2000 Presidential Election results in the state of Florida, which word was used for the 'partially punctured holes in ballot sheets that were regarded as invalid', variously referred to as hanging, dimpled or pregnant?

Answers on page 66

21. Which French term can be applied to both the main course or dish in a meal, or the most valuable item in a collection of artworks?

22. What is the modern name of the city known as New Orange from 1673 to 1674, following its temporary recapture by the Dutch?

23. Sir Winston Churchill had two other Christian names. What were they?

24. Paresthesiae – experienced usually after long periods of immobility or as a symptom of some neurological diseases – is a sensation commonly referred to by which name?

25. What word for a lamentation, or a warning against the morals of the times, is taken from the name of a Hebrew prophet?

26. Which British author, who died in 1992, wrote the story 'The Company of Wolves', which was adapted for the screen by the director Neil Jordan?

27. 210 mm x 297 mm are the standard dimensions of which common paper size?

28. Which Hollywood actor's five wives were, in order, Margaret Sullavan, Frances Ford Brokaw (formerly Seymour), Susan Blanchard, Afdera Franchetti and Shirlee Mae Adams?

29. The French phrase *tant mieux*, often used to mean 'I'm glad to hear that', literally means 'so much the better'. What is the converse phrase meaning 'that's too bad', or 'so much the worse'?

30. The Warwickshire town of Rugby stands on which river?

31. Tenochtitlán, located on the site of what is now Mexico City, was the capital of which ancient people?

32. Which gas, whose chemical formula is CH_4, is also known as 'fire damp'?

33. At the start of which fairy tale, collected by the Grimm Brothers, does a miller foolishly boast that his daughter can spin straw into gold?

34. Which term for the simultaneous occurrence of events which appear meaningfully related, but have no discoverable causal connection, was used in 1983 as the title for a bestselling album by the rock group The Police?

35. The flightless nocturnal bird the kakapo – *Strigops habroptilus* – is an endangered species belonging to which order of birds?

36. In 1712, Jane Wenham, of Walkern in Hertfordshire, is thought to have been the last person in England to be convicted of what?

37. Which institution, with its headquarters near the Tower of London, is responsible for lighthouses, light vessels, buoys and beacons around the coasts of England, Wales, the Channel Islands and Gibraltar?

38. 'Mountain of light' is a translation of which Farsi phrase, most familiar as the name given to the diamond acquired by Britain in 1849 when the Punjab was annexed?

39. During the Vietnam War, what was the name of the surprise attack by the Viet Cong and the North Vietnamese Army against the American and South Vietnamese forces during the Lunar New Year celebrations in 1968?

40. Which famous, and sometimes scandalous, figure from twentieth century music was born Maria Anna Sophie Cecelia Kalogeropolous in the USA in 1923?

Answers on page 66

Answers to Quiz 6

1. Tweet

2. Coalbrookdale. The Iron Bridge, the first of its kind anywhere, was built in 1779.

3. The planet Uranus. The royal name never really caught on.

4. The (body) louse

5. Chicago – the cow belonged to a Mrs O'Leary, and has entered American mythology.

6. Elizabeth

7. The Gibbon – and, one might add, the Funky.

8. Xenon

9. Aga Khan

10. Stonehenge

11. *Green Eggs and Ham* by Dr Seuss. Theodor Seuss Geisel is said to have completed the book in response to a challenge issued by his editor, Bennett Cerf, to write a story using no more than fifty different words.

12. Kanchenjunga

13. The Ambassadors. Perhaps its most famous feature is the distorted image of a skull at the bottom.

14. Music – both in song and dance. It's a form of folk music usually with a fast tempo and played on instruments that include a piano accordion and washboard. It evolved in Louisiana.

15. Nemesis

16. Sir Edward Heath

17. Loganberry. After James H. Logan.

18. Table. Mensa's founders were Roland Berrill, a barrister, and Dr Lance Ware, a scientist and a lawyer.

19. Foxing

20. Chads. 'Hanging chads' were incompletely punched paper ballots. 'Pregnant' or 'dimpled' chads were paper ballots that were dimpled, but not properly pierced.

21. *Pièce de résistance*

22. New York (City). It had been founded as New Amsterdam in the early 1600s, and became British in 1664.

23. Leonard Spencer

24. Pins and needles

25. Jeremiad

26. Angela Carter

27. A4

28. Henry Fonda

29. *Tant pis*

30. The Avon

31. The Aztecs

32. Methane

33. Rumpelstiltskin

34. Synchronicity

35. Parrots (*Psittaciformes*). The name kakapo is derived from the Maori word for night – because it's nocturnal.

36. Witchcraft. She was sentenced to death by hanging but was given a royal pardon and lived out her days on the estate of the Earl and Countess Cowper in Hertingfordbury.

37. Trinity House

38. Koh-I-Noor

39. Tet Offensive

40. Maria Callas. A rival to Jackie Kennedy for the affections of Aristotle Onassis, she died a virtual recluse in Paris in 1977.

Quiz 7

1. Which wall, that marked the northern limits of Roman Britain, was abandoned near the end of the second century AD?

2. The Scotland international Billy Bremner is associated with which then-top-flight football club in the English league, which he captained during the late 1960s and early 1970s?

3. Of which iconic household item, chiefly associated with the 1960s, did its inventor once say, 'If you buy [it] you won't need drugs'?

4. According to the Book of Genesis, what was 300 cubits long, 50 cubits wide and 30 cubits high?

5. Which clergyman, known to posterity through his diaries, lived at Clyro in Radnorshire during the 1870s?

6. At the end of 2012, BBC Radio 2 conducted a poll among its listeners to find out which was their favourite no.2 hit of all time – in other words, the best record ever to stall at no.2 without reaching no.1. The triumph of 'Vienna' by Ultravox in the poll may have owed a lot to a 'sympathy vote' – because it was denied the no.1 place at the time by a record many felt didn't deserve to be there. What song was it that held 'Vienna' down at no.2?

7. Which viral disease is known in France as 'La Rage'?

8. *Strygidae* and *Tytonidae* are the two major families of which order of birds?

9. In a sporting context, the letters E.C.B. are the usual abbreviation for the England & Wales Cricket Board. But if a current news report about the financial world refers to the E.C.B., what do the letters stand for?

10. At a height of 893 metres or 2,930 feet above sea level, the summit of which hill in Cumbria is the highest point on the Pennine Way?

11. Which standard unit of energy traditionally represents the amount of heat required to warm one pound of water by one degree Fahrenheit?

12. The white wines of the appellations Vouvray, Saumur and Sancerre are all produced in the valley of which French river?

13. Which remote location in Russia suffered an enormously powerful unexplained explosion, possibly from some form of incoming cosmic fragment, in 1908?

14. The *Vitruvian Man*, a drawing showing the proportions of the human body, is often reproduced and was used for many years in the title sequence of the Granada TV programme *World In Action*. Which artist did the drawing?

15. In the study of grammar, when you list the different forms of a verb according to person and tense, you are said to 'conjugate' it. What do you do to a noun, when you list its various forms according to case and number?

16. Which BBC television reporter's dispatches from famine-torn Ethiopia in late 1984 prompted Bob Geldof to write and record the song 'Do They Know It's Christmas'?

17. The abbreviation ULCC is used for an ocean-going oil tanker measuring around 415 meters in length. What do the letters ULCC stand for?

18. 'I now pronounce you men and wives' is the closing line of which 1954 film musical?

19. Who, at Tokyo in 1964, became the first British woman to win an Olympic gold medal in a track and field athletics event?

20. What was Che Guevara's Christian name?

Answers on page 72

21. 'Woolsorters' disease' is a term first recorded in around 1880, to describe a form of which bacterial infection?

22. Which Russian physiologist wrote 'Conditioned Reflexes' published in 1927, and 'Lectures on Conditioned Reflexes' of 1928?

23. What sort of underwear, first introduced to the UK in 1938, was advertised with the slogan 'Like the Spitfire – scientifically built to fit the man'?

24. Dunmore Park in Stirlingshire contains a large folly in the shape of which fruit?

25. 'When the blazing sun is gone, / When he nothing shines upon, / Then you show your little light.' These are the opening lines of the little-known second verse of which familiar nursery rhyme?

26. Born Saloth Sar in the 1920s, how is the notorious former leader of the Khmer Rouge known to history?

27. The Brynmor Jones Library, where the poet Philip Larkin worked for thirty years, is at which university?

28. In Greek legend, Pygmalion was the king of which island?

29. Gaping Ghyll, White Scar Cave and Malham Cove can all be found in which of England's National Parks?

30. Fuelling conspiracy theories of a 'curse' of sorts, especially among rock stars, Brian Jones, Jimi Hendrix, Janis Joplin, Jim Morrison, Kurt Cobain and Amy Winehouse were all the same age when they died. What age?

31. In music, what does the Italian instruction *da capo* mean?

32. Which acclaimed film director first came to prominence as the only American-born member of the Monty Python comedy team?

33. The name of which alkaline earth metal derives from the mining location in Scotland where the mineral was discovered?

34. The seaside resort of Brighton was known by what name in the 18th century, the name being shortened following the growth in its popularity after regular visits by the future George IV?

35. 'We have lingered in the chambers of the sea / By sea-girls wreathed with seaweed red and brown / Till human voices wake us, and we drown.' These are the closing lines of which poem by T. S. Eliot?

36. The constellation Crux is more commonly known by which two-word English name?

37. Which term, derived from the Italian for 'shoulder', refers to 'a line of fruit-trees whose branches are pruned and trained into formal patterns against a wall or fence'?

38. Which traditional Japanese ceremonial activity is known by the name *Cha-no-yu*?

39. What is the name of the geological period during which the coal measures were laid down?

40. Which characteristic essentially distinguishes those mammals known as monotremes?

Answers on page 72

Answers to Quiz 7

1. The Antonine Wall. Septimius Severus refortified the structure in the early part of the third century AD, but little attempt was made to defend it thereafter.

2. Leeds United. Under legendary manager Don Revie, he is regarded by many as Leeds's greatest-ever star.

3. The lava lamp. Developed by the British inventor Edward Craven Walker.

4. Noah's Ark. It equates to 450 feet x 75 feet x 45 feet.

5. (Robert Francis) Kilvert. Surviving sections of his diaries were first published in the 1930s.

6. 'Shaddap You Face', the novelty hit by Joe Dolce

7. Rabies (accept Hydrophobia/lyssa)

8. Owls. The *Tytonidae* are the barn owls, of which there are some ten species; the *Strygidae* comprise most of the remaining owl species.

9. European Central Bank

10. Cross Fell. It's the highest point in England outside the Lake District.

11. British Thermal Unit. It is the equivalent of 1,055 joules.

12. The Loire

13. Tunguska. The Tunguska explosion is estimated to have been a thousand times more powerful than the atomic bomb dropped on Hiroshima.

14. Leonardo Da Vinci

15. Decline it

16. Michael Buerk

17. Ultra Large Crude Carrier

18. *Seven Brides for Seven Brothers*

19. Mary Rand/Bignal. She won gold in the long jump.

20. Ernesto

21. Anthrax. It's contracted by inhaling dust containing *Bacillus anthracis* and usually affects the skin and/or lungs. Those involved in the wool-sorting trade were very susceptible to it because of the dust in the fleeces.

22. (Ivan Petrovich) Pavlov

23. Y-Fronts

24. A pineapple

25. 'Twinkle, Twinkle, Little Star'. The next line goes 'Twinkle, twinkle, all the night'. There are five verses in all in the original poem by Jane Taylor, only the first of which is ever performed or printed in books of nursery rhymes.

26. Pol Pot

27. University of Hull

28. Cyprus

29. Yorkshire Dales

30. 27

31. 'From the top' or 'From the beginning'

32. Terry Gilliam. Born in Minneapolis, he now has British citizenship.

33. Strontium. After Strontian.

34. Brighthelmstone. Earlier known as Bryghneston, Brighthempston.

35. 'The love song of J. Alfred Prufrock'

36. Southern Cross

37. Espalier

38. (Japanese) tea ceremony/'The Way of Tea'. The tea is thought to have been used as a way of combatting drowsiness during meditation.

39. Carboniferous

40. They lay eggs. Only the platypus and the echidnas are extant members of the order.

Quiz 8

1. The phrase 'BRIC nations' refers to a group of countries whose economies and influence are growing, and predicted to keep growing, during the 21st century. What do the letters BRIC stand for?

2. Decaying uranium finally becomes an isotope of which metal?

3. *Le Manège Enchanté* was the original French title of which classic children's television series?

4. What financial enterprise began in a coffee house in Tower Street, London, in the 1680s, before moving to bigger premises near Lombard Street?

5. Which itinerant ballet company, directed by Sergei Diaghilev and widely regarded as the greatest ballet company of the 20th century, performed in many countries between 1909 and 1929?

6. In which range of hills are the Wookey Hole caves?

7. Which British actor and comedian directed his first Hollywood feature in 2009, called *The Invention of Lying*?

8. What is the chemical formula for Ozone?

9. In 1981, a book by twelve-year-old Patrick Bossert became one of the fastest selling books of all time. Its contents provided a means of solving which problem?

10. Recorded as an entry in his diary, 'God grant my eyes may never behold the like,' is a sentiment reflecting John Evelyn's reponse to which historical event?

11. The Rainbow Bridge, a natural arch of pink sandstone, crosses Lake Powell in which US state?

12. In the Hindu religion, what is a Sadhu?

13. Bob Paisley steered which football club to six league titles and three European Cups during nine years as manager?

14. According to the humorous book of British history *1066 and All That,* by Sellar and Yeatman, which Parliament was 'so-called because it had been sitting for such a long time'?

15. The sequel to Robert Louis Stevenson's *Kidnapped* takes its title from the girl the hero David Balfour falls in love with. What's its title?

16. What stretch of water separates the Isle of Anglesey from the Welsh mainland?

17. The host used in the sacrament of Holy Communion, the Indian chapati, and the matzo traditionally eaten during the Jewish feast of the Passover, are all forms of what type of bread?

18. Which old fashioned phrase for nudity, familiar from a song featured in a film with Danny Kaye, is thought to have been first popularised by its use in George du Maurier's novel *Trilby* in the 1890s?

19. Which chemical element has as its symbol the single letter P?

20. Delphi, home of the Oracle of legend, lies on the slopes of which Greek mountain, which was itself sacred to the Muses?

Answers on page 78

21. The Treaty of Paris in March 1856 formally ended which war?

22. The Morrison Formation, a geological feature of the western United States, is the American continent's richest source of fossil remains of what type of creatures?

23. The swimwear known as a bikini acquired its name because the word 'bikini' was in the news at the time of its introduction in 1946. Can you explain why?

24. *Buteo buteo* is the taxonomic name of which large bird of prey, widespread in Britain and Europe?

25. The film known simply as *Star Wars* on its first release in 1977 became Episode 4 in the eventual sequence of films, and acquired a subtitle. Can you give me the subtitle?

26. What two-word term is used for 'a synthetic androgen that selectively enhances the growth of skeletal muscle'?

27. The branch of chemistry known as organic chemistry involves the study of the compounds of which element?

28. In popular fiction, what profession is common to both Irene Adler, the New Jersey-born beauty who outwits Sherlock Holmes in Conan Doyle's *A Scandal in Bohemia*, and Bianca Castafiore, the victim of jewel theft in the Tintin adventure *The Castafiore Emerald?*

29. Which body was created in the UK in 1995 to assume many of the roles and responsibilities formerly undertaken by the National Rivers Authority, Her Majesty's Inspectorate of Pollution and the waste regulation authorites of England and Wales?

30. The carbonated soft drink generally known in the US as cream soda is flavoured with pods from plants of which genus?

31. In 1964, the American theoretical physicist Murray Gell-Mann coined which word for a group of subatomic particles regarded, along with leptons, as basic constituents of matter?

32. Bhadrapada, Asvina and Kartika are months in the calendar of which religion?

33. For what sort of event would an epithalamium be written?

34. What two-word term is widely used as the US equivalent to what the British would call 'positive discrimination'?

35. *Jane Eyre* is the best-known of Charlotte Brontë's four completed novels. Can you name ONE of the other three?

36. Two of the United States of America have names which, in common pronunciation, end with a silent 'S'. Which two?

37. What was the traditional subject of the type of wall painting, often seen in medieval churches, known as a 'Doom'?

38. Known for his drawings in black ink, influenced by the style of Japanese woodcuts and emphasizing the grotesque, the decadent, and the erotic, who was the first art editor of *The Yellow Book*, an influential literary periodical published in London in the 1890s?

39. In English folklore, a 'tod' is a traditional name for which animal?

40. The name of which Italian dairy product means 'recooked'?

Answers on page 78

1. Brazil, Russia, India, China. Often used in the context of economic power moving away from traditional G7 nations – these are also sometimes referred to as 'the Big Four'.

2. Lead

3. *The Magic Roundabout*

4. Lloyds

5. The Ballets Russes. Dissolved after Diaghilev's death in 1929. In 1932 Colonel Wassily de Basil and his associate René Blum revived the company under the name Ballet Russe de Monte Carlo.

6. The Mendips

7. Ricky Gervais

8. O_3

9. Rubik's Cube. *You Can do the Cube* sold 500,000 copies in four weeks, and 1.5m overall, being the global best seller of 1981.

10. The Great Fire of London

11. Utah

12. Holy Man, sage, or ascetic

13. Liverpool, 1974-83

14. The Rump Parliament

15. *Catriona*

16. Menai Strait

17. Unleavened bread. Essentially there being no raising agent such as yeast or baking soda.

18. 'In the altogether' – the Danny Kaye record was 'The King's New Clothes', but the original tale was 'The Emperor's New Clothes'.

19. Phosphorus. Not, of course, potassium, which is K.

20. Mount Parnassus

21. The Crimean War. It declared the Black Sea to be neutral territory, out of bounds to warships, and forbade any sort of fortifications on its shores.

22. Dinosaurs. The sedimentary deposits in the Morrison Formation were laid down in the late Jurassic period, the peak of dinosaur activity.

23. Bikini Atoll was the site of an atomic bomb test by the USA. Bikini Island and Atoll are in what's now Micronesia, in the Pacific Ocean. The 'bikini' swimsuit was advertised just days after the first, much-publicised, bomb test.

24. The Buzzard

25. *A New Hope*

26. Anabolic steroid

27. Carbon

28. Opera singer/diva

29. The Environment Agency

30. Vanilla

31. Quark(s). He won the Nobel Prize for Physics in 1969.

32. Hinduism

33. A wedding. It's a celebratory song or poem.

34. Affirmative action

35. *Shirley/Villette/The Professor*

36. Illinois and Arkansas

37. The Last Judgement

38. Aubrey Beardsley. He died of tuberculosis when he was just 25.

39. A fox, as in Beatrix Potter's *The Tale of Mr Tod*

40. Ricotta

Quiz 9

1. What name is given in reproductive biology to a certain type of cell, two of which merging with one another produce a zygote – examples being sperm and egg cells?

2. The five 'Leatherstocking Tales' of the 19th century American novelist James Fenimore Cooper are *The Pioneers, The Prairie, The Pathfinder, The Deerslayer* and which other novel, first published in 1826?

3. In 1598, the Edict of Nantes finally defined freedom of worship for which French religious group, who had to suffer its revocation in 1685 by Louis XIV?

4. Which term – first used in 1976 in Richard Dawkins' *The Selfish Gene* – is used to refer to a so-called 'unit of cultural information' passed between minds through imitated use?

5. At approximately 192 km, which is the longest river in Scotland?

6. According to Philip Larkin's poem 'Annus Mirabilis', in which year did sexual intercourse begin?

7. Which British actor's prominent roles encompass Lennie Price in *Two Way Stretch* in 1960, and Wilf Mott in *Dr Who* in the 21st century?

8. $C_5H_9N_3$ is a chemical formula for which biogenic compound, released by the immune system during allergic reactions?

9. Which bird, sometimes known as the 'sea swallow', has varieties including the Sooty, the Arctic and the Sandwich?

10. What name is generally given to the palaeoanthropological theory – advanced by geneticists in the 1980s – that all living humans share a single ancestor, a hypothetical woman living in eastern Africa between 150 and 200 thousand years ago?

11. Benjamin Franklin, Percival Lowell, Ralph Waldo Emerson, Edgar Allan Poe and Paul Revere were all born in which city, historically known as the 'Athens of America'?

12. What was King George VI's first name?

13. What traditional custom takes place in the Derbyshire villages of Tissington and Youlgreave, amongst others, said to be associated with the worship of water deities?

14. What is the name of the French village, outside Paris, where Monet spent the last years of his life, painting his famous *Waterlilies* series?

15. George Bingham was in overall charge of the cavalry at Balaclava: he was the 3rd holder of which title, that was made infamous by the 7th holder, declared legally dead in the 1990s?

16. Which Austrian physicist is responsible for the naming of the 'ratio of the speed of a body or fluid to the local speed of sound', particularly commonly applied in relation to aircraft?

17. The invention of which perfume is credited to Giovanni Maria Farina, who moved from Italy to Germany in the early eighteenth century to manufacture it?

18. Which musical instrument was patented in Hawaii in 1917?

19. The Indri, aye-aye and fossa are animal species native to which country?

20. Although credited to three different acts, the early 1970s hit songs 'In a Broken Dream', 'Cindy Incidentally' and 'You Wear It Well' all featured lead vocals by whom?

Answers on page 84

21. Who was the man who ruled Cuba in the 1940s and again in the 1950s when he was overthrown by Fidel Castro?

22. Working on principles developed by Michael Faraday, what name is given to a machine or generator that transforms mechanical energy into electrical energy?

23. With a book and lyrics by Glenn Slater, which Andrew Lloyd Webber musical is a sequel to *The Phantom of the Opera*?

24. John Milton, Isaac Newton, Henry VIII and Benjamin Franklin are among the most famous names said to have suffered from which form of arthritis, brought on by the defective metabolism of uric acid?

25. 'Comparisons are odorous' is a characteristic malapropism spoken by which Shakespearean character?

26. Which small island in the River Thames is linked by a footbridge to the Embankment at Twickenham?

27. Which Russian composer's second piano concerto in C minor is heard on the soundtracks of the 1945 film romance *Brief Encounter* and the 1955 Billy Wilder comedy *The Seven Year Itch*?

28. Which spice, used in natural or powdered form, is derived from the dried membrane that covers nutmeg?

29. Which two-word phrase is used for the boundary of a black hole with the rest of the universe?

30. Which mythical beast was said to have a lion's head, a goat's middle and a dragon or serpent's tail?

31. What name is given to the oldest known fossil bird of the late Jurassic period?

32. What was the nationality by birth of Marie Antoinette, whose husband ascended the French throne as Louis XVI in 1774?

33. Although its name derives from the Provençal word for capers, what is actually the main ingredient of the dish Tapenade?

34. Which film directed by David Lean, based on a classic novel, did one critic say 'does for snow what his *Lawrence of Arabia* did for sand'?

35. A 'cordwainer' is an archaic term for an artisan who manufactured what type of goods?

36. To distinguish him from his father the second President, the sixth President of the United States is almost always referred to using which distinctive middle name, from his great grandfather?

37. The Ounce is an alternative name for which animal that lives in the mountains of Central Asia?

38. Which dry apple brandy shares its name with the department of north-west France where it is made?

39. Which international organisation, whose aims are the education and stimulation of retired members of the community, was founded in Toulouse in 1973?

40. What name is given to non-volatile computer memory that can be electrically erased and reprogrammed, which is primarily used on memory cards, memory sticks and the like?

Answers on page 84

Answers to Quiz 9

1. Gamete
2. *The Last of the Mohicans*
3. The Huguenots
4. Meme
5. The Tay
6. 1963. 'Between the end of the Chatterley ban and the Beatles' first LP.'
7. Bernard Cribbins
8. Histamine
9. The Tern
10. The Eve Hypothesis. Not identical with the 'Out of Africa' model which also proposes a restricted origin for mankind in time and space, but merely points to that continent as its location.
11. Boston
12. Albert ('Bertie'). He took the same regnal name as his father, George, in order to suggest a return to stability following his brother's abdication.
13. Well dressing
14. Giverny
15. Lord Lucan (Earl of Lucan)
16. Ernest Mach (1838-1916). Mach 1 is equal to the speed of sound in a given medium, and the number varies with the local conditions such as temperature and the density of the medium.
17. Eau de Cologne
18. The Ukulele. Introduced by the Portuguese in the 1870s.
19. Madagascar
20. Rod Stewart
21. Fulgencio Batista y Zaldivar
22. Dynamo
23. *Love Never Dies*
24. Gout
25. Dogberry (in *Much Ado About Nothing*)
26. Eel Pie Island

27. Sergei Rachmaninov. In *The Seven Year Itch*, Marilyn Monroe's character, Candy Kane, confesses, 'Every time I hear it, I go to pieces.'

28. Mace

29. Event Horizon

30. Chimera

31. Archaeopteryx

32. Austrian. She was born in 1755, the daughter of Francis I and Maria Theresa.

33. Olives. It's a puree made from black olives, capers, and anchovies pounded together with olive oil.

34. *Doctor Zhivago*

35. Shoes, boots and other articles in soft leather. Literally, a worker in cordovan leather.

36. Quincy (John Quincy Adams). The great grandfather was Colonel John Quincy.

37. The snow leopard

38. Calvados

39. University of the Third Age (U3A). Founded by Pierre Vellas, there are no qualifications: it is studying for pleasure. Brought to the UK in 1983 by Peter Laslett.

40. Flash (memory)

Quiz 10

1. Which elementary particles, believed to be one of the basic building blocks of matter, are divided into six types: Up, Down, Top, Bottom, Strange and Charm?

2. Which fictional villain, later the subject of a musical by Stephen Sondheim, made his first appearance in 'The String of Pearls', a story which first appeared in *The People's Periodical* in 1846?

3. Marie van Goethem – a 14-year-old dance student at the Palais Garnier in Paris – became the subject of an iconic work by which French artist?

4. In which county of Ireland is Knock, the village celebrated as the site of a series of visions of the Virgin Mary in August 1879?

5. What is a Devon rex?

6. The 'Otto Cycle' is the name given to the function of which type of engine?

7. In classical mythology, who, collectively, were Stheno, Euryale and Medusa?

8. Which fictional group began its adventures 'on a Treasure Island' in 1942 and ended them 'Together Again' in 1963?

9. Which country became known as 'The Cockpit of Europe' because it has so frequently been the battleground of Europe?

10. What is the name for a triangle which has three sides of differing lengths?

1. In biology, what is the name for the point of contact between one neurone and another, the junction across which a nerve impulse passes from an axon terminal to a neuron, muscle cell, or gland cell, also known as a neuronal junction?

2. In art, what is the generally used French term for an object found by an artist and displayed as it is, or sometimes with minimal alteration?

3. 'Oeil de boeuf', or 'bull's eye', is a French term referring to a 17th century type of which architectural feature?

4. 'Rehearsal for Disaster' is the title of the first chapter of which novel by Paul Gallico, filmed in 1972 with a cast including Gene Hackman, Shelley Winters and Ernest Borgnine?

5. Which Arabic term is used as a title of respect, for one who knows the Koran by heart?

6. What is the collective term for the four largest moons orbiting Jupiter?

7. Given a licence in 1962, the oral vaccine widely used against poliomyelitis takes its name from which Polish-born American microbiologist who developed it in 1955?

8. Of which larger family of animals is the badger a member?

9. Derived from the Old French for a coin, what word is used to denote the fineness of material such as silk?

20. How many years separated London's 19th century Great Exhibition, and the 20th century's Festival of Britain?

Answers on page 90

21. 'Urchin' is a Middle-English word for which common insectivorous mammal native to mainland Britain?

22. Which English king instituted the Order of the Garter in 1348?

23. What name is given to the protecting and nourishing fluid in which a baby develops in the womb?

24. Paralysis agitans is a medical term for a degenerative disorder of the central nervous system, now more usually referred to by the name of which English doctor, who published the first detailed description of the condition in 1817?

25. The Hindu god Ganesh or Ganesa is depicted as having the head of which animal?

26. *Dead Cert*, published in 1962, was the first novel by which crime writer?

27. Batavia, a Roman name for the Netherlands, was the capital of the Dutch East Indies; post-independence, how is the city known today?

28. The Stevie Wonder hit song 'Happy Birthday' was written as a tribute to which public figure?

29. Depending on their activities, which scatologically-named insect is grouped into either 'rollers', 'tunnelers' or 'dwellers'?

30. 'The Tell-Tale Heart' and 'The Cask of Amontillado' are among the stories collected under the title *Tales of Mystery and Imagination*, the best known work of which American writer?

31. Which actress, in a film entitled *Klondike Annie*, utters the quip that when choosing between two evils 'I always pick the one I've never tried before'?

32. In the human body, which membranous sac surrounds the heart?

33. Which US physicist gave his name to zones of highly energised charged particles, trapped at high altitude in the Earth's magnetic field?

34. The characters Buttons and Baron Hardup traditionally appear in which pantomime?

35. Jewish people of 'Sephardic' descent have ancestors that were resident in which part of Europe, from the Middle Ages until their persecution and mass expulsion from those countries in the last decades of the 15th century?

36. Jody Scheckter, Jacques Lafitte and Jochen Rindt were prominent competitors in the 1970s in which international sport?

37. By what name do we now know the element produced in the 18th century by Henry Cavendish and described by him as 'inflammable air'?

38. Which silent film star became known as 'The Great Stone Face', because of his deadpan demeanour?

39. What name is given to the unsuccessful attempt by Mao Zedong between 1958 and 1961 to hasten the process of industrialization and the improvement of agricultural production in China?

40. *Arrangement in grey and black* was the original title, when it was first exhibited in 1872, of an American painting now much better known by what name?

Answers on page 90

1. Quarks. The six types are known as 'flavours'.

2. Sweeney Todd

3. Edgar Degas. His wax models of her being cast in bronze.

4. County Mayo

5. A breed of cat

6. Four-stroke engine, after German engineer Nikolaus Otto, who introduced it in 1876.

7. The Gorgons

8. (Enid Blyton's) Famous Five – the five being siblings Julian, Dick and Anne, cousin George (Georgina) and Timmy, a mongrel dog.

9. Belgium

10. Scalene

11. Synapse

12. *Objet Trouvé* (literally a 'found object')

13. Window

14. *The Poseidon Adventure*

15. Hafiz

16. Galilean moons/satellites. Discovered by Galileo Galilei in January 1610. They derive their names from the lovers of Zeus: Io, Europa, Ganymede and Callisto.

17. (Albert Bruce) Sabin. Jonas Salk's injected vaccine, introduced earlier, had proved less reliable.

18. Weasel Family (Mustelidae)

19. Denier

20. 100 years. The Great Exhibition was held in Crystal Palace in 1851. The Festival of Britain was in 1951 and marked the centenary of the Great Exhibition.

21. The Hedgehog. Hence the name 'sea-urchin' for a marine creature that looks like a hedgehog.

22. Edward III

23. Amniotic fluid (liquor amnii)

24. James Parkinson

25. Elephant

26. Dick Francis (Richard Stanley Francis)

27. Jakarta

28. Dr Martin Luther King Jr. Stevie Wonder was instrumental in getting King's birthday, 15th January, declared a national holiday in the USA.

29. Dung Beetle. Rollers are noted for rolling dung into spherical balls, burying it and laying a single egg on it. Tunnelers tunnel under the dung and drag down pieces to be compacted in a brood mass. Dwellers leave it where it is and construct brood balls in situ.

30. Edgar Allan Poe

31. Mae West. The film dates from 1936.

32. Pericardium

33. James Van Allen. They're known as the Van Allen belts.

34. Cinderella

35. Spain/Portugal. The Iberian Peninsula, in other words.

36. Formula One

37. Hydrogen

38. Buster Keaton. The nickname is also applied to fellow actor Keanu Reeves, and legendary American TV presenter Ed Sullivan.

39. The Great Leap Forward (*Da Yu Jin*)

40. *Whistler's Mother*

MODERATE

The next 35 quizzes are closer to what you'd expect in a broadcast edition of *Brain of Britain*: a real mixture of difficulty level. See how you get on.

Quiz 11

1. Which month, known as the windy month, was the sixth month of the French Revolutionary calendar, and lasted from around 20th February to 21st March?

2. Alberto Juantorena, Quincy Watts and Michael Johnson are among those who have won Olympic gold in which athletics event?

3. Which children's story by Roald Dahl was first adapted for the London stage in 2011 with songs by the musician and comedian Tim Minchin?

4. One of the four kings in a standard English pack of cards is depicted without a moustache – supposedly, originally, it was missed off because of poor copying. Which king is it?

5. Which artist became the first President of the Royal Academy in 1768?

6. Of which British Prime Minister is the Labour politician Douglas Jay quoted as saying that 'he never used one syllable where none would do'?

7. In a chemistry laboratory, what is the purpose of a Kipp's apparatus?

8. Which two provinces in the North East of France, annexed by Bismarck in 1871, were returned to France by the Treaty of Versailles after the First World War?

9. Which is the only one of the Seven Wonders of the Ancient World whose exact location remains unconfirmed by archaeology?

10. The adjective pelagic, often used to describe certain types of bird, comes from a Greek word meaning what?

11. Which powerful Italian organised crime ring, whose name is possibly derived from a local word for 'thief', is based in Calabria but has links and operatives all over the world?

12. In the children's television drama series *Grange Hill*, what was the name of the long-serving head teacher played by Gwyneth Powell?

13. Although it's used in casual speech to mean the dim and distant past, in law the phrase 'time immemorial' relates very precisely to a particular calendar year. Which one?

14. Which Dutch sprinter, who won the 100 metres and 200 metres at the 1948 London Olympics, was nicknamed 'The Flying Housewife'?

15. The medal of the Order of the British Empire for Gallantry was superseded in September 1940 by the introduction of which other honour?

16. In Jonathan Swift's *Gulliver's Travels*, what's Gulliver's first name?

17. What name, also meaning a particular time of day, is sometimes given to the hot and dry southern states of Italy, including the islands of Sicily and Sardinia?

18. Which North American city is served by George Bush International Airport?

19. Which novelty swing dance, derived from the Charleston, was named following Charles Lindbergh's crossing of the Atlantic in 1927?

20. Which part of the British Isles has a parliament called the Court of Chief Pleas?

Answers on page 98

21. Which type of theatre derives its name from a Latin word meaning 'a player of many parts'?

22. Apatosaurus is the name by which scientists now refer to the dinosaur formerly known as the Brontosaurus. The name Brontosaurus means 'thunder lizard' – but what does the name Apatosaurus mean?

23. Windermere is the largest of the lakes in the English Lake District, and the largest natural lake in England. Which is the second largest?

24. In Morse code, the most commonly occurring vowel and the most commonly occurring consonant are represented respectively by a single dot, and a single dash. Which letters are these?

25. Which athlete and politician became the first person to be named BBC Sports Personality of the Year, in 1954?

26. The comic playwright born Jean Baptiste Poquelin in 1622 is better known by what pen-name?

27. Which pioneering jazz pianist, who came to prominence as part of the 'be-bop' movement in the 1940s, had the unusual middle name 'Sphere'?

28. In the care label symbols found on clothes, what is indicated by a square with a circle inside it, crossed out?

29. A painting of 1599 by Caravaggio depicts a scene from the Old Testament, in which the Hebrew widow Judith beheads an Assyrian commander, after having calculatedly seduced him and made him drunk. What's his name?

30. The heavy black-brown mineral cassiterite is the principal ore of which metallic element?

31. The toxic quinolizidine alkaloid, that became the suspected agent of poisoning in the Daphne du Maurier novel *My Cousin Rachel*, is present in the seeds of which tree, grown for its hanging clusters of golden flowers ?

32. Which Scottish monarch was killed at the Battle of Flodden Field in 1513?

33. In an early printed book, where would you find the 'explicit'?

34. Which artist did the writer Gore Vidal call 'a genius with the IQ of a moron'?

35. Which Latin phrase meaning 'come with me' is often used to describe a personal handbook, carried for use when needed?

36. The cran, equal to 37½ gallons, is used commercially to measure the volume of which commodity?

37. The comedian Frankie Howerd's role as Pseudolus, in the London production of Stephen Sondheim's *A Funny Thing Happened On The Way To The Forum*, led to a TV comedy series which was written for him, and directly inspired by that show. What was its title?

38. The four American Presidents whose faces are carved into Mount Rushmore in South Dakota are Lincoln, Washington, Theodore Roosevelt and which other?

39. The Canadian physician Frederick Banting won the Nobel Prize in Physiology or Medicine in 1923, for his work with his colleague Charles Best, that made possible the treatment of which common condition?

40. The Drury Lane Theatre, on 28th September 1745, saw the first recorded public performance of which now very familiar piece of music?

Answers on page 98

Answers to Quiz 11

1. Ventose
2. 400 metres
3. *Matilda*
4. The King of Hearts
5. Sir Joshua Reynolds
6. Clement Attlee
7. Production of gases. It consists of a series of three glass chambers stacked on top of one another, like an hourglass with three compartments.
8. Alsace and Lorraine. Their chequered history lies behind the highly-symbolic decision to site the European Parliament in Strasbourg, the capital of Alsace.
9. The Hanging Gardens of Babylon
10. The (open) sea
11. The 'Ndrangheta
12. Mrs (Bridget) McClusky
13. 1189 – before the reign of Richard I
14. (Fanny) Blankers-Koen
15. The George Cross
16. Lemuel
17. Mezzogiorno ('midday')
18. Houston, Texas. It's named after the father, not the son.
19. Lindy Hop
20. Sark
21. Pantomime
22. Deceptive Lizard – because part of its fossilised skeleton resembled that of another creature when first unearthed
23. Ullswater. Rutland Water and Kielder Water, both man-made, are larger than Ullswater.
24. E and T
25. Christopher Chataway
26. Molière
27. Thelonious Monk

28. Do not tumble dry

29. Holofernes

30. Tin

31. Laburnum

32. King James IV

33. At the end – the word refers to the last words of a text

34. Andy Warhol (in *The Observer*, 18th June 1989)

35. *Vade Mecum*

36. Fish – especially Herring, when freshly caught

37. *Up Pompeii*

38. Thomas Jefferson

39. Diabetes. They discovered the function of insulin.

40. 'God Save The King'(/Queen)

Quiz 12

1. Which English singer-songwriter, who died tragically young in 1974, released only three albums during his lifetime, *Five Leaves Left*, *Bryter Later* and *Pink Moon*, largely ignored at the time but all now acknowledged as classics?

2. 'A Cream Cracker Under the Settee' was the title of the last of Alan Bennett's acclaimed 1988 series of television monologues, *Talking Heads*. Which actress performed it?

3. 'Aqua fortis', the Latin for 'strong water', was a name used archaically for which acid?

4. What common process is known to botanists as 'positive geotropism'?

5. The viral disease epidemic parotitis, most commonly afflicting children between the ages of 5 and 15, is commonly known by what name?

6. What name is given to the long sleeveless outer vestment worn by priests, and normally distinguished by the liturgical colour appropriate to the mass being celebrated?

7. The Rev. Canon Chasuble D.D. is a vicar in which of Oscar Wilde's comedies?

8. Which naturalist and physician was responsible for giving us our biological name *Homo sapiens*?

9. Alphabetically, which is the last book of the Old Testament?

10. Which 14th century manuscript, consisting of more than fifty poems including some attributed to a bard who lived as early as the 6th century, inspired the title of an LP by the rock band Deep Purple?

11. Claire Tomalin, whose biography of Charles Dickens was published in 2011, is also the author of an acclaimed biography of Dickens' mistress, published twenty years earlier with the title *The Invisible Woman*. What was that mistress's name?

12. Patrick Troughton, Richard Greene, Michael Praed and Jonas Armstrong have all appeared in television dramas playing which medieval figure?

13. Which London railway terminus is depicted in W. P. Frith's painting of 1862, entitled *The Railway Station*?

14. What term is used in archaeology to refer to the physical material – such as soil or sediment – in which cultural artefacts or fossils are embedded?

15. The organisation CSETI, founded in the USA in 1990 by Steven M. Greer, is dedicated to the furtherance of human understanding of what phenomenon?

16. In 1985, the zoologist Dian Fossey was murdered while making a study of mountain gorillas – in which African country?

17. Which European capital city got its ancient name from the Latin word for mud?

18. 'The book of my enemy has been remaindered / And I am pleased. / In vast quantities it has been remaindered / Like a van-load of counterfeit that has been seized'. These are the opening lines of the title poem of which writer's book of collected verse?

19. In physics, what is the anti-particle to the electron called?

20. In the 17th century, Nicholas Lanier became the first person to hold what post at the English royal court?

Answers on page 104

21. Certain insects have 'stridulatory organs'. Can you explain what these are?

22. In Greek legend, what did the craftsman Epeius fashion from timbers cut from the slopes of Mount Ida?

23. 'A Satyr Against Reason and Mankind' is a poem by which courtier of Charles II, who has been portrayed on film by Johnny Depp, and whose debauched lifestyle earned him the reputation of 'the wickedest man in England'?

24. When the Republic of China was declared in 1912, who was named its first provisional President?

25. In which city in France was Joan of Arc burned at the stake in 1431?

26. In the Beatles' 1964 film *A Hard Day's Night*, which Irish-born actor, by then already familiar from television, was cast as the grandfather?

27. The area known as The Hamptons, in Suffolk County, an exclusive summer retreat for wealthy Americans, is at the eastern end of which island?

28. *From Doon with Death*, first published in 1964, was the first novel of which British crime writer?

29. Which year of the 20th century saw the start of the First Arab-Israeli War, the publication of the Kinsey report into Sexual Behaviour in the Human Male and the assassination of Mahatma Gandhi?

30. Which common three-letter word was originally an abbreviation of a two-word Latin phrase meaning 'excitable crowd', a meaning which it often retains?

31. According to tradition, who was shot dead at Mann's saloon in August 1876, holding, in a poker game, two eights and two aces, the combination of cards becoming known as 'the dead man's hand'?

32. Which branch of mathematics was developed by John Von Neumann with later collaboration by Oskar Morgenstern?

33. Which director-general of the BBC introduced on air the radio broadcast of the abdication speech made by Edward VIII on 11th December 1936?

34. Which district of New York City is situated north of 96th Street in Manhattan?

35. Which transition metal, which shares its name with a major London theatre, has atomic number 46 and atomic mass of 106.4?

36. Which force created to preserve public order in London, originally numbering only six men, was founded by Henry Fielding in the 1740s, and lasted until being finally disbanded in the 1830s?

37. At 636 metres, which is the highest point in the Peak District?

38. The composer Richard Rodgers had two astronomically successful partnerships in his career. Can you name the two lyricists with which he scored his major hits?

39. What is the name of the man-eating water monster who plagues the hall of King Hrothgar in the Anglo-Saxon epic poem *Beowulf*?

40. The so-called 'underground cathedral', housed in a former mine in Wieliczka in South-Eastern Poland, consists of a series of large-scale sculptures in which material?

Answers on page 104

Answers to Quiz 12

1. Nick Drake
2. (Dame) Thora Hird
3. Nitric Acid
4. The tendency of plant roots to grown downwards. Negative geotropism, you may not be surprised to learn, is the tendency of shoots to grow upwards.
5. Mumps
6. Chasuble
7. *The Importance of Being Earnest*
8. Carl Linnaeus. Father of the taxonomic naming system used for all living things.
9. Zephaniah. In terms of the actual ordering of the Old Testament it comes between Habukkuk and Haggai.
10. *The Book of Taliesin*. Kept at the National Library of Wales. Deep Purple released their record of the same title in 1968.
11. Ellen (Nelly) Ternan. She was an actress, twenty-seven years younger than Dickens, for whom he left his wife Catherine in 1858.
12. Robin Hood
13. Paddington
14. Matrix
15. Extra-terrestrial intelligence – or words to that effect. The letters stand for the Centre for the Study of Extra-Terrestrial Intelligence.
16. Rwanda. Her story was told in a film, *Gorillas in the Mist*, in which Dr Fossey was played by Sigourney Weaver.
17. Paris. *Lutetia*, from *lutum*, mud.
18. Clive James
19. Positron
20. Master of the King's Musick
21. Organs that produce sound when rubbed together – such as the wings of crickets
22. The Trojan horse
23. (John Wilmot, 2nd Earl of) Rochester
24. Sun Yat-Sen

25. Rouen

26. Wilfred Brambell. His role as Albert Steptoe was already well-established, having first been seen in 1962.

27. Long Island in New York State

28. Ruth Rendell

29. 1948

30. Mob (from *mobile vulgus*)

31. Wild Bill Hickok, real name James Butler Hickok. The saloon was at Deadwood in South Dakota Territory.

32. Game Theory

33. Lord Reith

34. Harlem

35. Palladium

36. The Bow Street Runners

37. Kinder Scout

38. Lorenz Hart and Oscar Hammerstein II

39. Grendel. They are also plagued by Grendel's mother.

40. Salt

Quiz 13

1. The British singer Brinsley Forde, who fronted the reggae band Aswad, began his showbusiness career as a teenager as part of the ensemble cast of which children's TV programme?

2. The vineyards of Chateauneuf-du-Pape are in the valley of which major French river?

3. The world's first purpose-built airport, officially opened in 1920, was located in, and named after, which London suburb?

4. In the human body, the masseters are pairs of muscles, located where?

5. Which Scottish-born novelist, who died in 2006, based her best-known fictional character on a real person named Christina Kay, who was her schoolteacher when she was eleven?

6. Which name is shared by the 18th century author of *The State of the Prisons in England and Wales* and the man who served as Prime Minister of Australia between 1996 and 2007?

7. What name was given between 1925 and 1961 to the Russian city which had previously been known as Tsaritsyn and would later be called Volgograd?

8. Which American journalist and sage, in a publication entitled *A Book of Burlesques*, defined Puritanism as 'the haunting fear that someone, somewhere, may be happy'?

9. Shostakovich's opera *Katerina Ismaylova*, produced in 1962, was a revised version of which earlier work, which had been condemned and banned by Stalin in the 1930s?

10. In physics, what name is given to the principle, formulated by Werner Heisenberg, that states the impossibility of specifying precisely both the position and simultaneous momentum of a particle?

11. If something is described as amygdaloid, it means it is shaped like what?

12. A John Masefield novel of 1926, called *Odtaa*, is an adventure story set in a South American state during a revolution. What do the five letters of its title, ODTAA, stand for?

13. Which character in Shakespeare has the most lines in a single play without being the character named in its title?

14. In a survey in the early 2000s to find the most frequently played pop songs ever on British radio, both the top place and the runner-up spot were taken by songs containing the word 'Fandango' in their lyrics. Can you name them both?

15. Which one of the castles that form the group known as the 'Iron Ring', built in the 13th century by Edward I on the Welsh coast, stands on the island of Anglesey?

16. The last two individuals of which species of seabird were thought to have been discovered in June 1844 on Eldey Island, south-west of Iceland, by a group of Icelandic fishermen who subsequently killed them?

17. The word 'myriad' is derived from the ancient Greek for a specific number. Which number?

18. Which Finnish athlete, nicknamed the 'Flying Finn', won gold medals in both the men's 5,000 metres and 10,000 metres, at two successive Olympic Games in 1972 and 1976?

19. Someone called Mr Chicken was the last known private resident of which famous address?

20. Which Italian fashion designer coined the term 'shocking pink'?

Answers on page 110

21. In a 1946 newspaper article, who wrote about an imaginary pub called 'The Moon Under Water', which for him summed up the ideal features of an English public house?

22. *Cardiac Arrest, Bodies* and *Line of Duty* are among the hit TV series created by which British television writer, producer and former doctor?

23. Which Johannesburg suburb – the location of Lilliesleaf Farm, where African National Congress leaders were arrested in 1963 – lent its name to the trial of Nelson Mandela and others, who were charged with 221 acts of sabotage?

24. Where in the human body would you find Bowman's capsules, named after the 19th century English surgeon and histologist Sir William Bowman?

25. Eustasy is a phenomenon currently much occupying oceanographers and environmentalists. What is eustasy?

26. When it started as a single division in 1888, how many teams contested the very first English Football League?

27. Dirty, Snoopy, Biggo-Ego and Awful are among the names considered, but rejected, for which group of cartoon characters?

28. Which actress, having the good fortune to be bilingual, was able to dub her own voice for her character, Fiona, in the French release of the 1994 film *Four Weddings and a Funeral*?

29. According to the American humourist Will Rogers, 'The Income Tax has made more liars out of the American people than...' what?

30. What were Eric Morecambe and Ernie Wise's real surnames?

31. The ornate pink 18th century palace known as Hawa Mahal, or the Hall of the Winds, is a landmark of which Indian city?

32. The pioneering British scientists Sir Joseph Banks, Sir William Herschel and Sir Humphry Davy all died within a few years of one another – in which decade?

33. Which bestselling novel, first published in 1972, includes chapters entitled 'The Departure', 'The Crow and the Beanfield' and 'The Story of the King's Lettuce'?

34. The sum of the internal angles of a triangle is 180 degrees: what is the sum of the internal angles of a hexagon?

35. The first winner of the Booker Prize, on its inauguration in 1969, was a writer who also happened to be the Controller of BBC Radio Three at the time. The winning novel was called *Something to Answer For*. Who was the writer?

36. Arundel Castle in West Sussex is the principal seat of which member of the nobility?

37. On a standard grand piano keyboard of 88 keys, how many are black?

38. If Eros is no.433, Vesta is no.4, Mathilde is no.253 and Johncleese is no.9618 – what are they all?

39. In botany, the adjective 'nyctanthous' describes what type of plants?

40. The 1980s television sitcom *'Allo 'Allo* parodied characters and situations from which slightly earlier BBC drama series, set in Nazi-occupied Belgium?

Answers on page 110

Answers to Quiz 13

1. *(Here Come) The Double Deckers*. It was first screened in 1971.

2. The Rhône

3. Croydon

4. The face (accept jaw) – they are used in chewing and raising the lower jaw

5. (Dame) Muriel Spark – the character was Miss Jean Brodie

6. John Howard (the earlier one giving his name to the Howard League for Penal Reform)

7. Stalingrad

8. H. L. Mencken

9. *Lady Macbeth of the Mtzensk District*

10. The (Heisenberg) Uncertainty Principle or Principle of Indeterminacy

11. An almond

12. 'One damn thing after another' (Yes, really…)

13. Iago – in Othello. He has 1117 lines to Othello's 888.

14. 'Bohemian Rhapsody' (by Queen) and 'A Whiter Shade of Pale' (by Procol Harum)

15. Beaumaris

16. The Great Auk

17. Ten thousand

18. Lasse Viren

19. Downing Street

20. Elsa Schiaparelli

21. George Orwell

22. Jed Mercurio

23. Rivonia

24. The kidneys

25. The process of global change in sea levels

26. Twelve. They were Accrington, Aston Villa, Blackburn Rovers, Bolton Wanderers, Burnley, Derby County, Everton, Notts County, Preston North End, Stoke City, West Bromwich Albion, Wolverhampton Wanderers.

27. The Seven Dwarfs – in the 1937 Disney Film *Snow White and the Seven Dwarfs*

28. Kristin Scott Thomas. She received the OBE in 2003 and was admitted to the French *Légion d'Honneur* in 2005.

29. Golf

30. Bartholomew and Wiseman

31. Jaipur

32. The 1820s – 1820, 1822 and 1829 respectively

33. *Watership Down* by Richard Adams

34. 720 degrees

35. P. H. Newby (Howard Newby)

36. The Duke of Norfolk

37. Thirty-six

38. Asteroids

39. Those which flower at night. Evening primrose is an example.

40. *Secret Army*

Quiz 14

1. In which book of the Bible will you find the story of Samson and Delilah?

2. In physics, what name is given to the fourth state of matter, which displays distinct properties that are quite different from those of solids, liquids and gases?

3. Because of an association with a particular piece of Handel's music, the main character Pip in Dickens' *Great Expectations* is given the nickname 'Handel' by his friend Herbert Pocket. Which piece of music is it?

4. The peculiarly-named thoroughfare 'Whip-Ma-Whop-Ma-Gate' is to be found in which English city?

5. Which two politicians' names were combined in the word 'butskellism', a term denoting a pragmatic agreement over a policy between two opposing parties?

6. 'Woke up one morning half asleep, with all my blankets in a heap' are the opening words of which pop song, the first ever to be played on Radio 1?

7. What's the name of the soldier with whom Tolstoy's Anna Karenina falls in love, their affair tragically ending in her death?

8. Which term for a megalith is derived from the Welsh words for 'long stone'?

9. In physics, which term is used to describe a particular temperature and pressure at which three different phases of one substance – normally solid, liquid and gas – can co-exist?

10. The Marquis de Sillery has been credited with being the first man to ship which drink to London, some time in the 17th century?

11. Decaying uranium finally becomes an isotope of which metal?

12. Which English horse racecourse at one time alternated with Silverstone as the venue for the British motor racing Grand Prix?

13. Legend has it that the weather on St Swithin's Day determines the weather for the next forty days. On which date does St Swithin's Day fall?

14. Edith Cavell, Dietrich Bonhoeffer, Raoul Wallenberg, Martin Luther King Jr, Robert Kennedy, Nelson Mandela, Dame Cicely Saunders and Aung San Suu Kyi are the eight subjects of *Courage: Eight Portraits*, a book published in 2007 by which politician?

15. Two of the best-remembered poets of the First World War, Siegfried Sassoon and Wilfred Owen, met in 1917 whilst being treated for shell-shock at which hospital in Edinburgh?

16. In physics, the term 'magic numbers' refers to the numbers of protons or neutrons generally present in a stable nucleus. What are the first two magic numbers?

17. Thomas Gainsborough's painting of the young Jonathan Buttall, now to be found in the Huntington Art Gallery in California, is usually known by what name?

18. Which incident in a Shakespeare play prompted Dr Johnson to write that he was 'so shocked by [it] that I know not whether I ever endured to read again the last scenes of the play till I undertook to revise them as an editor'?

19. 'Hidden beneath a layer of creamy, golden-crusted haricot beans in a deep, wide earthen pot, [it] contains garlicky pork sausages, smoked bacon, salt pork, a wing or leg of preserved goose, perhaps a piece of mutton, or a couple of pig's feet, or half a duck, and some chunks of pork rind.' This rich-sounding concoction is how Elizabeth David described which rustic traditional French dish?

Answers on page 116

20. Linus Pauling is the only man to have won two Nobel Prizes in different disciplines. Which two?

21. Pianosa, an island off the west coast of Italy, is the setting for which novel first published in 1961?

22. Which English word meaning 'self-denying' or 'temperate of appetite' is unusual in containing all five vowels, used once each, in alphabetical order?

23. What was the stage-name of the music hall star born George Edward Wade in Herne Hill in 1869, and most closely associated with the song 'If You Were The Only Girl In The World'?

24. While he was in prison for his part in a riot, in the 1780s, William Addis fashioned the first commercially successful example of a now-common household implement, out of bone and animal hair. What implement?

25. 'Ol' Blood and Guts' is a nickname associated with which US Army General of the Second World War?

26. The only time tanks have been deployed against the public in mainland Britain was in January 1919 in George Square – in which city?

27. The singer and broadcaster Guy Garvey fronts which British rock band?

28. Although it's not the state capital, which is the largest city in the US state of Nebraska?

29. 'The Old Lady of Threadneedle Street', an affectionate term for the Bank of England, was coined in a caption to a cartoon of 1797 by which satirical artist and illustrator?

30. In the 1930s Mahatma Gandhi led a symbolic protest march against the government's tax on which commodity?

31. Following the death of its composer, which unfinished opera was completed in 1926 by Franco Alfano?

32. Which technological innovation, invented in 1876, was described by Ambrose Bierce as 'an invention of the devil which abrogates some of the advantages of making a disagreeable person keep his distance'?

33. In a phrase coined by the 18th century poet Edward Young, what do you do if you 'join the great majority'?

34. In September 2008, the US government announced it was taking control of two huge mortgage companies in order to help shore up the economy: one was called Fannie Mae, what was the other called?

35. In 1911, the poet Guillaume Apollinaire was questioned as a suspect by French authorities investigating which major crime?

36. *Garrulus glandarius* is the Latin name of which common member of the crow family?

37. What is the title of Damien Hirst's controversial artwork featuring a lamb in formaldehyde, first seen in public in 1994?

38. Which small type of French cake was supposedly named by Louis XV in honour of his father-in-law's cook?

39. In a cultural initiative of the Austrian Presidency of the EU in 2006, typical cakes or sweetmeats from all [then] 27 of the member countries were presented in cafés. Belgium contributed waffles, Cyprus baklava and Italy tiramisu. What was chosen to represent the UK?

40. Which five-letter word, now familiar in a quite different context, is used in archaeology for 'a monumental gateway to Egyptian temples or palaces, built in stone and usually decorated with relief figures and hieroglyphs'?

Answers on page 116

Answers to Quiz 14

1. Judges
2. Plasma
3. 'The Harmonious Blacksmith'. Pip grew up in a blacksmith's forge.
4. York. One theory is that it was so-called because cattle were 'whipped in' on their way to slaughter in the nearby butcheries of The Shambles.
5. Richard Austen 'Rab' Butler and Hugh Gaitskell
6. 'Flowers in the Rain' by the Move
7. Count Vronsky
8. Menhir
9. The triple point
10. Champagne
11. Lead
12. Aintree
13. 15th July
14. Gordon Brown
15. Craiglockhart (War) Hospital. The building still stands but is now part of Napier University.
16. 2 and 8
17. The *Blue Boy*
18. The death of Cordelia in *King Lear*
19. Cassoulet
20. Chemistry and Peace
21. *Catch-22* by Joseph Heller
22. Abstemious
23. George Robey
24. A toothbrush
25. General George S. Patton
26. Glasgow. It was known as 'Bloody Friday' – when a general strike in the city was crushed.
27. Elbow
28. Omaha. The capital is Lincoln.

29. James Gillray

30. Salt

31. Puccini's *Turandot*

32. The telephone

33. Die ('Death joins us to the great majority'). It is one of the synonyms for death which Monty Python's Parrot Sketch fails to include.

34. Freddie Mac

35. The theft of the *Mona Lisa*. The real perpetrator was an Italian house-painter, and former worker at the Louvre, called Vincenzo Peruggia.

36. The Jay

37. *Away from the Flock*

38. Madeleine – after Madeleine Paumier. The father-in-law was the King of Poland.

39. Shortbread

40. Pylon

Quiz 15

1. What name is given to the zone, or those parts of the Earth and its atmosphere, able to support life?

2. The architect Frank Matcham specialised in the design of what sort of building?

3. Which two Greek words, meaning 'the image of a King', formed the title of the collection of writings supposedly composed by the incarcerated Charles I, and published on the day of his burial in 1649?

4. Which British racing driver was killed in a road accident off the racing track, just months after winning the world driver's championship in 1958?

5. Which branch of mathematics takes its name from the Latin word for a pebble?

6. How many gallons of beer are there in a firkin?

7. The koala bear is not a bear. To which family of animals does it belong?

8. Discovered in 1787 by William Herschel, what's the largest moon of Uranus?

9. The mythological lovers Pyramus and Thisbe, whose story is performed by the mechanicals in Shakespeare's *A Midsummer Night's Dream*, belonged to which ancient civilisation?

10. In which borough of New York will you find the city's Botanical Gardens, and the Poe Cottage, the last home of the writer Edgar Allan Poe before his mysterious death in 1849?

11. In Poe's story 'The Cask of Amontillado', what is the not-very-fortunate fate of the character Fortunato?

12. What was the title of the film western, directed by John Huston and released in 1961, that featured Clark Gable and Marilyn Monroe, both in the final roles of their careers?

13. Violet Gibson was known for her attempt to assassinate which prominent figure in 1926?

14. In an allusion to his ancestor Edward the Confessor, which of the eight later King Edwards was nicknamed 'Edward the Caresser'?

15. Describing whose funeral, in New York in 1974, did Alastair Cooke write: 'When the ten thousand people inside were asked to stand and pray, there was a vast rustling sound as awesome, it struck me, as that of the several million bats whooshing out of the Carlsbad Caverns in New Mexico at the first blush of dawn'?

16. In which German city will you find a statue by Gerhard Marcks which shows 'a cock standing on a cat standing on a dog standing on a donkey'?

17. What was the name of the Russian coalminer lauded by the Communist regime, whose name became a byword for prodigious (and highly improbable) feats of productivity?

18. *Sunflower*, *Surf's Up* and *Holland* were consecutive LP releases, in the early 1970s, by which multi-million-selling pop group?

19. Which is the only one of the chemical elements known as the halogens that is liquid at normal room temperatures?

20. The opening line of every episode of which US television police series, which originally ran from 1951-59, was: 'Ladies and gentlemen, the story you are about to see is true. The names have been changed to protect the innocent'?

Answers on page 122

21. Harry Longabaugh was the real name of which figure from the Wild West?

22. The coccyx, the bony lower end of the spinal column, takes its name from an ancient Greek word for which bird?

23. Who was the first British Prime Minister to appear in a *live* television broadcast?

24. The three spires of which English cathedral are nicknamed the 'Ladies of the Vale'?

25. A 'Decembrist' was a name given to a member of a revolutionary group called the 'Northern Society', opposed to the accession of which Russian Tsar in 1825?

26. The music of the 1883 opera *Lakmé*, containing the 'Flower Duet' which often appears among the most popular classical pieces in surveys, was composed by whom?

27. Although she's universally known as Anne Frank, the name 'Anne' is actually a pet-name or abbreviation of the diarist's actual first name, which was – what?

28. In cell biology, what name is usually given to the jelly-like matter within the cell, but outside the nucleus, which contains the organelles of the cell and in which protein synthesis takes place?

29. Often changing his name to reflect the development of his various styles, which Japanese artist, born in 1760, is best known for the woodblock print *The Great Wave Off Kanagawa*?

30. When Margaret Thatcher won the leadership of the Conservative Party in February 1975, she stood against four male candidates and won almost twice as many votes as her nearest rival in the ballot, 146 to his 79. Who was that runner-up?

31. Which old Spanish coin was initially worth two pistoles?

32. Which physicist and mathematician, born in 1642, described himself as 'like a boy playing on the seashore ... whilst the great ocean of truth lay all undiscovered before' him?

33. *Critical Path* and *Operating Manual for Spaceship Earth* are works by which American architect and environmentalist who died in 1983?

34. If a regular rectangular box has sides of 5 centimetres, 6 centimetres and 8 centimetres, what is its volume in cubic centimetres?

35. Which book ends with the line: 'It was not till they had examined the rings that they recognised who it was'?

36. The wives of which jazz musician, who was married no fewer than eight times, included the actresses Lana Turner and Ava Gardner, and the novelist Kathleen Winsor?

37. 'God is my oath' or 'God is my abundance' is the literal meaning of which girls' name in common use?

38. *The Logic of Scientific Discovery*, originally published in 1934, is the English title of a seminal work by which Austrian-born British philosopher?

39. Fallingwater, a private house built above the Bear Run Stream in rural Pennsylvania, is the work of which great American architect?

40. Pythias, the ward of Hermias of Atarneus, married which Greek philosopher in the city of Assos around 345 BC?

Answers on page 122

1. Biosphere

2. Theatres/music halls. The London Coliseum is a notable example of his work.

3. *Eikon Basilike*

4. Mike Hawthorn

5. Calculus

6. Nine

7. Marsupials

8. Titania

9. Babylon/The Babylonians

10. The Bronx

11. He is bricked up in a cellar and left to die

12. *The Misfits*

13. Mussolini. She was the daughter of Lord Ashbourne. The single shot she fired, in the Piazza del Campidoglio in Rome, left Mussolini with a bandaged nose.

14. Edward VII

15. Duke Ellington's

16. Bremen. The statue depicts the 'Bremen Town Musicians' of the Grimm Brothers' fairy tale.

17. (Alexei) Stakhanov (in English, a person notable for amazing output is still sometimes called a 'Stakhanovite')

18. The Beach Boys

19. Bromine

20. *Dragnet*

21. The Sundance Kid

22. Cuckoo

23. Neville Chamberlain – on returning from Munich in 1938

24. Lichfield

25. Nicholas I

26. Leo Delibes

27. Annelies. She was Annelies Marie Frank.

28. Cytoplasm, or Cytosol

29. (Katsushika) Hokusai

30. William Whitelaw. (The other runners were Jim Prior, Sir Geoffrey Howe and John Peyton.)

31. A Doubloon

32. Isaac Newton

33. Richard Buckminster Fuller

34. 240 cubic centimetres

35. *The Picture of Dorian Gray* by Oscar Wilde

36. Artie Shaw

37. Elizabeth. Common and royal use, you might say.

38. (Sir) Karl Popper

39. Frank Lloyd Wright

40. Aristotle. She bore him one daughter before she died at an early age.

Quiz 16

1. Which children's writer and illustrator, whose family fled Hitler's Germany in the 1930s, created the bestselling children's books *The Tiger Who Came to Tea* and the series about a forgetful cat called Mog?

2. Based on a folk tune, the orchestral work *Five Variants on Dives and Lazarus* was written in 1939 by which English composer?

3. Lavrentiy Beria, executed in 1953, was the head of which organisation during the Second World War?

4. Which King of England reigned between the years 978 and 1016, succeeding his father Edgar and his half-brother Edward?

5. Which journal, still in existence, was founded in 1823 by the Devon-born MP, coroner and social health reformer Thomas Wakley?

6. Lady Jane Grey got married shortly before she became Queen of England in July 1553 – so what was her actual married name at the time of her death?

7. Which Irish Taoiseach signed the Hillsborough Agreement in 1985?

8. In the *Spiderman* series of Marvel comics, Peter Parker is a freelance photographer for which newspaper?

9. In the classic board game of *Cluedo*, the plant toxicologist Dr Orchid was introduced to the cast of suspects in 2016, becoming the first new character in the game for more than sixty years. Which of the six original characters did she replace?

10. The 'Droeshout engraving', the 'Janssen bust' and the 'Chandos portrait' are all believed to be likenesses of which historical figure?

11. In Australian Rules football, how many points are awarded for a goal?

12. Which famous 20th century novel opens with these words: 'To the red country and part of the grey country of Oklahoma the last rains came gently, and they did not cut the scarred earth'?

13. In 2008, in genealogical research for the BBC television programme *Who Do You Think You Are?*, which political figure discovered a hitherto-unsuspected blood tie to the British Royal Family?

14. The villages of Reeth, Gunnerside and Keld are to be found in which of the North Yorkshire dales?

15. What is an 'Eton crop'?

16. The 'address' of a site on the worldwide web is often referred to as its 'URL'. What do the letters URL stand for in this context?

17. What's the surname of the brother and sister, both noted Hollywood actors, who played a pair of fictional siblings in the 2001 film thriller *Donnie Darko*?

18. In the 1930s, the Nazi regime justified its drive for expansion of its territory by the argument that the country was over-crowded and needed 'living space' to give its people a comfortable life. What German word meaning 'living space' was used in this context?

19. In a novel of 1889, the best-known work of its author who was born in the West Midlands, there is a comical incident in which the protagonists manage to lose their way in the Hampton Court maze. Which novel is that?

20. According to legend, the ninth-century Pope officially known as Pope John the Eighth was unique in what respect?

Answers on page 128

21. Which of the Seven Wonders of the Ancient World was to be found at Halicarnassus in present-day Turkey, which was also the birthplace of Herodotus?

22. Somersby Rectory in Lincolnshire was the birthplace, in 1809, of which English poet?

23. As opposed to plankton – minute aquatic organisms which drift – which word describes the ecological division of aquatic animals that swim actively and by their own efforts?

24. What nationality was the 20th century composer Gerald Finzi?

25. The word 'Pavonine', sometimes applied to a dandy or flamboyantly-dressed person, actually means 'having the appearance of, or being similar to' – what?

26. In which 19th century novel does the hero meet up with two conmen who call themselves the Duke of Bridgewater and 'Looy the Seventeen'?

27. A classic and much-reproduced newspaper cartoon from the First World War features the caption 'Well, if you knows of a better 'ole, go to it.' Who drew the cartoon?

28. Which two-word term was coined by Thomas Rymer, the author of *Tragedies of the Last Age Considered*, to describe the idea that, in a work of literature, good characters should be rewarded and evil characters punished?

29. What name was given to the first-ever line of the London underground, opened in January 1863 and running originally from Bishop's Road to Farringdon Street?

30. Which silver-white metalloid element, discovered by Franz Joseph Muller von Richtenstein in 1782, has the atomic number 52 and takes its name from the Latin word for 'earth'?

31. Casey Kasem, in addition to being one of America's most popular disc jockeys, was also known for providing the voice for which cartoon character created by Hanna-Barbera?

32. On which of the twenty or so Hawaiian islands will you find the modern State capital, Honolulu, as well as the former base of the US Pacific Fleet at Pearl Harbor?

33. The principle that 'Entities are not to be multiplied beyond necessity' is known by what name?

34. The Indian-born British physician Ronald Ross was the first to identify the means of transmission of which deadly disease?

35. Which writer's first published novel *The Grass Is Singing* dates from 1950?

36. Two Italian composers wrote operas called *La Bohème*, both based on episodes from an 1851 book by Henri Murger. Puccini's is the better known; who wrote the other?

37. In which decade of the twentieth century were the following phrases first recorded in the Oxford English Dictionary: nouvelle cuisine, paternity leave, no-go area, and passive smoking?

38. Living in Manchester, the Irish sisters Mary and Lizzie Burns became successively the mistresses of which philosopher who married the latter on her deathbed in 1878?

39. Which artist was commissioned by *The Strand* Magazine to illustrate the first series of the Sherlock Holmes stories by Sir Arthur Conan Doyle?

40. Which British pop group had eight Top Ten hits in a row in the early 1970s, all of whose titles were deliberately misspelled?

Answers on page 128

Answers to Quiz 16

1. Judith Kerr
2. Ralph Vaughan Williams
3. The NKVD or The People's Commissariat for Internal Affairs – the Soviet secret police
4. Ethelred II ('The Unready')
5. *The Lancet*
6. Lady Jane Dudley. Her husband was Lord Guilford Dudley, who had his head cut off about an hour before her own execution.
7. Dr Garret FitzGerald
8. *The Daily Bugle*
9. Mrs White
10. William Shakespeare
11. Six – a player can also score a 'behind' for one point
12. *The Grapes of Wrath* by John Steinbeck
13. Boris Johnson
14. Swaledale
15. A hairstyle – a very short, slicked-down version of the crop hairstyle, especially popular in the 1920s when it was worn by Josephine Baker among others.
16. Uniform Resource Locator
17. (Jake and Maggie) Gyllenhaal
18. *Lebensraum*
19. *Three Men in a Boat* by Jerome K. Jerome
20. She was female. Otherwise known as 'Pope Joan', she supposedly ruled for two years, but was killed by a furious mob when she went into childbirth during a procession.
21. The Tomb of Mausolus
22. Alfred, Lord Tennyson
23. Nekton
24. British/English – born in London in 1901, he was probably best known for his settings for voice and piano of the poetry of Hardy, Milton and Wordsworth.
25. A peacock

26. *The Adventures of Huckleberry Finn* – by Mark Twain. 'Looy' hasn't quite grasped the nickname of his partner in crime, and refers to him as the 'Duke of Bilgewater'.

27. (Charles) Bruce Bairnsfather

28. Poetic Justice

29. The Metropolitan Line

30. Tellurium – from *tellus*

31. Shaggy (in the *Scooby Doo* cartoons)

32. Oahu

33. Occam's Razor or The Law of Parsimony or The Principle of Economy. It gets its name from the English medieval philosopher William of Occam.

34. Malaria – by mosquitoes of the genus *Anapholes*

35. Doris Lessing

36. Leoncavallo

37. The 1970s (1975, 1973, 1971, and 1971 respectively)

38. Friedrich Engels

39. Sidney Paget. It was Paget who gave Holmes his famous deerstalker hat.

40. Slade. Their hits included: 'Take Me Bak Ome', 'Mama Weer All Crazee Now' and 'Cum On Feel The Noize'. They eventually started spelling their titles correctly, and (coincidentally or not) that marked the start of their commercial decline.

Quiz 17

1. The films *Strangers on a Train* and *The Talented Mr Ripley* are based on stories by which American writer?

2. The boxer James J. Corbett, who won the World Heavyweight title in 1892 from John L. Sullivan, was known by what nickname?

3. Another famous person often known by the same nickname, the singer Jim Reeves, was killed in a plane crash near Nashville in the summer of 1964 – and two years later an unreleased 'demo' recording he had made was dusted off, with a new instrumental backing, to give him a posthumous no.1 hit. What was the song's title?

4. What's the name of the plumed serpent god of the Aztec and Toltec civilisations, associated with the morning and evening star?

5. What term is applied to the average period of the revolution of the Earth with respect to fixed stars, a unit of time longer than a conventional year by twenty minutes and twenty three seconds?

6. *A Love Supreme*, *Crescent* and *Giant Steps* are among the albums of which jazz saxophonist, who died in 1967?

7. Rising to just over 1,700 feet, the hill known as Dunkery Beacon is part of which English National Park?

8. The French film director Claude Berri won many awards for his two-part interpretation of the novels of Marcel Pagnol in the 1980s, both films noted for their beautiful cinematography and generous budgets. The first part was entitled *Jean de Florette*; what was the title of the second?

9. *Trouble at Willow Gables* is the title of a pastiche novel set in a girls' school, written, but never published during his lifetime, by which respected poet and novelist?

10. In the electromagnetic spectrum, what is found between X-rays and visible light?

1. *Assault On A Queen* was a 1966 adventure film starring Frank Sinatra, that was a critical and box-office flop. Who, or what, was the Queen mentioned in the title?

2. Mary Queen of Scots' motto, *En ma fin git ma commencement*, which she embroidered on her cloth of estate, is echoed by the final line in a poem of 1940 – by which writer?

3. Lipase, an enzyme which catalyses the breakdown of fats into fatty acids and glycerol in the small intestine, is secreted by which organ of the body?

4. What was the name of the London thoroughfare, renamed Milton Street In 1830, which Dr Johnson described as having been home to 'writers of small histories, dictionaries, and temporary poems'?

5. In which European city did the architect Walter Gropius found the Bauhaus school of design in 1919?

6. In medicine, what is measured by a spirometer?

7. In Iraq, the rivers Tigris and Euphrates unite before they flow into the The Gulf. What is the name of the waterway formed by their union?

8. 'How Tom Brangwen Married A Polish Lady' is the title of the opening chapter of which 20th century English novel?

9. Which word, meaning a handsome and promiscuous man, was originally the name of a character in Nicholas Rowe's play of 1703, *The Fair Penitent*?

20. In 2010 a man known as Comrade Duch became the first person ever to be convicted for the systematic and horrifying crimes against humanity committed in the 1970s, in which country?

Answers on page 134

21. What, specifically, is feared by those who have the condition acrophobia?

22. To which writer is the quotation attributed: 'An archaeologist is the best husband any woman can have – the older she gets, the more interested he is in her'?

23. In fish, the lateral line system is a sensory organ used by the fish for what purpose?

24. Rising to 14 and a half thousand feet, in the Sierra Nevada of California, which is the highest mountain in the contiguous United States – in other words, outside Alaska?

25. Which name comes next in the following sequence: Heinrich Brüning, Franz von Papen, Kurt von Schleicher – ?

26. Which resonant acronym was widely used for the committee set up by the Republican Party in the early 1970s, to re-elect Richard Nixon as President of the United States?

27. Which sparsely-populated island, roughly midway between the Orkneys and mainland Shetland, lends its name to the shipping forecast sea area in whose waters it lies?

28. The adjective 'diphyodont' refers to which characteristic of mammals?

29. Which British Prime Minister was the last to have been born in the 19th century?

30. What mishap befell the canvas entitled *Le Bateau*, by Henri Matisse, when it was initially displayed at the New York Museum of Modern Art in 1961?

31. Which fruit derives its name from an old Aztec word for a testicle?

32. 'Sparrow' is the literal meaning of the name of which Chinese game?

33. Frank Sinatra and Donna Reed both won acting Oscars, and Fred Zinnemann was named Best Director, for which 1953 adaptation of a novel by James Jones?

34. What was the name of the primeval supercontinent believed to have existed some 250 million years ago, and which split into the two land masses known as Gondwanaland and Laurasia?

35. Which country made Jonas Furrer its first President in 1848, and has changed its President on an annual basis ever since?

36. The title of a 1966 Jerry Herman Broadway musical, and that of a Jane Austen novel first published in 1815, are anagrams of one another. Can you name them both?

37. Who was the widow of the Roman tributary, King Prasutagus?

38. The Revolution and the New Power Generation were names given to backing bands of which musician at different stages of his career?

39. Koplik's Spots, occurring in the mouth as bluish-white specks on the inner side of the cheeks, are an early symptom of which viral disease?

40. What was the name of the successor to Mohammed, known as al-Siddiq or 'the Upright', who became the first caliph of the Muslim world in the year 632?

Answers on page 134

1. Patricia Highsmith

2. 'Gentleman Jim'

3. 'Distant Drums' – written by Cindy Walker

4. Quetzalcoatl

5. A sidereal year. It is sometimes defined as 365.256 mean solar days.

6. John Coltrane

7. Exmoor

8. *Manon des Sources/Manon of the Spring*. The films starred Gérard Depardieu and Yves Montand.

9. Philip Larkin

10. Ultraviolet Light

11. (The ocean liner) *The Queen Mary*. The plot involved Sinatra, and partners-in-crime, salvaging a wrecked German U-boat and using it to hijack the liner. The film is perhaps only memorable for a score by Duke Ellington.

12. T. S. Eliot. It means 'In my end is my beginning' – which is the final line of 'East Coker', the second of his Four Quartets.

13. The pancreas

14. Grub Street. It's still there, close to Moorgate Station.

15. Weimar

16. Lung capacity

17. The Shatt-al-Arab

18. *The Rainbow* by D. H. Lawrence

19. Lothario

20. Cambodia. His real name was Kang Kek Iew. He admitted responsibility for the torture and execution of thousands of inmates in Cambodia's notorious prisons.

21. Heights

22. Dame Agatha Christie – who was married to the archaeologist Sir Max Mallowan for 44 years

23. Sensing movement, or pressure changes in the water – from predators and other objects it needs to be aware of.

24. Mount Whitney. Extraordinarily, its summit is only 76 miles from the lowest point in the whole of North America, in Death Valley.

25. Adolf Hitler. They were successive Chancellors of Germany in the 1930s.

26. C.R.E.E.P. (the Committee for the Re-election of the President). Its members were heavily implicated in the Watergate scandal and, although internally it was known as the C.R.P., its enemies preferred the expanded form, C.R.E.E.P.

27. Fair Isle

28. The development of two successive sets of teeth during their lifetime

29. Harold Macmillan (born 1894)

30. It was hung upside down. Nobody noticed for 47 days.

31. Avocado

32. Mah-Jong

33. *From Here to Eternity*

34. Pangaea

35. Switzerland

36. *Mame* and *Emma*

37. Boudicca/Boadicea

38. Prince

39. Measles

40. Abu Bakr

Quiz 18

1. Alexei Leonev was the first man, and Edward H. White the first American, to do what?

2. Which two actors played the Likely Lads, Terry and Bob, in the BBC television sitcoms of the 1960s and 70s?

3. Only one whole square number under 100 is the sum of the preceding two square numbers. Which number?

4. Which small tool, used for boring holes, shares its name with a cocktail containing lime juice and either gin or vodka?

5. In Scandinavian mythology, Urd, Verdandi and Skuld were three giant goddesses who presided over the fates of both men and gods. How were they known collectively?

6. Although usually known for her roles in musical extravaganzas, which actress won her only Best Actress Oscar for her dramatic role in the film *Kitty Foyle* in 1940?

7. The art movement exemplified by 20th century Dutch artists such as Piet Mondrian, Gerrit Rietveld and Theo van Doesburg, is often known by what Dutch name?

8. Firzan, meaning 'counsellor', was the original Arabic name for which chess piece?

9. In October 2008, the first UN-sanctioned auction for nearly ten years took place in Southern Africa – of which substance?

10. The serial killer Patrick Bateman is the narrator of which controversial and globally-successful novel of 1991?

11. Which soft felt hat, with a low crown and wide brim, supposedly derives its name, in a punning way, from the fact that it doesn't have a 'nap'?

12. Including the innermost, how many rings are there in a standard archery target?

13. In the 1975 ITV dramatisation of *The Naked Civil Servant*, which actor played Quentin Crisp?

14. The 'Big Three' meeting at Yalta in the Crimea in February 1945, between Churchill, Roosevelt and Stalin, was the second conference between these three wartime leaders. Which Middle Eastern city hosted the first of their meetings in 1943?

15. The former John Street, in Hampstead in London, was renamed to reflect the street's association with which major poet who lived there between 1818 and 1820?

16. Blaisdon Red, Early Laxton, and Rivers' Early Prolific are varieties of which fruit?

17. What did the initials of the writer P. G. Wodehouse stand for?

18. Which Scottish border town gives its name to a regiment first mustered in 1650, which is the oldest Corps by continuous existence in the British Army?

19. To which great French cinema director did Steven Spielberg give a bit-part as a UFO expert, in the 1977 science-fiction film *Close Encounters of the Third Kind*?

20. Which English noun can mean both conscientious and industrious attention to a task, and a type of stagecoach?

21. In towns up and down the British Isles there are thoroughfares and squares with the street name 'The Butts'. Traditionally, this indicates that which activity once went on there?

Answers on page 140

22. In the opening chapters of which of Charles Dickens' novels is the corpse of a man named John Harmon found floating in the Thames, 'in an advanced state of decay, and much injured'?

23. Can you name the method of music education developed in the early 20th century by Emile Jacques Dalcroze, which uses movement to help the appreciation of music, and which gave its name to a pop group many decades later?

24. In botany, what defines a leaf, flower or fruit described as 'sessile'?

25. The so-called Black Box, the unit containing an aeroplane's flight and voice recorders, is usually painted what colour?

26. What's the family relationship between the writer of the screenplay of *Chitty Chitty Bang Bang*, and the writer of the recipe book *Voluptuous Delights – The Art of Eating a Little of What You Fancy*, published in 2008?

27. *The Great White Hope*, a 1970 film which starred James Earl Jones as a black boxer hounded for his relationship with a white woman, was based on the life of which real heavyweight champion?

28. What's the design on the jersey worn in the Tour de France cycle race by the rider designated 'King of the Mountains'?

29. Which state of the USA is the setting for Harper Lee's Pulitzer Prize-winning novel *To Kill a Mockingbird*?

30. What's the second letter of the Hebrew alphabet?

31. Reclaimed by India, by military force, fifty years ago in December 1961, the state of Goa was previously an enclave governed by which European country?

32. Which cocktail – made with white rum, lime juice and sugar syrup – takes its name from a beach resort near Santiago on the south coast of Cuba?

33. With a capacity of 150,000, the Rungrado May Day Stadium is reputedly the largest sporting venue in the world, and is situated in which East Asian country?

34. According to Daniel Defoe's *Tour of the Whole Island of Great Britain*, which town in County Durham contains 'nothing remarkable but dirt'?

35. According to *How To Be An Alien* by the Hungarian-born writer George Mikes, 'Continental people have sex lives; the English have…' what?

36. From 1821, Liberia was established by American interests as an African colony for freed slaves. Which African country was settled by the British for a similar purpose?

37. The writer and socialite Anne-Louise Germaine Necker, born in 1766, became one of the most celebrated figures in Paris before the French Revolution. Diplomats, writers, philosophers and even the Duke of Wellington fell under her spell. By what name does posterity remember her?

38. Of which Lerner and Loewe musical did Noel Coward say, 'It's about as long as *Parsifal* and not as funny'?

39. In a famous speech to the United States Congress in January 1941, Franklin Roosevelt outlined four basic freedoms: 'freedom of speech and expression', 'freedom of worship', 'freedom from want' – and which other?

40. What form of food poisoning gets its name from the Latin for a sausage?

Answers on page 140

Answers to Quiz 18

1. Walk in space – respectively, in March and June of 1965.

2. James Bolam and Rodney Bewes

3. 25 (which equals 9 + 16)

4. Gimlet

5. Norns

6. Ginger Rogers. Born Virginia Katherine McMath, the nickname by which she became known to the world was the result of her baby cousin's mispronunciation of 'Virginia' as 'Ginja' when she was small.

7. De Stijl ('The Style')

8. The Queen

9. (Elephant) Ivory

10. *American Psycho* by Bret Easton Ellis

11. The 'Wideawake' – popular in the American West, and widely associated with the Quaker movement in the 17th and 18th centuries.

12. Ten

13. John Hurt. ITV took on the series after the BBC proved too nervous to commission it, and it proved to be a memorable and much-talked-about TV event.

14. Tehran

15. John Keats – it's now called Keats Grove

16. Plum

17. Pelham Grenville – he was of course known to his friends as 'Plum'

18. Coldstream – the regiment is the Coldstream Guards

19. François Truffaut

20. Diligence. The stagecoach got its name in France, *diligence* having the connotation of speed and efficiency.

21. Archery

22. *Our Mutual Friend*

23. Eurythmics – also called eurhythmy, or sometimes Dalcroze after its inventor.

24. It has no stalk – but grows directly out of the stem of a plant

25. Bright orange

26. They are grandfather and granddaughter – Roald Dahl and Sophie Dahl respectively

27. Jack Johnson

28. White with red spots/polka dots

29. Alabama – in the fictional town of Maycomb

30. BET. Also, sometimes rendered as BETH or VET

31. Portugal

32. Daiquiri. The cocktail gets a mention in F. Scott Fitzgerald's *This Side of Paradise*, helping to induce hallucinations of a purple zebra amongst those who indulged too liberally in it.

33. North Korea. It's hard to be sure, because they won't let anyone from outside the country see it.

34. Darlington

35. Hot Water Bottles

36. Sierra Leone

37. Madame de Staël

38. *Camelot*

39. Freedom from fear

40. Botulism – the Latin word is *botulus*

Quiz 19

1. With the chemical formula Fe_2O_3, which ore is the world's most important source of iron?

2. The BBC Proms, founded in 1895, were held at which London venue until they moved to the Royal Albert Hall?

3. The 18th century portrait popularly known as *The Skating Minister* of the Edinburgh cleric the Reverend Robert Walker skating on Duddingston Loch, is by which painter?

4. Which ocean liner, the first ever to exceed a thousand feet in length, ended her days under the name of Lafayette while being converted into a Second World War troopship?

5. Which Holy Roman Emperor was one of the leaders of the Third Crusade in 1189, but drowned in a river before reaching the Holy Land?

6. Who was born at 17 Bruton Street, London W1, at 2.40 in the morning on the 21st April 1926?

7. A 'kit' is a tiny, high-pitched variety of which musical instrument used widely by dancing-masters between the 16th and 18th centuries?

8. Macfarlane Burnet, who discovered acquired immunological tolerance; Lawrence Bragg, a pioneer of X-ray crystallography and Howard Florey, who isolated and purified penicillin, are all Nobel laureates born in which country?

9. Which landmark of East Anglia owes its distinctive profile to the 14th century engineering work of Alan de Walsingham?

10. What's the present-day name of the capital city known until 1976 as Lourenço Marques?

11. Which form of transport was first developed in Yokohama in 1869 by the Reverend Jonathan Scobie, for the use of his invalid wife?

12. Which entertainer, whose real name was Daniel Patrick Carroll, was once described by Bob Hope as 'the most glamorous woman in the world'?

13. What is the Latin name for the element sodium, giving rise to its chemical formula Na?

14. The so-called 'Wicked Bible' was printed in 1631 by Barker and Lucas in Blackfriars in London, and its nickname arises from a misprint of some rather crucial words in Exodus chapter. What four-word phrase, in particular, is responsible for this Bible's notoriety?

15. Which word for a source of wealth, often associated with a large output from a mine, comes from a Spanish term for 'good weather'?

16. What is the name of the American golfer who, in 1971, became the first to win the UK, US and Canadian Opens in the same year?

17. The French term *houille blanche* and the German *weisse Kohle*, both literally meaning 'white coal', refer specifically to what?

18. In physics, what name is given to a tiny particle emitted from a radioactive nucleus during beta decay that specifically contains no charge?

19. *Oroonoko, or The Royal Slave*, is a work of fiction published in London in 1688, about an African prince tricked into slavery and barbarically killed, by a female writer about whom little is known. What was her name?

20. Cryophytes, a group of organisms which are most likely to be algae and fungi, thrive in which specific type of environment?

Answers on page 146

21. In 1974, after a rock concert in Boston, Massachusetts, the music critic Jon Landau wrote 'I saw rock and roll future, and its name is – ' With which name did he complete the sentence?

22. Hydrated magnesium silicate is often used in the home. By what everyday name do we know it in that context?

23. Now an archaic poetic term, a 'Palfrey' was a horse meant especially to be ridden by which group of people?

24. Heard in the US Supreme Court in 1893, the case of Nix v Hedden established that which edible crop was a vegetable and not a fruit?

25. Also a musical term for a florid melodic passage in music, what name is given to the posture in ballet where the dancer stands with one leg extended horizontally backwards, the torso extended forwards, and the arms outstretched?

26. In the 2005 Julian Barnes novel *Arthur & George*, George Edalji is a solicitor accused of multilating horses. Who is Arthur – the novelist whose investigations help acquit him of the charge?

27. Bernardo O'Higgins was the first President of which country?

28. Which species of North American pit viper gave its name to a Northerner sympathetic to the South, or opposed to Lincoln's policies, in the American Civil War?

29. The term 'dystrophy', as in muscular dystrophy, literally refers to a fault or defect in what function?

30. Franz Schubert's Ninth Symphony is known as the 'Great'; but which number is ascribed to his so-called 'Unfinished' Symphony?

31. If all of the characters in the Bible were listed alphabetically, who would come first?

32. In the BBC television situation comedy *Yes Minister*, by Antony Jay and Jonathan Lynn, to which fictional government department was Jim Hacker first appointed a Minister?

33. Which popular grape variety is used to produce the wines of Chablis?

34. Which humorous artist and musician often used to sign his name with a trademark signature in which the double 'f' in his surname was replaced by two treble clefs?

35. 'It's being so cheerful as keeps me going' was the catchphrase of the character Mona Lott, in which classic radio comedy show popular in the 1940s?

36. Which two-word phrase, indicating the tendency of writers and artists to ascribe human emotions and sympathies to nature, was coined by John Ruskin in the third volume of his work *Modern Painters*?

37. Which Spanish city has a name that literally means 'pomegranate'?

38. What's the name of the unfeasibly articulate and scheming toddler at the centre of the cartoon series *Family Guy*?

39. What name describes a mechanical model, usually clockwork, representing the motions of the planets around the sun, an example having been depicted in a famous 18th century painting by Joseph Wright of Derby?

40. Which American woman, who escaped from slavery in Maryland in the 1840s, is remembered for helping over 300 Southern slaves to freedom via the so-called 'Underground Railroad' of safe-houses?

Answers on page 146

Answers to Quiz 19

1. Haematite

2. The Queen's Hall – which was destroyed by bombing in 1941

3. Sir Henry Raeburn. The painting is one of the biggest attractions in the National Gallery of Scotland, and is widely used in the gallery's marketing.

4. The Normandie – regarded by some as the most beautiful liner ever built, she caught fire in New York harbour in 1942.

5. Frederick the First (Barbarossa)

6. The Queen

7. A violin. It's called a *Tanzmeistergeige* in German, literally a 'dancing-master's violin'.

8. Australia

9. Ely Cathedral – specially the octagonal 'lantern' tower he designed

10. Maputo – capital and chief port on Mozambique, formerly Portuguese East Africa.

11. The Rickshaw

12. Danny La Rue

13. Natrium

14. 'Thou shalt commit adultery'. Barker and Lucas were fined 300 pounds for their error, causing them complete financial ruin.

15. Bonanza

16. Lee Trevino. Trevino was struck by lightning in 1974.

17. Hydroelectric power

18. (A) neutrino

19. (Mrs) Aphra Behn

20. On snow and ice. Their name means 'that which grows on ice'.

21. Bruce Springsteen

22. Talc(um powder)

23. Women/female riders. Particularly a small saddle horse.

24. The tomato. Although the court agreed that a tomato is a fruit according to dictionary definition (Websters) the judgement to call it a vegetable was based on 'the common language of the people, whether sellers or consumers of provisions'.

25. Arabesque

26. Sir Arthur Conan Doyle

27. Chile

28. Copperhead

29. Nutrition

30. Eight

31. Aaron – brother of Moses

32. The Department of Administrative Affairs

33. Chardonnay

34. Gerard Hoffnung

35. *ITMA* (It's that man again)

36. Pathetic Fallacy

37. Granada. It's from that place name that we get the words 'grenadine', a cordial made from pomegranates, and 'grenade', an explosion device presumably named for its fruit-like shape.

38. Stewie (Griffin)

39. Orrery – named after Charles Boyle, 4th Earl of Orrery.

40. Harriet Tubman

Quiz 20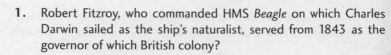

1. Robert Fitzroy, who commanded HMS *Beagle* on which Charles Darwin sailed as the ship's naturalist, served from 1843 as the governor of which British colony?

2. Which flower, referred to as 'gillyflower' in works by Shakespeare and Chaucer, was once used as a treatment for fevers and is now the symbol for Mothering Sunday?

3. 'Le Freak' was one of the best-known songs of which American group of the disco era, led by musicians Nile Rodgers and Bernard Edwards?

4. Which annual publication that first appeared in 1864 has been edited over the years by Charles Pardon, John Woodcock and Matthew Engel, among others, and featured an entry on the trial of Charles I in its first edition?

5. What's the name of the mythological snake, also sometimes called a cockatrice, an example of which is killed by Harry Potter in *Harry Potter and the Chamber of Secrets*?

6. *Plasmodium falciparum* and *Plasmodium vivax* are protozoan parasites that cause which disease, most common in the tropics and subtropics?

7. Which jazz trumpeter was the subject of the 1988 film documentary *Let's Get Lost*, released the year of his death?

8. In 1844, the architects Eugène Viollet-le-Duc and Jean-Baptiste Lassus were given the job of restoring which famous building?

9. Mount Toubkal, rising to 13,670 feet or 4,167 metres, is the highest peak of which mountain range?

10. Which team sport, that can be played indoors or outdoors, was devised by William Morgan in 1895, supposedly for middle-aged men who found basketball too vigorous?

11. Many German princes were known as Electors, such as Elector of Hanover – a title that referred to what special privilege or duty?

12. In which English county is the prehistoric monument known as the Rollright Stones?

13. Harald, son of Gorm the Old, who was King of Denmark in the 10th century, was known by what surname?

14. If a painting is described as a 'tondo', what shape must it be?

15. Which public-school-educated policeman, who made his debut on radio, also appeared in the *Eagle* comic during the 1950s?

16. A Möbius strip is a band or ribbon with only one face. What name is given to a bottle which is formed by passing the neck through the side to join a hole in the base, thus effectively creating a single side with neither an inside or an outside?

17. Which item of food is thought to have been first displayed in England in the London shop window of Thomas Johnson on 10th April 1633?

18. The names of which two signatories are generally used to identify the manifesto issued in London in July 1955, calling for scientists of the world to address together the problems of nuclear proliferation?

19. In which TV series of the 1980s – set '20 minutes into the future' – did the seriously injured investigative reporter Edison Carter have a copy of his mind downloaded onto a computer?

20. Maud Gonne was a muse to which poet and visionary writer, his love for her inspiring some of his best known works?

Answers on page 152

21. What is the name of the 264m tall volcanic neck in Wyoming in the USA, consisting of solidified lava, which was prominently featured in the Steven Spielberg film *Close Encounters of the Third Kind*?

22. What name, derived from the Hebrew meaning 'formless thing' or 'shapeless mass', is given in Jewish legend to an artificially created life being brought to life by supernatural means, and is also the title of a 20th century Gothic novel by Gustav Meyrinck?

23. Who commanded the joint French and Spanish fleet at the Battle of Trafalgar?

24. What is the English alternative name for the Ruwenzori mountain range in East Africa?

25. Derived from an old Norse word, a Cleg is another name for which insect?

26. *The Guardian's* obituary of the film director Irvin Kershner, who died in November 2010, begins with the following sentence: 'Chosen to direct [X], he turned in one of the best sequels – and highest box-office earners – of all time'. Which film title have we left out?

27. From Fred Perry in 1936 until 1997, no British male tennis player had reached a Grand Slam singles final. Which player broke that sixty-one-year drought?

28. Having four valence electrons, which element forms the most known compounds?

29. 'Clunton and Clunbury / Clungunford and Clun / Are the quietest places / Under the sun,' are lines from a poem published in the 1890s, naming villages in which English county?

30. With which Foreign Secretary did Lord Castlereagh, the then Secretary of State for War and the Colonies, fight a duel on Putney Heath in 1809?

31. Modern Tanzania consists of the former state of Tanganyika, along with three islands. Pemba and Mafia are two; which is the third?

32. Which TV weather forecaster was the subject of a novelty hit song by the Wearside band A Tribe of Toffs in 1988?

33. Which battle of the Vietnam War, fought by the United States and South Vietnam against North Vietnamese forces from 10th May until 20th May 1969, was made into a John Irvine directed film of 1987?

34. The Arctic gets its name from *Arktikos*, the ancient name for a constellation, which in turn derives its name from the Greek word *arktos* – meaning what?

35. Which Russian composer died on the same day as Joseph Stalin in 1953?

36. What name is given to the specific speed an object must achieve as a minimum, if it is rising against the pull of gravity, so that it will not return to the object exerting the gravitational field?

37. Which supposedly mystical word of seven Greek letters was used in ancient engravings on precious stones and amulets, and was also used as an album title by the rock group Santana?

38. Which word, taken from a name for the divine intoxicating drink of the gods in Hindu mythology, was used by Aldous Huxley for the drug that subdues the populace in the novel *Brave New World*?

39. In the game of backgammon, how many playing pieces are on the board at the beginning, in total?

40. In 1955, which Dutch artist created the children's character known in English as Miffy the rabbit?

Answers on page 152

Answers to Quiz 20

1. New Zealand. He was dismissed in 1846, apparently on account of his sympathy for Maori land claims.

2. Carnation

3. Chic. Bernard Edwards died in 1996, but Nile Rodgers has worked with many performers and is seen as one of the most influential figures in pop music over the past forty years.

4. *Wisden (Cricketers' Almanack)*. At first it was merely a statistical reference book and contained a number of non-cricketing facts, such as the aforementioned trial.

5. Basilisk

6. Malaria

7. Chet Baker

8. (The Cathedral of) Notre Dame de Paris

9. The Atlas Mountains

10. Volleyball

11. To elect the Holy Roman Emperor

12. Oxfordshire

13. Blue-tooth. He was baptised in 965 and tried to have Denmark converted to Christianity, but was driven from the country by his son Sweyn Forkbeard.

14. Round

15. P.C.49 (aka Archibald Berkeley-Willoughby)

16. A Klein bottle. Named after Felix Klein (1849-1925), the German mathematician who first described it.

17. Bananas

18. Bertrand Russell and Albert Einstein. Einstein signed two days before he died.

19. Max Headroom. 'Max Headroom' being the last words Carter glimpsed before his motorcycle crashed into a vehicle clearance height sign.

20. W. B. Yeats. Despite repeated offers, she refused to marry him. He went on to marry Georgie Hyde-Lees in 1917.

21. Devil's Tower

22. The Golem

23. (Admiral Pierre Charles Jean Baptiste Sylvestre, Comte de) Villeneuve. Following the battle, the admiral lay a prisoner in England until 1806. Returning to Paris, he stopped at Rennes to learn how Napoleon would receive him, and shortly afterwards was found dead in bed having apparently stabbed himself to death.

24. Mountains of the Moon. As mentioned by Ptolemy, and as such the supposed source of the Nile.

25. Horsefly also called Gadfly

26. *The Empire Strikes Back*

27. Greg Rusedski. He lost to Pat Rafter in the 1997 US Open final.

28. Carbon. More than all the other elements put together.

29. Shropshire – they're from A. E. Housman's *A Shropshire Lad*, though some may say these words pre-date Housman and that he took them from a local traditional rhyme.

30. George Canning. Both survived, although Canning was shot in the leg, Castlereagh only lost a button.

31. Zanzibar

32. John Kettley. 'John Kettley is a weatherman, and so is Michael Fish'.

33. Hamburger Hill. Also known as Ap Bia Mountain.

34. Bear. Referring to Ursa Major.

35. (Sergei Sergeyevich) Prokofiev. It has been reported that, as he lived near Red Square, for three days the throngs gathered to mourn Stalin made it impossible to carry Prokofiev's body out for the funeral service at the headquarters of the Soviet Composer's Union. Paper flowers and a taped recording of the funeral march from *Romeo and Juliet* had to be used, as all real flowers and musicians were reserved for Stalin's funeral.

36. Escape Velocity

37. Abraxas. The letters of the word are identified with the number 365.

38. Soma

39. Thirty – fifteen white, fifteen black

40. Dick Bruna. She's called Nijntje in the original Dutch, and there is a statue of her, standing in a square named after her, in Bruna's home town of Utrecht.

Quiz 21

1. What kind of performer would be most likely to use a swazzle?

2. *LHOOQ* is a bawdy title given to an artwork of 1919 by Marcel Duchamp, consisting of a reproduction of a very famous portrait, on whose face he had drawn a beard and moustache in pencil. Which portrait?

3. The dormant volcano Mount Rainier, and the National Park that bears its name, are to be found in which state of the USA?

4. The 1896 novel *Quo Vadis*, by Henryk Sienkiewicz, and the film adaptation of 1951, are set in Rome in the time of which Emperor?

5. Which former journalist on the *Atlanta Constitution* in Georgia wrote the stories which provided the basis for the 1946 Disney film *Song of the South*?

6. What criminal-sounding name is given to the broad-nosed marsh crocodile, found in parts of India and Sri Lanka and traditionally venerated in the Hindu religion?

7. In the binary system, what conventional number is expressed as 1111?

8. What is the name of the faun, the first inhabitant of the land of Narnia to be introduced in the novels of C. S. Lewis?

9. The ancient mathematician, Euclid; the chemist and chrystallographer Dorothy Hodgkin; and Naguib Mahfouz, the Nobel Prize-winning novelist, were all born in which country?

10. In a dramatic monologue by J. Milton Hayes, whose grave is tended by 'a broken-hearted woman' beneath the gaze of a 'one-eyed yellow idol to the north of Khatmandu'?

11. How many sides does a hendecagon have?

12. Whose acclaimed 2009 play *Jerusalem* centres around Johnny 'Rooster' Byron, a defiant drop-out living in a ramshackle mobile home, played in the original production by Mark Rylance?

13. According to a widely-quoted comment by the polyglot Holy Roman Emperor Charles V, he supposedly spoke Spanish to God, Italian to women and French to men. Which language did he reserve for his horse?

14. Players of which game compete for the Bermuda Bowl and the Venice Cup?

15. Whose 1966 recording of the song 'Bang Bang (My Baby Shot Me Down)' was memorably used on the soundtrack of the Quentin Tarantino film *Kill Bill Vol. 1*, and also sampled by the Audio Bullys in the hit 'Shot You Down'?

16. Hoopes' Process is an electrolytic technique of refining which metallic element, achieving a purity level as great as 99.99 per cent?

17. In the musical *Wicked*, based on the 1995 book by Gregory Maguire, in turn inspired by characters from L. Frank Baum's *The Wizard of Oz*, what's the name of the character known originally only as the 'Wicked Witch of the West'?

18. In the human body, the tongue is attached at the floor of the mouth to which U-shaped bone in the upper part of the throat?

19. Almond kernels, the stones of apricots and apple pips all contain traces of acidic compounds of which poison?

20. The physicist and astronomer Georges Lemaître, who was also a Roman Catholic priest, proposed which theory in 1933 which has since become widely accepted?

Answers on page 158

21. Popularised by an 1834 novel entitled *Ayesha*, a Turkish word for something worthless or empty came into common English usage, often as an exclamation ridiculing another person's words as contemptible nonsense. Which word?

22. Ben Macdui, Braeriach and Cairn Toul are summits rising to more than four thousand feet, in which much-visited Scottish mountain region?

23. The composer Rossini is said to have composed the overture to which of his operas in a mad rush on the day of its premiere, after being locked in a room at La Scala by the opera's infuriated Director?

24. Why has a horse called The Chase, which came first in a race at Haydock Park in August 1948, entered racing history?

25. With a density more than seven times that of air, which is the heaviest of the 'noble' gases?

26. Which voice-over artist, who died in 1985, provided the voice of Donald Duck in Walt Disney cartoons for over fifty years?

27. What term, derived from a Hindi word for 'spotted', was originally used for painted or stained calico imported from India, but is now commonly used for cotton cloth printed with coloured designs, and then usually glazed?

28. Which naval figure, who commanded the vessel the *Glatton* at the Battle of Copenhagen under Nelson in 1801, is better known to posterity for his part in an event that took place more than ten years earlier?

29. What name was used for any of the shanty towns built by the unemployed and destitute during the American depression of the 1930s, a famous example having been in New York's Central Park?

30. The motor car designer responsible for the Morris Minor and the Mini, Sir Alec Issigonis, was born in 1906 in which country?

31. Which island nation has – at approximately 2.4 m – the lowest maximum point of natural elevation of any country?

32. Its name derived from the name of the third wife of the Emperor Claudius, the 'Messalina complex' is a synonym for which more common term for a form of manic behaviour?

33. Traditionally served in umble pie, umbles are most usually the entrails of which animal?

34. In the *Super Mario Bros* series of video games, what's the name of Mario's brother?

35. In botany, what term is given to a variety of plants, all of which share the feature of their leaves being permanently orientated in a north-south direction, to take advantage of early and late sun, while avoiding the stronger midday sunlight?

36. At the court of King George I, who or what were nicknamed 'the Maypole' and 'the Elephant and Castle'?

37. For which London bank was T. S. Eliot working in 1922, when he published his great poem 'The Waste Land'?

38. In the classic Morecambe and Wise sketch featuring the conductor André Previn, what piano piece was Eric Morecambe playing with 'all the right notes, but not necessarily in the right order'?

39. In which capital city was André Previn born in 1929?

40. *The Hostage* and *The Quare Fellow* are plays by which irreverent 20th century Irish playwright who died in 1964?

Answers on page 158

Answers to Quiz 21

1. A Punch-and-Judy operator. It's the contraption that produces the distinctive buzzy voice of Mr Punch.

2. The *Mona Lisa*. The title *LHOOQ*, when read in French, sounds like *Elle a chaud au cul*, a phrase that means she has a keen sexual appetite.

3. Washington

4. Nero. He was memorably portrayed in the film by Peter Ustinov.

5. Joel Chandler Harris

6. Mugger – the name has nothing to do with the crocodile's violent habits, but comes from the Hindi word *magar.*

7. Fifteen (1x8, plus 1x4, plus 1x2, plus 1x1)

8. Mr Tumnus

9. Egypt

10. 'Mad Carew' – in the 1911 poem 'the Green Eye of the Little Yellow God'

11. Eleven

12. Jez Butterworth

13. German

14. (Contract) Bridge

15. Nancy Sinatra

16. Aluminium

17. Elphaba. Maguire formulated the name out of L. Frank Baum's initials.

18. The Hyoid bone

19. Cyanide. Fortunately, the body has a natural detoxin and apple seeds would have to be eaten in handfuls to do any harm.

20. The 'Big Bang' Theory of the origin of the universe. He referred to it as his 'hypothesis of the primeval atom'.

21. Bosh

22. The Cairngorms – all three are higher than the most famous mountain of the range, Cairn Gorm itself.

23. *The Thieving Magpie/La Gazza Ladra*

24. It was Lester Piggott's first winner – when he was twelve!

25. Radon

26. Clarence Nash. Often known as 'Ducky' Nash, for obvious reasons. He also did a bullfrog's voice in *Bambi*.

27. Chintz

28. Captain William Bligh – Master of the *Bounty* at the time of the mutiny in 1789.

29. Hooverville – after the then President, Herbert Hoover. New York's was built in a drained former reservoir of the city's water supply system. The largest of all the Hoovervilles was, in fact, in St Louis.

30. Turkey – in what's now the city of Izmir

31. The Maldives

32. Nymphomania

33. Deer

34. Luigi

35. Compass plants

36. The King's Mistresses. Respectively, Ehrengard Melusina von Schulenberg (later the Duchess of Kendal), who was rather skinny, and Charlotte Sophia Kelmans who was more generously built.

37. Lloyds. At one point the poem describes the multitude of City workers teeming across London Bridge, a sight Eliot must have seen on a daily basis.

38. Grieg's Piano Concerto

39. Berlin, as Andreas Priwin

40. Brendan Behan

Quiz 22

1. When Sir Alistair Pilkington developed the so-called 'Float Process' for the manufacture of glass, he used a molten bath or river of which metal to float the glass on?

2. Which 1760s novel by Horace Walpole is often credited with setting the fashion for supernatural romance?

3. *Kashrut* is that body of Jewish law relating to what in particular?

4. In Edgar Allan Poe's short story 'The Murders in the Rue Morgue', the violent murders of an old woman and her daughter turn out to have been committed by what kind of creature?

5. 'Dippermouth' was an early nickname for which jazz musician who died in 1971?

6. Which golfer, in 1988, became the first Briton to win the US Masters?

7. Which city was proclaimed the first capital of the united kingdom of Italy in 1861?

8. Very soon after the English Civil War, the philosopher Thomas Hobbes published his most famous work, a treatise in which he memorably described the life of men as 'solitary, poor, nasty, brutish and short'. Under what title did that treatise appear?

9. The bestockinged leg that appears in the foreground on posters for the 1967 film *The Graduate* was not, in fact, that of female lead Anne Bancroft, but belonged to a model and actress who was later to star as Sue Ellen in the hit TV series *Dallas*. Can you name her?

10. The Paris-based American photographer Emmanuel Rudnitsky, who died in 1976, was known professionally by which name?

11. In Freudian psychoanalytic theory, which component of the human personality is responsible for ethics and self-imposed standards of behaviour?

12. Which Labour MP, born near Halesworth in Suffolk and subsequently a leader of his party, resigned his parliamentary seat in 1912 to draw attention to the imprisonment of suffragettes?

13. 'An Orkney Wedding, with Sunrise' is one of the most popular orchestral pieces of which British composer, who made his home in Orkney for over forty years and died in 2016?

14. Betsy Ross, who lived between 1752 and 1836, is often credited with making the first what?

15. Lepenski Vir, now submerged by an artificial lake, is the site of a Mesolithic farming settlement in a valley of which European river?

16. Occurring throughout western Europe, what kind of creature is a 'Devil's coach horse'?

17. Who was the first unseeded player to win the Wimbledon Men's Singles title?

18. The elaborate buildings originally constructed in London for the Franco-British Exhibition of 1908 went by a collective nickname that's still in use, although the buildings are long gone. It's also remembered as the name of a sporting venue. What name is this?

19. What was once described by George Orwell as '…something halfway between a girls' school and a lunatic asylum'?

20. Which British rock group recorded a 1972 album with a cover depicting the model Amanda Lear taking a black panther for a walk?

Answers on page 164

21. In medicine, Naegele's Rule is a method used to estimate the probable date of the onset of which natural process?

22. Which 18th century novelist's eponymous heroes include Roderick Random, Peregrine Pickle and Humphry Clinker?

23. Which English painter, a member of the Camden Town Group, was briefly an actor with Sir Henry Irving's company and has also been suggested, most recently by Patricia Cornwell, as a suspect for the Jack the Ripper murders of 1888?

24. In 991 AD, Viking invaders defeated an Anglo-Saxon army at Maldon – on the shores of the Blackwater Estuary – in which modern English county?

25. The so-called Junius Pamphlet was a letter written in 1916 by which Polish-born Spartacist during a period of imprisonment?

26. The three stars named Delta, Epsilon and Zeta, fairly equally spaced in a straight line, together form which familiar feature of the night sky?

27. The actor Peter O'Toole portrayed the same English king in two very different films, a few years apart, in the 1960s. Which king?

28. Which eponymous Virginia Woolf character changes sex part-way through a novel?

29. Sometimes used in English sentences before a named individual or body, to indicate a respectful contradiction, which Latin word of four letters means 'in deference to' or 'with due respect'?

30. In Jonathan Swift's *Gulliver's Travels*, what absurd dispute was at the root of a long-running war between the nations of Lilliput and Blefuscu?

31. In the Bible, who was the third of Noah's sons after Shem and Ham?

32. In physics, what name is given to the observable effect whereby the course of a moving object appears to be deflected as a result of the rotation of the Earth?

33. What is the national epic poem of Finland (usually translated as 'Land of Heroes')?

34. Which commonly used religious word derives directly from the Greek adjective meaning 'anointed'?

35. *A Childhood at Green Hedges* by Imogen Smallwood is an account of the author's childhood as the youngest daughter of which children's writer?

36. Which English scientist developed the method of classifying fingerprints by patterns, a system – improved by the London Police Commissioner, Sir Edward R. Henry – that was introduced at Scotland Yard in 1901?

37. In a mix-up that was reported around the world, the Academy Award ceremony of 2017 was memorable for the wrong movie, *La La Land*, being announced as winner of the Best Picture Oscar. Which film actually won?

38. On which temperature scale – proposed in 1730 – is the freezing point of water set at 0° and its boiling point at 80°?

39. *Titus Groan*, the first novel in Mervyn Peake's 'Gormenghast trilogy', was first published in 1946. The other two novels followed in the 1950s. Can you name both of those other two?

40. According to a 2011 biography by his daughter Clare, Mervyn Peake was commissioned to create the logo for which publishing firm, best known for their paperbacks?

Answers on page 164

Answers to Quiz 22

1. Tin

2. *The Castle of Otranto*

3. Diet – determining what is, and what is not, kosher.

4. An orang-utan

5. Louis Armstrong – later known, of course, as 'Satchelmouth' or 'Satchmo'.

6. Sandy Lyle. Alexander Walter Barr Lyle.

7. Turin/Torino. The capital was moved to Florence in 1864-65 and then to Rome in 1870.

8. *Leviathan*

9. Linda Gray

10. Man Ray. Rudnitsky is alternatively spelled Radnitsky or Radnitzky.

11. The Superego

12. George Lansbury

13. Sir Peter Maxwell Davies

14. American Flag

15. The Danube. It's in modern Serbia, at the Iron Gates Gorge.

16. A beetle – also sometimes called a rove beetle or cock-tail beetle.

17. Boris Becker – in 1985. He was also the first German, and the youngest-ever player, to take the title at that date.

18. White City

19. The BBC

20. Roxy Music. It was their second LP, *For Your Pleasure*.

21. Childbirth – nine months and seven days being added to the date of the first day of the last known menstrual period.

22. (Tobias) Smollett

23. Walter Sickert

24. Essex. Perhaps confusingly, Essex then formed part of Wessex. The battle was chronicled in a long Old English poem.

25. Rosa Luxemburg – Junius being her chosen pseudonym.

26. The Belt of Orion. The three stars are also called Alnilam, Alnitak, and Mintaka.

27. Henry II. The films were *Becket* (1963) and *The Lion in Winter* (1969)

28. Orlando

29. *Pace*

30. Which end to open a boiled egg

31. Japheth

32. The Coriolis Effect. The effect can result in diverting a moving object to the right of its path in the Northern Hemisphere and to the left in the Southern Hemisphere. Named after the 19th century scientist Gaspard-Gustave Coriolis.

33. Kalevala

34. Christ

35. Enid Blyton

36. Francis Galton

37. *Moonlight*

38. The Réaumur Scale. From the French naturalist and physicist René Réaumur. Largely unused after 1790 except for taking temperatures of milk in some Italian dairies.

39. *Gormenghast* and *Titus Alone*

40. Pan (Books Ltd). Peake designed the little silhouette of the god Pan with his pipe at his lips. Amazingly, he declined the offer of a percentage on every book sold, and instead took a lump sum – the grand total of £10.

Quiz 23

1. Which British Labour politician once defined his foreign policy as '[being] able to take a ticket at Victoria Station and go anywhere I damn well please'?

2. In which field of the arts is the 'Prix Goncourt' awarded?

3. The Scottish football club long known simply as Morton Football Club now acknowledges its home town in its name: which town?

4. What is the British term for what an American would call a 'Plantar Wart'?

5. Warren Casey and Jim Jacobs were the writers of a stage musical first performed in 1971 which became one of the most-performed musicals in the world, especially in schools. What is it called?

6. Which small animal – brought to Europe from South America where it was domesticated for its meat – has been used since the mid-18th century in scientific research, being Robert Koch's chosen model in experiments that produced the first TB vaccine?

7. Which rank of the British Army – awarded to junior officers in cavalry regiments – shares its name with a brass band instrument commonly pitched in B flat?

8. Wittern, whitty, wiggen and quickbeam are all dialect names for which species of tree?

9. What is the motto of the Salvation Army?

10. Which novel by Robert Graves did Alexander Korda attempt to film in 1937, with Charles Laughton in the title role, although the project was abandoned after a few weeks' shooting?

11. The signing of which treaty in 1902 ended the Second Boer War?

12. Which Greek word, meaning union, refers to the proposed union of the island of Cyprus and Greece?

13. Which American musician, who remained unaware for decades that his records had made him a huge star in South Africa, was the subject of the 2012 documentary film *Searching for Sugarman*?

14. Which British reservoir was created in the 1970s by damming the river Gwash?

15. In the original 1982 book by Sue Townsend, how old specifically was Adrian Mole?

16. Which Canadian prairie province lies between Ontario to the east, and Saskatchewan to the west?

17. Blacksmith is a general term for a worker in iron, but what specific name is given to someone who shoes horses?

18. In jazz, what adopted forename is common to the drummer and bandleader born William Henry Webb, and the pianist whose real name is Armando Corea?

19. *Hippoglossus hippoglossus* is the Latin name for which common flatfish found in the North Atlantic?

20. Which town on the River Tweed has a ruined Cistercian abbey that is supposedly the burial-place of the heart – though not the rest of the remains – of Robert the Bruce?

21. In the 1400s, John Holland, Duke of Exeter, became Constable of the Tower of London. What instrument of torture is he credited with introducing there?

Answers on page 170

22. Which term, coined by Ludwig von Rochau in the 19th century, describes pragmatic politics based on material needs rather than moral ideals?

23. The Eastern European city known in German as Laibach is more widely known by what name?

24. The 15th century Chateau des Milandes, in the Dordogne region of France, was the home from the 1940s onward of which American singer and dancer, also prominent in the civil rights movement?

25. Who wrote the short story on which the much-admired film *The Shawshank Redemption* was based?

26. What is the scientific name for a plant that grows on another, but is not parasitic?

27. Which Italian footballer, the 1993 World and European Player of the Year, was known as the Divine Ponytail?

28. In tectonics, the oceanic plate on the Pacific coastline of South America is named after which ancient culture?

29. 'E.P.' and Hugh Selwyn Mauberley are personae adopted in each of two sections of a long work of 1920, itself named *Hugh Selwyn Mauberley*, by which American-born poet?

30. In legend, Leodegrance, King of Cameliard, is the father of which queen, whose marital infidelity is said to have brought her a life of penitence at an Amesbury nunnery?

31. The conductor Bernard Haitink, a former music director at both Glyndebourne Opera and the Royal Opera House Covent Garden, was born in which country?

2. What creatures does someone fear if he or she suffers from ailurophobia?

3. According to the Beaulieu National Motor Museum, which term should properly be used only to designate those vehicles manufactured between 1919 and 1930?

4. Who once wrote of the Holy Roman Empire – to give the standard English translation – 'This agglomeration which was called and which still calls itself the Holy Roman Empire was neither holy, nor Roman, nor an empire'?

5. Found also in tea, nuts, cocoa and spinach, which chemical compound of hydrogen, carbon and oxygen is present at toxic levels in the leaves of the rhubarb plant?

6. What is the name of a niche or slab in a Mosque that is used to indicate the direction of Mecca?

7. Can you name both of Bertie Wooster's aunts who appear regularly in the novels by P. G. Wodehouse?

8. Which London building, demolished in 1902, was known, with great irony, as the 'City College'?

9. *Paradise Regained*, which John Milton published as a sequel to *Paradise Lost* in 1671, deals with which episode in the New Testament?

10. When the first Penguin paperbacks were published, their jackets were colour-coded as to subject matter: orange for general fiction, blue for biography. What specific category was covered by the green-coloured paperbacks?

Answers on page 170

Answers to Quiz 23

1. Ernest Bevin

2. (French) Literature. Awarded by the Académie Goncourt each November for an outstanding work of imaginative prose.

3. Greenock. Morton Football Club came in to being in 1874 and, a long ago as July 1896, became a limited company with the title of The Greenock Morton Football and Athletic Company Limited.

4. Verruca

5. *Grease*. Filmed in 1978 with John Travolta, Olivia Newton John, and severa very successful new numbers.

6. The Guinea Pig. Its name, of course, is now used metaphorically to mea anyone or anything on which experiments are tested.

7. Cornet

8. Rowan or Mountain Ash

9. Blood and Fire

10. *I, Claudius* (and the sequel *Claudius The God*)

11. Treaty of Vereeniging

12. Enosis

13. (Sixto) Rodriguez

14. Rutland Water. England's largest reservoir by surface area, complete 1975.

15. Thirteen and three quarters (*The Secret Diary of Adrian Mole Aged 13¾*)

16. Manitoba

17. Farrier

18. Chick

19. The halibut

20. Melrose

21. The rack. Which became known, grimly, as 'The Duke of Exeter's Daughter

22. *Realpolitik*

23. Ljubljana. Capital of Slovenia.

24. Josephine Baker

25. Stephen King

26. Epiphyte

7. Roberto Baggio

8. Nazca. The culture was located on the southern coast of what is now Peru.

9. Ezra Pound

0. Guinevere

1. The Netherlands

2. Cats

3. Vintage. Veteran – up to 31st Dec 1904. Edwardian – from 1st Jan 1905-31st Dec 1918. Vintage – from 1st Jan 1919 to 31st Dec 1930.

4. Voltaire (in 1756)

5. Oxalic Acid

6. Mihrab (plural Maharib). Specifically it indicates the *qibla*, the direction of the Kaaba in Mecca, the cube-shaped building that is the most sacred site in Islam.

7. Agatha and Dahlia

8. Newgate Prison

9. Christ's Temptations in the Wilderness/40 Days in the Wilderness

0. Crime Fiction

Quiz 24

1. Which city was the capital of Pakistan from independence until the late 1950s?

2. According to legend, Captain Vanderdecken was in charge of which vessel on its voyage home from the East Indies port of Batavia?

3. Which medically-important chemical was fortuitously discovered by the American chemist and physician Samuel Guthrie when, in 1831, he combined alcohol with chlorinated lime in an effort to produce an economically viable pesticide?

4. Diaphoresis is the technical name for which bodily process?

5. Which period of geological time, the second period of the Palaeozoic era, is named after an ancient Welsh people because rocks formed during this time were first studied in Wales?

6. Which Canadian ice-hockey star was voted the Most Valuable Player to his team in the National Hockey League every year between 1980 and 1987?

7. From 1932 until the 1990s, Russia's fifth largest city, Nizhny Novgorod, was named after which writer born there in 1868?

8. Where would you find Humboldt's Sea and the Lake of Death?

9. In the book *Cider With Rosie*, by Laurie Lee, what was Rosie's (suitably bucolic) surname?

10. Which Labour MP – at the time the Shadow Chief Secretary to the Treasury – did David Cameron advise to 'Calm down, dear' at Prime Minister's Questions in April 2011?

11. Bernard de Launay became the first prominent casualty of the French Revolution when he was lynched and then decapitated at the hands of a mob on 14th July 1789. Which official post had he held immediately prior to his death?

12. According to the title of a children's book by E. Nesbit, who are Robert, Anthea, Jane, Cyril, the Lamb and the Psammead?

13. What was the name for the type of ancient Greek galley, usually used for combat because of its comparative power and speed, with three banks of oars on either side?

14. Which of the works of Gilbert and Sullivan, when first presented at the Savoy Theatre in January 1887, was billed as 'A New and Original Supernatural Opera in Two Acts'?

15. Which 19th century writer was known as the Sage of Chelsea?

16. The common at the Surrey village of Outwood is notable as the site of what is said to be the oldest working example in Britain of which type of structure?

17. Which city in the state of Uttar Pradesh was the scene of the first uprising of the Indian Rebellion, once known as the Indian Mutiny, in 1857?

18. The first BBC local radio station was launched on 8th November 1967 in which British city?

19. The French word for French is 'Français' and the German for German is 'Deutsch'. Which European language calls itself 'Shqip'?

20. In which country does a website originate if the suffix to the URL is .lk?

Answers on page 176

21. Which Spanish city, now better known as a tourist destination, was in 1881 the birthplace of Pablo Picasso?

22. In the Theban Myths, dramatized by Sophocles, who is the father of Antigone?

23. Laura Jesson and Alec Harvey are the central characters in which 1945 film?

24. Ceratopsian dinosaurs are so named because they had what physical feature?

25. Which cloaked-and-hatted crime fighter, popular on American radio and in comics during the 1930s, was played on air for a few months by Orson Welles and was associated with such lines as 'The weed of crime bears bitter fruit'?

26. 'Tent stitch', a fine, usually diagonal stitching used in embroidery, is also known by which French term?

27. Which writer, particularly noted for his portraits of low-life figures in downtown New York City, was on the staff of the New Yorker magazine until his death in 1996, and for the last 32 years of his life went into the office every day without producing a single piece of writing?

28. Which of the Seven Wonders of the Ancient World is said to have been the work of Chares of Lindos, who worked on it for twelve years?

29. In which city would you find Thor Heyerdahl's Kon-Tiki raft and the reed boat Ra II on permanent exhibition?

30. The Rosebay Willowherb has another name which relates to the reason why it used to be common on bomb sites. What is that other name?

31. Featuring the cross of Ypres, an oil lamp – known as the Lamp of Maintenance – is the emblem of which international charitable organisation?

32. Whose statue on Grafton Street in Dublin is known colloquially as 'The Tart with the Cart'?

33. Found mostly in Australia, what kind of creature is a taipan?

34. According to popular legend, what was the profession of Peeping Tom, the Coventry citizen struck blind for his impudent observation of the naked Lady Godiva?

35. Which writer founded the review *Les Temps Modernes* with Maurice Merleau-Ponty, Raymond Aron and her life-long companion Jean-Paul Sartre?

36. What is the name for the eastern part of the Sahara Desert, lying between the Nile and the Red Sea in north-eastern Sudan?

37. The hormones insulin and glucagon, which regulate blood sugar, are produced by which organ of the body?

38. Asser, a monk at St David's Abbey in Pembrokeshire, became the counsellor and biographer of which Anglo-Saxon monarch?

39. Famous for his report on the Profumo affair, who was the Master of the Rolls from 1962 to 1982?

40. Which publishing company, specialists in travel guides, began life in Koblenz in 1827, and lent their name (rather against their will) to a series of air raids launched against British cities in the Second World War?

Answers on page 176

Answers to Quiz 24

1. Karachi. Karachi was the first capital from 1947-59. Rawalpindi was the interim capital from 1959-67 whilst Islamabad was being built.

2. The Flying Dutchman

3. Chloroform. It is no longer used as an anaesthetic because much safer methods have been developed.

4. Perspiration/sweating. Especially to an unusual degree as a symptom of disease or a side effect of a drug. From the Greek *diaphorein* 'carry off, sweat out'.

5. Ordovician. Named after the Ordovices, a Celtic tribe from North Wales.

6. Wayne Gretzky. The trophy he won was the Hart Memorial Trophy.

7. (Maxim) Gorky

8. On the moon

9. Burdock

10. Angela Eagle

11. Governor of the Bastille. Six others from the prison garrison died with him along with Flesselles, president of the Paris committee.

12. *Five Children and It*

13. Trireme

14. *Ruddigore* – subtitled 'The Witch's Curse'. It was a satire on old-fashioned melodrama – and the composers' original spelling of the title, *Ruddygore*, had to be changed after offence was taken in some quarters.

15. Thomas Carlyle

16. A windmill. Dating from 1665, it is a post mill. Its sails rotate on the bough of a single oak tree.

17. Meerut

18. Leicester

19. Albanian

20. Sri Lanka

21. Malaga

22. Oedipus

23. *Brief Encounter*. They were played by Celia Johnson and Trevor Howard. Directed by David Lean, the film was based on Noel Coward's short play *Still Life*.

24. A horn. From Greek *keras*, *kerat-* 'horn' + *ops* 'face'.

25. The Shadow

26. Petit point

27. Joseph Mitchell

28. The Colossus of Rhodes

29. Oslo (in the Kon-Tiki Museum)

30. Fireweed

31. TOC-H. Hence the phrase 'dim as a Toc-H lamp'.

32. Molly Malone – as in the folk song 'Cockles and Mussels'

33. A (poisonous) snake

34. He was a tailor. Some versions of the story have him being struck dead after peeping from his shop window.

35. Simone de Beauvoir

36. Nubian Desert

37. Pancreas

38. Alfred the Great

39. Lord Denning

40. Baedeker. Between April and June 1942, Germany launched air attacks against English cities that had little strategic importance, but were picturesque and had buildings of historical interest. This was called the 'Baedeker Blitz' by the British as it was believed the German High Command were using Baedeker's guide as a means of identifying the targets.

Quiz 25

1. Knockaloe, the site of a major British internment camp for 'enemy alien' civilians living in the UK during both world wars, was established in which island off the coast of Britain?

2. The Edgware Road in London lies along the route of which ancient Roman road?

3. In Mozart's *The Marriage of Figaro*, whom does Figaro marry?

4. The Central Lobby at the heart of the Palace of Westminster; the Globe Theatre erected around 1599 at London's Bankside; and the centrepiece observatory of Wren's Flamsteed House at Greenwich, share what unusual architectural distinction?

5. *Wild Life in Suburbia*, an LP record released in 1959 consisting of the monologues of Edna and Sandy Stone, two philistine inhabitants of the Australian suburbs, is an early work by which humorist and writer?

6. What do the initials E. M. stand for in the name of E. M. Forster, the author of the novels *A Passage to India* and *A Room With a View*?

7. Stingray Bay was the original name of which location on the eastern coast of Australia?

8. What is the name of the stiff, full, white skirt traditionally worn by men in Albania and parts of Greece?

9. The 2015 film *Spotlight* is about a real-life investigation conducted by the *Boston Globe* newspaper into what issue?

10. Which beautiful youth of Greek legend provided the title of a poem by John Keats and also an 1880 novel by Benjamin Disraeli?

11. What is the literal meaning of the Urdu word *halal*, often encountered in connection with Islam?

12. Which chain of British comedy clubs takes its name from that of a type of medieval wandering minstrel?

13. In 1724, as part of the Hanoverian programme to make the still potentially volatile Highlands easier to control, which field-marshal and MP for Bath went there to supervise the construction of numerous bridges and metalled roads?

14. Which two French terms are used to describe the seizures characteristic of both the severe and the less severe forms of epilepsy?

15. The lamb is the symbol of which female saint, often placed at her side in religious paintings?

16. Which American horse breed gets its name from its ability to outdistance other breeds of horses in races of 440 yards or less?

17. Shakespeare's sonnets, first published together as a sequence in 1609, comprise how many poems?

18. *Still Crazy After All These Years*, in 1976, and *Fate For Breakfast*, in 1979, are among the solo albums of which former singing duo?

19. What title was first given to the chief minister of the Abbasid caliphs, subsequently to the chief minister of the Turkish sultan, and later to those of other Muslim states?

20. At a height of around 330 metres, Cleeve Cloud is the highest point in which English county?

Answers on page 182

21. Which crank-turned instrument, originally used to teach music in cloisters or monastic schools, can be referred to as a 'wheel fiddle' or *vielle à roue*?

22. Which novel by Robert Tressell, first published in an abridged form in 1918, has been called 'the workers' Bible' and is often said to have provided inspiration for the early Labour movement and the establishment of the welfare state?

23. The Queen has two Christian names apart from Elizabeth. What are they?

24. Which cricket ground, named after the Hampshire fast bowler who leased the land on which its pitches were established in the 1840s, is used to stage home matches played by the students of Cambridge University?

25. Astronomers have predicted that our Galaxy, the Milky Way, will collide in 4 billion years time with which other?

26. Who was the first criminal to be named Public Enemy No.1 by the FBI?

27. What was the subject of William Harvey's 1628 treatise generally known as *De Motu Cordis*?

28. Which director, born into an aristocratic Italian family, is noted, among other films, for *The Leopard* in 1963, and *Death in Venice* in 1971?

29. Which Arabic word for 'West' denotes the region of North Africa that embraces Morocco, Algeria, Tunisia and parts of Libya?

30. In the most popular versions of the traditional rhyme, one magpie is for sorrow and two for joy. What do six magpies bring?

1. Much of Russia's oil and gas is exported to the West via Ventspils, the largest port in which other European country?

2. Which character created by Jules Verne has been played on film by Herbert Lom and James Mason?

3. Captain Hawdon, a retired military officer, does law-writing under the name of Nemo, in which novel by Charles Dickens?

4. How many acres are there in a square mile?

5. What phrase colloquially used to mean 'keep quiet' derives from a Navy signal for all hands to turn in?

6. Which Connecticut businessman, a failed iron manufacturer, developed a process for the vulcanisation of rubber using sulphur under intense heat, and patented the method in 1844?

7. Which is the largest of the Society Islands?

8. Which Welsh equestrian won individual European Championships in 1961, 1967 and 1969, Olympic bronze in 1960 and 1968, and was individual World Champion in 1970?

9. What term describes the point at which a celestial object in orbit around the Earth, such as the Moon, makes its closest approach to Earth?

0. In 1816, the French physician Dr R. T. E. Laënnec devised which medical instrument, its original form being a wooden or metal tube with expanded ends?

Answers on page 182

1. Isle of Man. It even had its own post office and railway link.

2. Watling Street. The main Roman road north.

3. Susanna

4. They were all built as octagons

5. Barry Humphries

6. Edward Morgan

7. Botany Bay

8. Fustanella

9. Child abuse in the Catholic Church

10. Endymion

11. According to religious law

12. Jongleurs

13. (George) Wade. The bridges, constructed of 40 large stones each, were known as Wade Bridges.

14. Grand Mal/Petit Mal

15. St Agnes, the patron saint of virgins

16. Quarter horse

17. 154

18. (Paul) Simon & (Art) Garfunkel

19. Vizier

20. Gloucestershire. It's in the Cotswolds.

21. The Hurdy-Gurdy. Known to have existed from the 12th century. The original instrument was so cumbersome it required two players.

22. *The Ragged-Trousered Philanthropists*

23. Alexandra Mary

24. Fenner's. He was Francis Phillips Fenner.

25. Andromeda. Researchers came to this conclusion after using the Hubble Space Telescope between 2002 and 2010 to painstakingly track the motion of Andromeda as it inched along the sky. Andromeda, roughly 770,000 parsecs (2.5 million light years) away, is the nearest large spiral galaxy to the Milky Way.

26. John Herbert Dillinger. In June 1934. The FBI offered a reward of $10,000 for his capture – but he had become a folk-hero to many Americans disillusioned with failing banks and hapless Depression-era government.

27. The circulation of the blood in animals

28. Luchino Visconti

29. Maghreb or Maghrib

30. Gold. '… Three for a girl, four for a boy / Five for silver, six for gold / Seven for a secret never to be told.'

31. Latvia

32. Captain Nemo. In the films *Mysterious Island* and *20,000 Leagues Under the Sea*.

33. *Bleak House*

34. 640

35. 'Pipe Down'

36. Charles Goodyear. The process retained the elasticity of rubber while making it stronger and more waterproof.

37. Tahiti. The Society Islands (French: *Îles de la Société* or officially *Archipel de la Société*) are a group of islands in the South Pacific Ocean.

38. David Broome. He was also voted BBC Sports Personality of the Year for 1960.

39. Perigee

40. The stethoscope. He improvised a paper tube to listen to a young woman's heart so as not to have the embarrassment of placing his head on her chest.

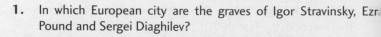

1. In which European city are the graves of Igor Stravinsky, Ezra Pound and Sergei Diaghilev?

2. 'Goodbye, Farewell, Amen' was the title of the last episode of which American TV series?

3. Which 1959 novel by Günter Grass, which features Oskar Matzerath, a boy who refuses to grow up, is generally seen as an allegory of Germany throughout its early 20th century history?

4. No.1 Carlton Gardens has been whose official residence in London since the 1940s?

5. Who was the first official Poet Laureate, appointed in 1668 and dismissed for refusing to take the oath of allegiance during the Glorious Revolution?

6. What's the name of the limestone plateau in the north of County Clare in Ireland, featuring a network of caves and underground waterways as well as prehistoric burial sites, which is also of importance to botanists as one of the most varied plant habitats in the whole of the British Isles?

7. The feast of Candlemas occurs on the second day of which month?

8. Which figure from South American history gives his name to the currency of Venezuela?

9. Who once said to Anton Chekhov: 'Shakespeare's plays are bad enough, but yours are even worse'?

10. When making bookings online it is often necessary to enter letters or digits from a distorted image, to ensure that the response is by a human rather than a computer. By what rather contrived acronym is this test known?

11. Some thirty years before the much-publicised cloning of Dolly the sheep in the late 1990s, the British biologist John Gurdon successfully cloned what type of creature?

12. Which Labour Government White Paper of 1969 was designed to harmonise labour relations and was issued by Barbara Castle as Secretary of State for Employment?

13. In 2007, which bestselling writer was appointed President of the Campaign to Protect Rural England?

14. Bluebell, Black Rock, Cuckoo Maran and Araucana are hybrid varieties of which creatures?

15. From which port did the Spanish Armada set sail in 1588?

16. Which British crystallographer became, in 1964, the third woman to be awarded the Nobel Prize for Chemistry, and in 1965 was admitted to the Order of Merit, the first woman to be so honoured since Florence Nightingale?

17. In the only outdoor public statue of him in London, sculpted by Francis Bird, which monarch is represented above the north gate entrance to St Bart's Hospital, surmounted by reclining figures symbolising lameness and disease?

18. Who, collectively, were Denny Doherty, John Phillips, Michelle Phillips and Cass Elliot?

19. Which royal palace in West Lothian, begun in the 1420s by James I of Scotland, became in 1542 the birthplace of Mary Queen of Scots?

20. A goitre is the enlargement of which gland?

Answers on page 188

21. The South African port which is the largest city of Kwa-Zulu Natal, and the name of a fishing village in East Lothian on Scotland's east coast, popular with tourists, are anagrams. Can you give me the names of both?

22. The actor Lee Van Cleef is perhaps best known for his role as the 'Bad' guy in the film *The Good, the Bad and the Ugly*, but he also made a much earlier screen appearance as a villain in which classic western of 1952?

23. Which Royal personage was the subject of the caricature by James Gillray, published in 1792, with the title *A Voluptuary Under the Horrors of Digestion*?

24. When would you be likely to hear the sound of a nautophone?

25. What type of mammal is a klipspringer?

26. What is the full correct title of the body who annually hand out the 'Oscars'?

27. In Wagner's 'Ring Cycle' of operas, who is the father of the Valkyries?

28. Which book's publication in 1987, and the government's unsuccessful attempts to suppress it, led to Section 2 of the 1911 Official Secrets Act being replaced under a new 1989 act?

29. Which instantly recognisable television characters were originally designed in 1963 by BBC staff member Raymond P. Cusick?

30. Which 20th century British politician was the only one of the century to hold all four great offices of state: Chancellor, Foreign Secretary, Home Secretary and Prime Minister?

31. What adjective is officially used to describe the water in bodies such as the Baltic Sea, which is not as saline as the open ocean due to the volume of fresh water that flows into it?

32. Which English poet married Erika – the daughter of the German writer, Thomas Mann – in 1935, in order to secure her a British passport?

33. In materials engineering, what is the term for the point when a body is permanently deformed through stress?

34. Now located 20 kilometres from the Estonian border, which city was the scene of the abdication of Tsar Nicholas II in 1917?

35. To the nearest 1%, what percentage of the air we breathe is oxygen?

36. Although most of the original James Bond stories of Ian Fleming are narrated in the third person, one of the novels is largely told from a female point of view. Which one?

37. Which 13th century Gothic cathedral was traditionally the setting for the coronation of most French kings?

38. For which Italian club did Paul Gascoigne play between leaving Tottenham Hotspur in 1992, and his return to British football with Rangers in 1995?

39. During the late 1800s, which cult religion was briefly practised by Native American tribes in the South Western United States, in the hope of ridding their lands of white settlers?

40. Which American writer and publisher, in editorial charge of *Cosmopolitan* magazine for over thirty years from 1965, wrote the influential book *Sex and the Single Girl*?

Answers on page 188

Answers to Quiz 26

1. Venice

2. M*A*S*H. It was two hours long and gained America's biggest-ever TV audience at its time.

3. *The Tin Drum/Die Blechtrommel*

4. The Foreign Secretary

5. John Dryden

6. The Burren

7. February

8. Simon Bolivar. The currency is the bolivar, equal to 100 centimos.

9. (Leo) Tolstoy

10. CAPTCHA. Standing for Completely Automated Public Turing test to tell Computers and Humans Apart

11. A frog. His work has been enormously important in the development of stem cell medicine, and he was awarded the Nobel Prize in Physiology or Medicine in 2012.

12. 'In Place of Strife'

13. Bill Bryson, OBE

14. Domestic chickens

15. Lisbon

16. Dorothy Hodgkin. She helped to determine the structure of penicillin in the 1940s, and of vitamin B12. Among her students at Oxford was one Margaret Roberts.

17. Henry VIII. He had refounded the building as a hospital in 1546.

18. The pop group, The Mamas and the Papas

19. Linlithgow Palace. It was largely ruined by fire in 1740s, but remains a tourist attraction.

20. Thyroid. The majority of cases of goitre are caused by iodine deficiency.

21. Durban and Dunbar

22. *High Noon*

23. The Prince of Wales/Prince Regent – later George IV. It depicts him as he has been seen in the popular imagination ever since, bloated and decadent.

24. When it is foggy – it's a high-pitched signal used on buoys and lightships and operated remotely at such times.

25. An antelope. Rock-dwelling, native of southern Africa.

26. The Academy of Motion Picture Arts and Sciences

27. Wotan. Not Odin. In Wagner's tale, Brünnhilde is one of the Valkyries, who are born out of a union between Wotan and Erda, the personification of the Earth.

28. *Spycatcher*. Written by former secret serviceman, Peter Wright.

29. The Daleks *(Dr Who)*. Terry Nation was responsible for the idea of the Daleks, but Mr Cusick gets the credit for their original design. The staff designer Cusick replaced was Ridley Scott. I wonder what happened to him? Bill Roberts built them.

30. James Callaghan

31. Brackish. The Baltic Sea's catchment area is almost four times larger than the sea itself.

32. W. H. Auden. She was a lesbian actress and journalist.

33. Yield point/yield strength

34. Pskov

35. 21%

36. *The Spy Who Loved Me*

37. Reims (Rheims)

38. (Società Sportiva) Lazio

39. The Ghost Dance. It was believed that the dance would bring back the spirits of the tribal ancestors to help in the struggle against the white man.

40. Helen Gurley Brown

Quiz 27

1. Planula, polyp, ephyra and medusa are stages in the life cycle of which type of invertebrate?

2. The *Dandy* and the *Beano* were both first published in which decade?

3. Which range of hills shares its name with the house in Liverpool in which John Lennon lived from 1945 to 1963?

4. In which US state is Bill and Hillary Clinton National Airport?

5. Which wading bird, a member of the Sandpiper family, shares its name with a unit of speed?

6. The title of John Wyndham's science fiction novel *The Kraken Wakes* was inspired by a 19th century poem which includes the lines: 'Far, far beneath in the abysmal sea, / His ancient, dreamless, uninvaded sleep / The Kraken sleepeth.' Who wrote the poem?

7. Also called the malar or malar bone, what is the more common name for the zygomatic bone?

8. The memoirs of which prominent 19th century figure were burnt after his death by his friends, including publisher John Murray, being judged too salacious for publication?

9. In an expedition of 1865, following six previous failed attempts, Edward Whymper succeeded in climbing which mountain?

10. In which 20th century play does the main character speak the line: 'Don't clap too hard, it's a very old building'?

11. What was the name of Peter Cook's satirical nightclub that opened in October 1961 in Greek Street, London?

12. The 1993 film *Dark Blood* had to be abandoned three weeks from completion after one of its stars died at the early age of 23. Who was he?

13. The traditional American dish, the 'Rocky Mountain oyster', consists of which part of a calf?

14. Which lake, with a maximum depth of nearly 260 feet, is the deepest in the English Lake District?

15. The Latin for a feather, 'pinna' is a term applied to which feature of the anatomy in humans and other mammals?

16. Which Indian cricketer in 2011 became the first ever to reach a career score of 15,000 runs in Test cricket?

17. Complete this sentence from St Matthew's Gospel: 'If the blind lead the blind…'

18. The Butler Bill, approved by Governor Austin Peay in the state of Tennessee in March 1925, prohibited which educational practice?

19. In the Ordnance Survey 1:50,000 Landranger Series of maps, what type of building is indicated by a pink triangle?

20. If you followed a sign in Milan that said 'Cenacolo Vinciano', what would it lead you to?

Answers on page 194

21. The Leeds-born comedian Steve Delaney created the character of which out-of-work variety performer, in a Radio 4 comedy series first broadcast in 2005 and later adapted for a TV show?

22. What was the name of the peasants' revolt that took place in Northern France in the summer of 1358, which has since become a word synonymous with peasant uprisings in general in both English and French?

23. James Gordon Bennett Jr was a Scottish-born newspaper owner who is famed for backing whose expedition to Africa in 1869?

24. In chemistry, what is defined as a negative logarithm of the hydrogen ion activity in a solution?

25. The name of which British city literally means 'the homestead of the people of Snot'?

26. The British folk singer Sydney Carter, who died in 2004, is best remembered for his composition of which Christian song, adapted from a Shaker hymn and becoming particularly popular with children?

27. Which date did Mark Twain describe thus: 'This is the day upon which we are reminded of what we are on the other three hundred and sixty-four'?

28. A recording of Mahler's *Song of the Earth*, with the Vienna Philharmonic and Bruno Walter, is among the final and most famous recordings of which British singer who died young from cancer in 1953?

29. The distinctive memorial tomb to Oscar Wilde in Père Lachaise cemetery in Paris was the work of which sculptor?

30. The Sylvian fissure is a prominent, deep-seated lateral cleft dividing parts of which organ of the human body?

31. The kalong, native to East Asia, is the largest species of which mammal of the suborder Megachiroptera?

32. Robben Island was the most famous of the prisons to house Nelson Mandela, but in which prison did he spend the last few years of his sentence?

33. What is the literal meaning of the word 'protein'?

34. In which sport do teams compete for the Vince Lombardi Trophy?

35. Which three countries have land borders with Cambodia?

36. What is the literal meaning of the word *Schutzstaffel*, the term for the militant branch of the Nazi Party, usually abbreviated to 'S.S.'?

37. The Royal estate at Balmoral stands on which river?

38. In 1943, Maria Dickin instituted a medal bearing her name to honour the gallantry of what kind of participants in war and civil defence?

39. Which well-loved antiques expert, who died in 1985, has a surname shared with the name of a drink made of wine, most commonly port, mixed with hot water, spiced and sugared?

40. Which American state is the setting for the annual Berkshire Music Festival?

Answers on page 194

Answers to Quiz 27

1. Jellyfish

2. 1930s (1937 and 1938 respectively)

3. Mendips

4. Arkansas. It's the airport that serves the city of Little Rock.

5. Knot

6. Alfred, Lord Tennyson

7. Cheekbone

8. Lord Byron

9. Matterhorn (known in French as Mont Cervin, in Italian as Monte Cervino). Whymper's successful ascent ended tragically when four of the party fell to their deaths on the way down.

10. *The Entertainer* by John Osborne. The line is spoken by fading song-and-dance-man, Archie Rice.

11. The Establishment

12. River Phoenix

13. The testicle(s)

14. Wastwater

15. The (external) ear or auricle. Its purpose is to 'collect' sound in the tunnel it helps to form.

16. Sachin Tendulkar. On 8th November 2011, against the West Indies in New Delhi.

17. '…both shall fall into a pit.' Matthew ch 15, vv 13-14

18. The teaching of Evolution Theory in state schools

19. A youth hostel

20. *The Last Supper* – the painting by Leonardo in Santa Maria delle Grazie

21. Count Arthur Strong

22. The Jacquerie (Jacquards). The revolt became known as the Jacquerie because the nobles derided peasants as 'Jacques' or 'Jacques Bonhomme'

23. Sir Henry Morton Stanley (born John Rowlands). James Gordon Bennett raised the *New York Herald*'s profile on the world stage when he provided the financial backing for the 1869 expedition by Henry Morton Stanley into Africa to find David Livingstone.

24. The pH value/pH scale. pH is a measure of the acidity or basicity of an aqueous solution. Expressed as pH = -log10 [H+].

25. Nottingham. The name was formerly Snotengaham and Snotingeham – Snot being the name of a person in this case.

26. 'Lord of the Dance'

27. 1st April

28. Kathleen Ferrier

29. Sir Jacob Epstein

30. The brain. It separates the frontal and parietal lobes from the temporal lobes.

31. (Fruit) Bat. It's also known as the Malay flying fox.

32. Victor Verster Prison. In 1982 he was transferred from Robben Island to Pollsmoor Prison, then to Victor Verster in Dec 1988, until his release in Feb 1990.

33. 'Of first importance'

34. American Football. It's the trophy awarded to the winners of the Super Bowl.

35. Thailand, Laos and Vietnam

36. Protection Squad. Guard detachment, defence staff, Hitler's personal bodyguard.

37. The Dee

38. Animals. 32 carrier pigeons, 18 dogs, 3 horses and a rat-catching ship's cat called Simon were the first recipients of the Dickin Medal. Maria Dickin was also the founder of the PDSA.

39. Arthur Negus. The drink Negus was an 18th and 19th century hot punch, invented by Colonel Francis Negus.

40. Massachusetts. It's held in the 'Berkshires', a range of wooded hills in Massachusetts.

1. In which sport would you find a peg, a rover and a baulk line?

2. Which phrase, referring to the young people who came of age during the First World War, was popularized by Ernest Hemingway, who used it as one of two contrasting epigraphs for his first novel *The Sun Also Rises*?

3. Which Derbyshire village, through the self-sacrificing decision to isolate itself from the outside world, lost hundreds of its inhabitants to the plague after an infected parcel of cloth was delivered there from London in September 1665?

4. Can you name either one of the two cousins who collaborated to write detective fiction under the name of Ellery Queen?

5. Which branch of philosophy concentrates on questions of right and wrong, good and bad, virtues and vices, and rights and obligations?

6. Species of which bird of prey include the black-shouldered, the brahminy, the hook-billed, the letter-winged and the red, the last of those being the only species found in Britain?

7. The South Pacific island group that was named the New Hebrides by Captain Cook, and was known as such until 1980, now has what name?

8. William Makepeace Thackeray's novel *Vanity Fair* originally appeared in monthly parts, beginning in 1847 – with illustrations by whom?

9. Which Italian painter, in 1334, became city architect and surveyor of Florence Cathedral, for which he designed the free-standing bell-tower or campanile?

10. What word, now with a more general usage, is used to describe decoration in classical and later architecture consisting of representations of fruit and flowers suspended in swags?

11. Which short-lived movement in British poetry of the 1970s and 80s – hinging on familiar objects or occurrences being described in unfamiliar terms – got its name from the first book published by the poet Craig Raine?

12. Which Saracen military leader commanded the victorious forces at the Battle of Hattin in 1187?

13. Living wild in small herds in parts of South America, guanacos belong to which genus of mammals?

14. On a Plimsoll line, on the side of a ship, the two letters TF appear against the line marker at the very top. What do these letters TF stand for?

15. The composer Franz Lehar, whose works include the light operas *The Land of Smiles* and *The Merry Widow*, was born in which country?

16. Which controversial American novelist shot and killed his wife Joan Vollmer, supposedly during a drunken game, in Mexico City in 1951?

17. Which is the only lake in the English Lake District actually to have the word 'Lake' as part of its name?

18. Bengal gram, a staple pulse of the Indian subcontinent, is more commonly known in the West by what name?

19. Which female MP, the member for Jarrow on the Tyne, led the so-called 'Crusade' from that town to London, to protest about the lack of jobs, in October 1936?

20. Which British track athlete, a native of Jarrow, set new world records in no fewer than three distance events within nineteen days in 1985 – the 1,500 metres, the mile, and the 2,000 metres?

Answers on page 200

21. Anna Mary Robertson, an American artist who began painting seriously at the age of 67 after a life as a farmer's wife, is remembered by what more familiar name?

22. Which term describes a gemstone – particularly a diamond – that has been cut, usually with a total of 58 facets?

23. LtCol Arthur Martin-Leake, Capt. Noel Chavasse, and Capt Charles Upham, are the only people to have achieved what military distinction?

24. 'Someone told me that each equation I included in the book would halve the sales.' Which best-selling book of 1988 was its author describing?

25. Who, together, were George and James Loveless, James Hammett, James Brine, and Thomas and John Stanfield?

26. In a suit of armour, which part of the body is protected by a 'vambrace'?

27. Which Roman building, commissioned by the Emperor Hadrian in the 2nd century AD, became the first pagan temple in Rome to be rededicated as a Christian church in the year 609?

28. Which well-known exhibit in the British Museum did a drunken member of the public smash to pieces in 1845?

29. The name of the man who, in 1873, became land agent for an absentee landlord in County Mayo, has entered the language. What was his name?

30. In which calendar year was the National Lottery in its current form first introduced in the UK?

31. Thought to derive from the Latin word for a magpie, what name is given in medicine to a compulsion to eat unconventional or normally-inedible substances?

32. The town of Blenheim – the site of the battle fought in August 1704 during the War of the Spanish Succession – is now in Germany but was, at the time, in which European state?

33. Who said, in the year 2000: 'I'm doing pretty well considering. In the past, when anyone left the Royal Family they had you beheaded'?

34. What is the surname of the American father and son – Eliphalet and Philo – who are credited with the 19th century invention and manufacture of repeating rifles and the first typewriter ?

35. A gurdwara is the name for a place of worship in which religion?

36. The firework display in 1749 to celebrate the peace of Aix-la-Chapelle, for which Handel wrote the *Music for the Royal Fireworks*, took place in which of London's parks?

37. Which two actors played the unlikely *Twins* in the 1988 Hollywood comedy of that title directed by Ivan Reitman?

38. The Uspallata Pass, which has been overlooked since 1904 by a statue called 'Christ of the Andes', is the principal route through that mountain range between which two countries?

39. What was the stage name of the dancer Marie Dolores Eliza Roseanna Gilbert, mistress of King Ludwig I of Bavaria?

40. In which modern French region, celebrated in the title of a First World War song, are the *départements* of Aisne, Oise and Somme?

Answers on page 200

Answers to Quiz 28

1. Croquet

2. The Lost Generation. The precise epigraph is 'You are all a lost generation', attributed to Gertrude Stein 'in conversation'.

3. Eyam. The Riley Graves, where members of Eyam's Hancock family are buried, remain as a memorial to the village's dead.

4. Frederic Dannay and Manfred B. Lee. These in turn were pen-names for Daniel Nathan and Manford Lepofsky. Ellery Queen was also the name of the detective character in the stories.

5. Ethics or moral philosophy

6. Kite

7. (The Republic of) Vanuatu

8. The author himself

9. Giotto (di Bondone)

10. Festoon

11. The Martian school / Martianism. After the book *A Martian Sends a Postcard Home*. Craig Raine was one of its principal exponents, as was Martin Amis, whose name is an anagram of 'Martianism'.

12. Saladin

13. Llama. Family *camelidae*.

14. Tropical fresh (water). The displacement of a ship is affected by the water temperature – and the other extreme, the lowest mark on the ship's side, has the letters WNA, for Winter North Atlantic.

15. Hungary

16. William S. Burroughs. He was apparently attempting to shoot a tumbler from her head, William Tell-style.

17. Bassenthwaite Lake – all of the others have either the name 'mere' or 'water', which mean the same thing – as in Windermere, Ullswater, Derwentwater, Grasmere, etc.

18. The chickpea

19. Ellen Wilkinson. Another of her achievements as a minister, perhaps less well remembered, was the introduction of free school milk.

20. Steve Cram. His world record mile time, of 3 minutes 46.32 seconds, stood for eight years.

21. 'Grandma Moses'

22. A brilliant

23. Won the Victoria Cross twice

24. (Stephen Hawking's) *A Brief History of Time*

25. The Tolpuddle Martyrs – the six farm labourers prosecuted in 1834 when they formed a local branch of an agricultural labourers' union. They were sentenced to seven years' transportation, but freed after a public campaign.

26. The (Fore)arm

27. The Pantheon

28. The Portland Vase – a priceless Roman vase dating from the lifetime of Christ. A museum craftsman tried to piece it together again, but thirty-seven tiny fragments were missing, and remained so for the next hundred years. It has now been restored using modern adhesives.

29. Capt. Charles Cunningham Boycott. Because of evictions from his estates, local men refused to work for him and local shopkeepers refused to serve him. The campaign was so successful that he had to be placed under police protection.

30. 1994. The first draw was on 19th November.

31. Pica. *Pica pica* is the taxonomic name for a magpie. The condition can occur during childhood, pregnancy or illness.

32. Bavaria

33. Sarah Ferguson (Sarah, Duchess of York)

34. Remington

35. Sikh(ism). The most well-known gurdwara of the Sikhs is the Harmandir in Amritsar, Punjab, India, otherwise known as the Golden Temple.

36. Green Park

37. Arnold Schwarzenegger and Danny DeVito

38. Argentina and Chile

39. Lola Montez. Although billed as a Spanish dancer, and thought of as half Spanish, she was in fact Irish.

40. Picardy – as in 'Roses of Picardy'

Quiz 29

1. In the Ptolemaic dynasty of Egypt, which regnal number is applied to the queen Cleopatra, who ruled in two periods from 51 BC to her death in 30 BC?

2. Guided walks from Arnside to Kents Bank cross which notoriously dangerous part of the British coastline?

3. Which mammal, common to the United States, has the taxonomic name *Mephitis mephitis*?

4. What or who is assessed using an Apgar score?

5. What technical term is applied to liquid precipitation which consists of drops with a diameter of between 0.2 and 0.5 mm?

6. Which two Russian cities are the end-points of the Trans-Siberian Highway?

7. With a total of 31 by the time of his death in 1997, which orchestral conductor has won more Grammy Awards than any other artist?

8. 'What is written without effort is generally read without pleasure,' and 'No man but a blockhead ever wrote except for money,' are assertions attributed to which 18th century writer?

9. The layout of the streets of which capital city was designed by the architect Pierre Charles L'Enfant?

10. Which British magazine, founded by Budapest-born Stefan Lorant in 1938, pioneered a style of 'photo-journalism with a conscience' that, in its heyday, attracted a huge readership?

11. Which explorer gave the Pacific Ocean its name?

12. Which compound, once commonly used in the manufacture of felt hats, was responsible for the prevalence of St Vitus's Dance, and other neurological conditions, among workers in the hat-making industry?

13. Who played the part of 'The Ringo Kid' in the 1939 film western *Stagecoach*, directed by John Ford?

14. In the works of Homer, which Greek island is the home to Odysseus, the story about his delay in returning there being a key element of the epic?

15. Which motor sport developed in the US in the 1920s when cars were modified to enable moonshine runners to outpace the authorities during prohibition?

16. Which colour takes its name from the common term for hydrated basic copper aluminium phosphate?

17. In the 1955 novel by Vladimir Nabokov, what's Lolita's real first name?

18. The subject of many of her husband's portraits, Jacqueline Roque became the second wife in 1961 of which painter, then aged 79?

19. As recounted in an old Scottish ballad, which hero was shipwrecked on his return voyage from Norway near the island of Papa Stronsay, with everyone on board being lost?

20. Drop, lancet, horseshoe, ogee and parabolic are all types of which architectural feature?

21. What two-word term, popularised as a disparaging phrase by George Bush Senior during his first Presidential election campaign, is often used for an ill-advised policy or promise to reduce taxes while maintaining government spending levels?

22. Covering just one square mile in area, what is the name of the small island located between Malta and Gozo?

Answers on page 206

23. Still used by some Scandinavians, which Swedish name served as the original official designation for the Finnish capital, Helsinki?

24. Which private detective, created by Mickey Spillane, appeared in ten novels beginning with *I, the Jury* in 1947?

25. The description of fox-hunting as 'the unspeakable in full pursuit of the uneatable' first appeared in which play, first performed in 1893?

26. What was the title of the composition with which the English composer Sir John Tavener first came to prominence in the late 1960s, a 'dramatic cantata' on a Biblical theme, released on the Beatles' Apple record label?

27. All captive examples of which popular pet animal are thought to be descended from a female captured at Aleppo, Syria, in 1930?

28. Diagnosed with a multiple personality disorder in the 1950s, Christine Costner-Sizemore inspired which Hollywood film, directed by Nunnally Johnson in 1957?

29. Ephilides is a medical term used to refer to which condition, associated in particular with a fair skin?

30. Which prominent journalist and commentator was punched on live television by the writer and musician Desmond Leslie in 1962?

31. In 1810, which German dramatist published *Zur Farbenlehre*, a scientific treatise on his theory of light and colour?

32. What was the middle name of the 29th President of the United States, Warren G. Harding?

33. 'Space isn't remote at all. It's only an hour's drive away, if your car could go straight upwards' – an observation made in 1979 by which British astronomer whose works of science fiction began with *The Black Cloud*?

34. Which form of alternative medicine has it origins in an Iowa 'magnetic studio' where, in 1895, Daniel Palmer claimed to have restored a client's hearing by realigning a vertebra in his spine?

35. Which comet, first observed in 1786, has a period of about 3.3 years and is the single most frequently observed of all such bodies?

36. Which influential and politically-radical New York hip-hop band won acclaim for its albums *It Takes a Nation of Millons to Hold Us Back* and *Fear of a Black Planet*, and was inducted into the US Rock and Roll Hall of Fame in 2012?

37. *Knights, Wasps, Clouds, Birds* and *Frogs* all provide titles of plays by which Ancient Greek playwright?

38. The only authentic canvas of Jane Austen from life is to be found in the National Portrait Gallery. Who painted it?

39. Which name, now more familiar in a medical context, was used by the British scientist J. J. Thomson to refer to the negatively-charged sub-atomic particles – now called electrons – whose existence he postulated in 1897 after experiments with cathode ray tubes?

40. The Order of the Elephant, founded in the first half of the 15th century, is the highest honour bestowed by which European country?

Answers on page 206

1. Seven(th)

2. Morecambe Bay. The speed of advancing tides across the sands of the bay make the walk potentially treacherous.

3. (Striped) Skunk. 'Mephitis' means literally 'a noxious or poisonous exhalation from the earth'.

4. (The health of) a new-born baby

5. Drizzle

6. St Petersburg and Vladivostok

7. Sir Georg Solti

8. Samuel Johnson

9. Washington DC. A new capital city named after George Washington was founded in 1791 to the east of a pre-existing settlement at Georgetown

10. *Picture Post.* Which finally ceased publication in 1957.

11. Ferdinand Magellan

12. Mercuric nitrate, also known as mercury (II) nitrate or mercury dinitrate – $Hg(NO_3)_2$. The use of mercuric nitrate in felt-making was banned in the 1940s.

13. John Wayne. It was the film that made him a star.

14. Ithaca

15. Stock Car Racing. Often known as NASCAR, after the National Association for Stock Car Auto Racing, the sanctioning body for stock-car racing in North America.

16. Turquoise

17. Dolores (Dolly)

18. Pablo Picasso

19. Sir Patrick Spens

20. Arch

21. Voodoo economics

22. Comino

23. Helsingfors

24. Mike Hammer

25. *A Woman of No Importance* by Oscar Wilde. I've often thought 'the inedible' would have been better.

26. *The Whale*

27. The hamster/Golden hamster

28. *The Three Faces of Eve*. Sizemore (who died in 2016) also called herself Eve White. Joanne Woodward won an Academy Award as Best Actress in the film role.

29. Freckles

30. Bernard Levin. On an episode of *That Was The Week That Was*. Levin had given an unfavourable review to a play in which Leslie's wife Agnes Bernelle was appearing.

31. Johann Wolfgang von Goethe

32. Gamaliel

33. (Sir) Fred Hoyle

34. Chiropractics

35. Encke's Comet

36. Public Enemy

37. Aristophanes

38. Her sister Cassandra. One writer describes it as 'little better than a daub', but it's all there is.

39. Corpuscles

40. Denmark. There is a similar chivalric order in Thailand, with a name usually translated as the Order of the White Elephant.

Quiz 30

1. Who won her first Best Actress Oscar at the ceremony in 1934 and her last in 1982?

2. The Philadelphia-born novelist Owen Wister is credited with the successful creation of which genre of literature?

3. Captain Matthew Webb was the first man to swim the English Channel, but he was drowned many years later in 1883 while attempting what feat?

4. The porcupine is a member of which order of mammals?

5. Informally observed in Ireland on 6th October each year, Ivy Day commemorates the death in 1891 of which nationalist?

6. Although it's now acknowledged as historically unreliable, if not pure fiction, the *History of the Kings of Britain* was for many centuries an important source of information about early British history, and provided Shakespeare with the story of King Lear. Which 12th century churchman was its author?

7. The name of which 18th century French finance minister is commemorated in the term used to describe a type of profile portrait, at its peak of popularity immediately prior to the invention of photography ?

8. The study of how force produces motion is known as Dynamics. What is the corresponding word for the study of how forces interact with each other to produce equilibrium?

9. Sak'art'velo is the local name for which former Soviet republic?

10. Who is the Greek god of the marriage ceremony, who also appears in the final scene of Shakespeare's *As You Like It*?

11. Who first published his American Dictionary of the English Language in 1828?

12. What nickname is shared by the most lucrative opium-growing region of South-East Asia, and the part of Cheshire known for the elaborate homes of stockbrokers and Premiership footballers?

13. Native to Africa and southern parts of Asia, which horny-plated, edentate mammal – the only extant genus of the order Pholidota – is also known as the scaly anteater?

14. Complete this line from Tom Stoppard's play *Rosencrantz and Guildenstern Are Dead*: 'Eternity is a terrible thought. I mean...'

15. Which position has been held by Trinle Gyatso and Thupten Gyatso, and is currently held by Tenzin Gyatso?

16. A version of the Geneva Bible, first printed in 1579, is often known by which other less refined name?

17. Which British pop group, most successful during the early 1980s, had three members with the surname Taylor, none of them related to one another?

18. The drug warfarin prevents blood clotting by inhibiting the action of which vitamin?

19. In 1913, which Bengali poet and philosopher became the first Asian winner of the Nobel Prize for Literature?

20. 'Knisper! Knasper! Knusper!' is the German equivalent of which famous advertising slogan?

Answers on page 212

21. The 'Bilby' is a mammal native to which country?

22. Which common name for the flowering plant *Matthiola longipetala* reflects its tendency to emit a sweet and heady odour after the sun has gone down?

23. *Wodwo* and *Lupercal* are among the original books of poetry published by which 20th century Poet Laureate?

24. In astrophysics, what term is used for the likely source of the universe's expansion according to the Big Bang theory, its existence predicted to occupy the space at the centre of a black hole – and that point in space-time at which the known laws of physics break down?

25. Which product, invented by Georges de Mestral, is a contraction of the French for 'hooked velvet'?

26. What was the screen name of Hungarian-born László Loewenstein, who first achieved international recognition as a child murderer in the 1931 film *M*, and went on to play a Japanese detective in eight Hollywood films between 1937 and 1939?

27. The Oort Cloud, proposed by Dutch astronomer Jan Oort in 1950, is composed of what?

28. In its original context, which sentence immediately follows this: 'Religion is the sigh of the oppressed creature, the sentiment of the heartless world, and the soul of soulless conditions'?

29. The name of the group Ian Dury & the Blockheads is well-remembered, but early in his career Dury was featured in a band whose name drew affectionate inspiration from the streets of London. What was that name?

30. Which four European Union countries share land borders with Italy?

31. The wild plant *Rubus fruticosus* and its variants, widespread in Britain, produce which commonly-eaten fruit?

32. Who was the last British monarch to lead his troops into battle?

33. What is the national instrument of Japan, a 13-string zither similar to the Chinese *guzheng*?

34. Vertigo is a medical condition causing dizziness, and is often associated with being in a high place, but what is the specific term for the fear of high places?

35. Released in 1937, which Marx Brothers film followed *A Night at the Opera* released some two years earlier?

36. OPEC, the Organization of Petroleum Exporting Countries, was established as a permanent body in the 1960s, in which South American city?

37. In the 'Mr Creosote' scene from the film *Monty Python's The Meaning of Life*, what item of food finally makes the obese restaurant patron explode?

38. Which city and seaport of Norway has a medieval cathedral where Norwegian sovereigns have been crowned since early times?

39. In which sport could you compete for the Coupe Aéronautique Gordon Bennett?

40. Which archangel, prominent in the story of Christ, is also the guide of the prophet Muhammad on his 'night-journey' or al-Miraj in Islamic belief?

Answers on page 212

1. Katharine Hepburn. Miss Hepburn also won the award in 1968 and 1969.

2. The Western. The first critically-recognized Western was Wister's novel *The Virginian*, published in 1902.

3. Swimming the rapids below Niagara Falls

4. Rodents/Rodentia

5. Charles Stewart Parnell. Sprigs of ivy are sported in the buttonholes of those remembering him.

6. Geoffrey of Monmouth

7. (Etienne de) Silhouette

8. Statics

9. Georgia

10. Hymen

11. (Noah) Webster

12. The Golden Triangle. Cheshire's 'Golden Triangle' includes the towns of Knutsford and Alderley Edge.

13. The Pangolin. There are seven species within the genus, all known as pangolins.

14. '…where's it going to end?'

15. Dalai Lama

16. The 'Breeches Bible'. Because it refers to Adam and Eve making themselves 'breeches' made from fig leaves in Genesis 3:7. It pre-dates the publication of the King James Bible by thirty-two years.

17. Duran Duran. John, Roger and Andy.

18. Vitamin K

19. (Rabindranath) Tagore/Thakur

20. 'Snap! Crackle! Pop!', advertising Rice Krispies.

21. Australia. Also, Tasmania and New Guinea. It's a marsupial, similar to a rat with large ears, pointed nose and long tail.

22. Night-scented Stock

23. Ted Hughes

24. Singularity

25. Velcro

26. (Peter) Lorre. The Japanese detective was Mr Moto.

27. Comets. As many as 10 trillion comets may be contained in the Oort Cloud.

28. 'It is the opium of the people.' From Karl Marx's posthumously published introduction to *A Contribution to the Critique of Hegel's Philosophy of Right*.

29. Kilburn and the High Roads

30. France, Switzerland, Austria and Slovenia

31. The Blackberry

32. George II

33. The Koto. The Kin, a slightly different instrument, can be written the same way as the Koto in the Japanese language.

34. Acrophobia

35. *A Day at the Races*

36. Caracas. Venezuela, Iran, Iraq, Kuwait, Saudi Arabia and Venezuela were the five founding members.

37. A wafer-thin mint

38. Trondheim (Nidaros Cathedral)

39. Ballooning

40. Gabriel/Jibreel

Quiz 31

1. The Boathouse in Laugharne, on the Taf Estuary in Carmarthenshire is now a museum dedicated to which writer?

2. How is the colour silver referred to in heraldry?

3. A perfect number is 'a number the sum of whose integral divisors including 1 but excluding itself, is that number itself'. The smallest perfect number is 6. What is the only other perfect number below 100?

4. *Pagan Papers* and *The Golden Age* are among the early works of which Scots-born children's writer, whose most enduring book was first published in 1908?

5. In 1653, Cromwell dismissed MPs of the Long Parliament with the words, 'You have sat here too long for any good you have been doing. Depart, I say, and let us have done with you. In the name of God, go!'. 287 years later, in 1940, which individual was the target of Leo Amery when he used the same words?

6. Kibo (or Uhuru), Mawenzi and Shira are the three most prominent peaks of which extinct volcanic mountain whose summit was first reached in 1899?

7. The town of Fray Bentos, best known for the industrial production of meat extract, is located in which South American country?

8. Which town on the river Wansbeck is the seat of the local government headquarters of Northumberland?

9. US Patent No. 6,812,392, filed in 2002, describes a mechanised device for tightening the heads of conga drums, and thus tuning them. According to the patent, the inventor of the device was a legendary Hollywood actor, who was also, in his spare time, a keen exponent of the conga drum. Who was that actor?

10. At King Arthur's round table, for whom was the seat called the 'Siege Perilous' reserved?

1. 'I was born in the year 1632, in the city of York, of a good family' are the opening words of which novel?

2. Which branch of the Roman Army, originally a small escort which accompanied an army commander, was established as a permanent force under Augustus and became closely involved in imperial politics, their support of crucial importance for any new emperor?

3. Which word, from the French for 'light of hand', means cunning deception or trickery?

4. Following the territorial disputes between New York and New Hampshire, in the 1770s, the 'Green Mountain Boys' became the militia of which newly declared 'republic', which was ultimately allowed into the United States as the 14th state in 1791?

5. The Barbary Ape, much loved by visitors to Gibraltar, is not actually an ape, but a tailless species of which genus of monkey?

6. What was the name of the peerage which Anthony Wedgwood (Tony) Benn disclaimed in 1963?

7. In stories by Norman Hunter, what is the name of the absent-minded professor who is always building crazy impractical machines?

8. Ram Das, the 16th century religious leader and the fourth guru of Sikhism, founded which holy city around the 'pool of nectar'?

9. Which fluid, deriving its name from the Latin word for 'egg', lubricates and cushions joints in the human body during movement?

20. Which football manager is credited with saying, 'A football team is like a piano. You need eight men to carry it and three who can play the damn thing'?

Answers on page 218

21. The congenital condition protanopia affects which of the senses?

22. The scientific name of which cultivated vegetable is *Allium porrum*?

23. The Jewish Festival of Lights, Hanukkah, commemorates the re-dedication of the temple after the victory of which army?

24. The 1956 summer Olympic Games were held in Melbourne, but because of Australian quarantine laws the equestrian events were held somewhere else. Where?

25. Which British rap star first came to international prominence when his first album *Boy in da Corner* won the 2003 Mercury Music Prize?

26. What is the modern English name for the headland that Bartholomeu Dias originally called *Cabo das Tormentas*, or 'Cape of Tempests' when rounding it for the first time in 1488?

27. Which well-known and much-anthologised 18th century poem is believed to have been at least partly written in the graveyard of the church at Stoke Poges in Buckinghamshire?

28. Sfax is the second largest city in which African country?

29. Who, in 52 BC, united the Gauls in an ultimately unsuccessful revolt against Roman forces during the last phase of Julius Caesar's Gallic Wars?

30. Okhrana is an informal name for the organisation founded in 1881 as the secret police force of which imperial power?

31. In the Albert Memorial, designed by George Gilbert Scott and standing opposite the Royal Albert Hall, which book is Prince Albert holding on his knee?

52. Which globally popular cartoon strip had its origins in an earlier strip called *Li'l Folks* that first appeared in a Minnesota newspaper in 1947?

53. *Troglodytes troglodytes* is the taxonomic name for the wren. But which mammal has the designation *Pan troglodytes*?

54. What is the name of the 18-mile-long shingle bank in Dorset that separates the Fleet lagoon from the sea?

55. With words by Samuel F. Smith, which enduring US patriotic song shares its melody with the British national anthem?

56. Which major road – one of the highest paved roads in the world – connects Islamabad in Pakistan to Kashgar in China?

57. On the Rowley Mile racecourse in Newmarket there stands a statue of a horse who was unbeaten in 18 races and whose name lives on in racing. What was the horse's name?

58. Since 1984 an annual festival has been staged at the Cornish town of Camborne, in celebration of the achievements of which engineer who was born nearby?

59. Which team game, invented in the early 1900s by Nico Broekhuysen, derives its name from the Dutch word for 'basket'?

60. Which agricultural system sees the seasonal movement of people with their livestock over relatively short distances, typically to higher pastures in summer and to lower valleys in winter?

Answers on page 218

Answers to Quiz 31

1. Dylan Thomas

2. Argent

3. 28. Which is the sum of its factors, i.e. 1+2+4+7+14. The next one i 496.

4. Kenneth Grahame. His best-known work was *The Wind in the Willows*.

5. Neville Chamberlain. The phrase 'In the name of God, go!' is now popularly quoted whenever anyone is suggesting that a politician o other public figure should resign.

6. Kilimanjaro. The mountain was the first climbed by the German geographer, Hans Meyer and Austrian mountaineer Ludwig Purtscheller.

7. Uruguay

8. Morpeth

9. Marlon Brando

10. The finder of the Holy Grail

11. *Robinson Crusoe* by Daniel Defoe

12. The Praetorian Guard

13. Legerdemain

14. Vermont

15. Macaque. Besides humans, they are the only primates to live freely in Europe.

16. Viscount Stansgate

17. Professor Branestawm

18. Amritsar (accept Ramdaspur). The pool or tank was called Amrita Sara – which translates as 'pool of nectar'.

19. Synovial Fluid

20. Bill Shankly

21. Sight. There is a loss of sensitivity to red light and a particular tendency to confuse reds with greens and bluish-greens.

22. Leek

23. The Maccabees. Hanukkah, Hebrew for consecration, is observed fo eight nights and days, starting on the 25th day of Kislev according to the Hebrew calendar.

24. Stockholm. It's hard to see how you could get much further away.

5. Dizzee Rascal

6. Cape of Good Hope. It was later renamed by John II of Portugal as 'Cape of Good Hope' because of the great optimism engendered by the opening of a sea route to India and the East.

7. Thomas Gray's *Elegy Written in a Country Churchyard*, first published in 1751.

8. Tunisia. It's a major port on the Mediterranean.

9. Vercingetorix. There is a statue to Vercingetorix created by the sculptor Aimé Millet in 1865, on the supposed site of the Battle of Alesia near Alise-Sainte-Reine.

0. (Tsarist) Russia. It was abolished after the February Revolution of 1917 – later to be superseded, as we know, by other secret police forces.

1. The Catalogue of the 1851 Great Exhibition. Albert had been the prime mover behind the enterprise.

2. *Peanuts*. *Li'l Folks* was the first comic strip by Charles M. Schulz and was a weekly panel that appeared mainly in Schulz's hometown paper, the *St. Paul Pioneer Press*, from June 1947 to January 1950.

3. Chimpanzee

4. Chesil Beach or Bank

5. 'America' or 'My Country 'tis of Thee'

6. Karakoram Highway (Karakoram Gonglu/Zhongba Gonglu)

7. Eclipse. He died in 1789 and the Eclipse Stakes is named after him.

8. Richard Trevithick. Trevithick had run his 'Puffing Devil' steam wagon up Camborne Hill on Christmas Eve 1801. 'Trevithick Day' is a one-day festival staged in April.

9. Korfball

0. Transhumance

Quiz 32

1. The St Scholastica's Day Massacre in 1355 took place in which English city?

2. The violinist and conductor Charles Williams composed 'Devil' Galop', a piece used as the title music for which radio serial, first broadcast in 1946?

3. Which Mediterranean island's southeastern tip is Cape Carbonara?

4. The tilt of the Earth's axis is referred to by the phrase 'the obliquity of the...' what?

5. What was bandleader 'Count' Basie's actual first name?

6. In which country will you find the Spitzkoppe, a mountain known locally as 'the Matterhorn of Africa'?

7. Which type of plant, popular as a flowering houseplant, is named after a US Minister to Mexico, who introduced it to the United States?

8. The words 'Cormac MacCarthy fortis me fieri fecit AD 1446' are inscribed on what?

9. 'Only Connect', now the name of a television quiz show, is also the epigraph to which novel by E. M. Forster?

10. Which African country takes its name from a Portuguese word for shrimps?

11. Which medical affliction that results in perceptual distortions of the size and shape of objects was identified by the psychiatrist John Todd in 1955, and named after a novel first published in 1865?

12. 'It is not enough to succeed. Others must fail', is a quote attributed to which American author who died in 2012 aged 86?

13. Which opera ends with Azucena's revelation that she threw the wrong baby into the fire?

14. Which flower, because of its strong smell, has a name meaning 'nose-twister'?

15. Otorhinolaryngology is the full title of the branch of medicine and surgery that specializes in the diagnosis and treatment of disorders of the head and neck, but derives its name from which three specific parts of the body?

16. *All That Fall* is a radio play first broadcast in 1957, commissioned by the BBC from which playwright who was later awarded the Nobel Prize for Literature?

17. In which major European art gallery will you find the 1812 Gallery, the Malachite Hall and the Hall of St George?

18. What should you expect to find inside a Warden pie?

19. In which city did Sally Gunnell win her Olympic 400 metres hurdles gold medal?

20. What name is given to the civilization known to have flourished in southern Mexico, generally considered the first Meso-American civilization?

21. Which record label, founded in New York in 1939 by Alfred Lion and Max Margulis, had its first success with a recording by Sidney Bechet, and went on to become associated with the 1950s be-bop of Thelonious Monk, Horace Silver, the Jazz Messengers and the MJQ?

Answers on page 224

Quiz 32

22. Christmas Island in the South Pacific – the site, from 1957, of various nuclear tests – is now represented on maps with a spelling more closely reflecting its native name. What is that revised spelling?

23. Which 1836 battle saw the capture of Mexican General Santa Anna and effectively marked the end of the Texas Revolution?

24. What does the abbreviation TNT stand for, when applied to the widely used explosive?

25. Which 1859 historical novel features chapters called: 'Knitting', 'Still Knitting' and 'The Knitting Done'?

26. Which city, the capital of the Philippines between 1948 and 1976, is named after the country's President between 1935 and 1944?

27. What five-word phrase is a recommended form of greeting to be used at the beginning of a letter written directly to the Queen?

28. A substance known as 'C90' is often used on film sets – for what purpose?

29. Which anarchic theatrical character was created by the French dramatist Alfred Jarry in the 1890s, his name being adopted by an alternative rock group from Ohio in the 1970s?

30. Which was the first professional football club for which Sir Stanley Matthews played?

31. Which British chemist, particularly noted for his work on plant pigments, alkaloids and other natural products, was awarded the Nobel Prize for Chemistry in 1947?

32. In astronomy, which term is used to describe the observable lengthening of the wavelength of light from an object as a result of that object's motion away from it?

33. Lake Wenham in Massachusetts became the most famous supplier of what commodity to Victorian Britain?

34. Which adjective, meaning 'completely honest and just', derives from the name of the son of Zeus and Europa?

35. The genre of Japanese painting called *Ukiyo-e*, characterised by screen paintings and wood block prints, which flourished during the Tokugawa period, is sometimes known in English as 'art of the…' what?

36. Named after the 19th century French scientist Jean Louis Marie Poiseuille, the poise is a standard unit used to measure which physical property of a liquid?

37. The book *Ten Days That Shook The World*, by the American journalist John Reed, is an account of which event?

38. An 'LED display' has been a familiar feature of electronic devices over the past fifty years or so. What do the letters LED stand for?

39. Malin Head, the northernmost point of mainland Ireland, is not in Northern Ireland. In which county of the Republic does it lie?

40. An 'Aubade', often found in the form of a love song or poem about lovers, refers to which specific time of day?

Answers on page 224

Answers to Quiz 32

1. Oxford
2. *Dick Barton (- Special Agent)*
3. Sardinia
4. Ecliptic
5. William (Bill)
6. Namibia
7. Poinsettia, after Joel R. Poinsett
8. The Blarney Stone. Nothing to do with the writer of bleak westerns.
9. *Howards End*
10. Cameroon
11. 'Alice in Wonderland Syndrome'
12. Gore Vidal
13. *Il Trovatore* by Verdi
14. Nasturtium
15. Ear, nose & throat. 'Oto' for ear, 'rhino' for nose and 'laryng' for throat.
16. Samuel Beckett
17. The Hermitage (in St Petersburg)
18. (Warden) pears. It's a pear pie coloured with saffron and spiced with mace, nutmegs, ginger, prunes, and sultanas.
19. Barcelona (1992). She also won a bronze in the 4x400 metres women's relay.
20. The Olmecs
21. Blue Note
22. Kiritimati. Its pronunciation is still remarkably close to that of the word 'Christmas'.
23. Battle of San Jacinto (river)
24. Tri-nitro-toluene. The name of the compound is properly 2-4-6-trinitrotoluene.
25. *A Tale of Two Cities* by Charles Dickens
26. Quezon City. The city was named after Manuel L. Quezón, who founded the city and developed it to replace Manila as the country's capital.

27. 'May it please Your Majesty.' The single word 'Madam' is also acceptable, according to protocol.

28. Fake/artificial snow. It's a cellulose powder that comes in various grades to imitate different types and severity of snow and frost.

29. Père Ubu

30. Stoke (City). It was also his last. His club footballing dates are Stoke City 1932-1947, Blackpool 1947-1961 and then Stoke City again 1961-1965, a career of over three decades.

31. (Sir) Robert Robinson. Not to be confused…

32. Red shift. So-called because the lengthening of wavelength 'shifts' the light towards the red end of the spectrum.

33. Ice. Lake Wenham ice was no different from ice found on any other lake, but it became so famous in the 1840s that ice from many other sources was passed off as coming from there.

34. Rhadamanthine

35. Floating World

36. Viscosity

37. The October Revolution/Bolshevik Revolution of 1917. It was first published in 1919.

38. Light-Emitting Diode

39. Donegal

40. Dawn (accept daybreak/early morning)

Quiz 33

1. In the 1982 children's novel by Michael Morpurgo set before and during the First World War, what is the name of the animal known as the 'War Horse'?

2. The sentence 'Colorless green ideas sleep furiously' was invented by which theoretical linguist to demonstrate that a sentence can be grammatically correct, but completely meaningless?

3. The first five chapters of which novel by H. G. Wells are entitled respectively: 'The Strange Man's Arrival', 'Mr Teddy Henfrey's First Impressions', 'The Thousand and One Bottles', 'Mr Cuss Interviews the Stranger' and 'The Burglary At The Vicarage'?

4. Arizona's Grand Canyon is the result of millions of years of erosion by which river?

5. The 18th- and early 19th-century artists Paul Sandby, Thomas Girtin and John Sell Cotman are most closely associated with which artistic medium?

6. Which innovative French film director was responsible for the films *J'accuse* in 1918, *La Roue* in 1922 and what is most often regarded as his masterpiece, *Napoléon* in 1927?

7. Which scientific process involves the lowering in temperature of a saturated solution without crystallization taking place, which then leads to the formation of a supersaturated solution?

8. Which of the shipping forecast areas of British coastal waters shares its name with the state capital of Delaware?

9. *The Ruffian on the Stair*, first broadcast in 1964, is a radio play by which English playwright, who died in 1967?

10. One Canada Square at Canary Wharf in London and the Petronas Towers at Kuala Lumpur are among the designs of which Argentinian-born American architect?

11. What middle name is shared by the former Conservative politician William Hague and the former US President Bill Clinton?

12. The Mercedes-Benz Museum on Mercedesstrasse, and the Porsche Museum on Porscheplatz, are in which major German city?

13. Which meteorological instrument was the invention of the 17th century Italian scientist Evangelista Torricelli?

14. The member of the animal kingdom thought to have the longest life-span of any on Earth, with some specimens thought to be 400 years old, *Arctica islandica* is a species belonging to which phylum of invertebrates?

15. In which US state is the vast majority of Yellowstone National Park?

16. The writer J. B. Priestley, the composer Frederick Delius and the painter David Hockney were all born in which city?

17. Who or what is the Witch of Agnesi?

18. The last prosecution for witchcraft in the UK took place in which decade?

19. What are the coronaria dextra and the coronaria sinistra?

20. Which region of France is formed by the delta between the 'Grand Rhone' and the 'Petit Rhone'?

21. In Boswell's *Life of Johnson*, which vegetable is being described when physicians in England advise it 'should be well sliced, and dressed with pepper and vinegar, and then thrown out as good for nothing'?

Answers on page 230

22. At which summer Olympic Games did Dick Fosbury win the gold medal in the high jump – using his revolutionary Fosbury Flop technique – to set a new Olympic record of 2.24 m?

23. Between the late 1880s and the early 1900s, which major philanthropist oversaw a survey with the umbrella title of *Inquiry into the Life and Labour of the People of London*?

24. The name of which French physicist was given to the radiations he first observed being given off by uranium compounds in 1896, the emissions now being distinguished as alpha, beta and gamma rays?

25. In which American city would you find the Mystics basketball team, the Nationals baseball team and the Capitals ice hockey team?

26. In 1782, the English portrait painter George Romney met his muse, and went on to paint over fifty portraits of her as various historical or mythological figures. Who was she?

27. *A Streetcar Named Desire* and *Death of a Salesman* won the Pulitzer Prize for Drama in consecutive years, in which decade?

28. Cullet is a waste version, with impurities, of which material?

29. The Reverend David Railton, latterly a vicar in Margate, is credited with the idea for what, inspired by his time serving as a chaplain in the First World War?

30. In Hindu thought, what are the Krita Yuga, the Treta Yuga, the Dwapara Yuga and the Kali Yuga?

31. Which Ukrainian Cossack leader is the title character of an historical tale by Nikolai Gogol and a rhapsody for orchestra by Leoš Janáček?

32. Although it's changed location a few times since, which great New York City jazz venue was to be found, during its heyday between 1949 and 1965, at 1678 Broadway?

33. What is the occupation of Mr Sludge, in an 1864 poem by Robert Browning?

34. The Spanish name for the percussion instruments known in English as the castanets, *castañuelas*, is derived from the diminutive form of *castaña*, the Spanish word for which nut?

35. To what was Benjamin Franklin referring, when he claimed that George III and his ministers had 'made thirteen clocks strike as one'?

36. Which score in darts is known as a 'bed and breakfast'?

37. In which Asian country will you find Tenzing-Hillary, also known as Lukla Airport, sometimes described as the most dangerous airport in the world?

38. According to the philosopher Søren Kierkegaard, 'the lowest depth to which people can sink before God is defined by the word…' what?

39. What would you conclude if you saw the name 'Alan Smithee' in the list of credits at the end of a Hollywood movie?

40. Claydon House in Buckinghamshire, once the home of Sir Harry Verney and his second wife Parthenope, contains a room dedicated to the memory of Parthenope's unmarried sister, who often visited the house. Which extremely well-known person was Parthenope's sister?

Answers on page 230

Answers to Quiz 33

1. Joey. The novel became an acclaimed stage show, and then a film by Stephen Spielberg.

2. Noam Chomsky

3. *The Invisible Man*

4. The Colorado

5. Watercolours/watercolour painting

6. (Abel) Gance

7. Supercooling. A liquid below its standard freezing point will crystallize in the presence of a seed crystal or nucleus around which a crystal structure can form. However, lacking any such nucleus, the liquid phase can be maintained all the way down to the temperature at which crystal homogeneous nucleation occurs.

8. Dover

9. Joe Orton

10. César Pelli

11. Jefferson. William Jefferson Clinton, original name William Jefferson Blythe III – Blythe being the surname of his father who died three months before he was born.

12. Stuttgart, which also contains the headquarters of both firms.

13. The Mercury Barometer

14. Molluscs (Mollusca). It's a clam – also known as the ocean quahog.

15. Wyoming

16. Bradford

17. A mathematical curve. The curve was studied by Maria Agnesi in the 18th century. The name 'witch' comes from a mistranslation of the word by which she referred to the curve, *versiera*, which can also colloquially mean a female devil or witch.

18. 1940s. Incredibly, in 1944, in Scotland, under the Witchcraft Act 1735

19. Arteries

20. The Camargue

21. A cucumber

22. 1968 (Mexico City)

23. Charles Booth. Not Henry Mayhew, whose famous study bearing the very similar title *London Labour & The London Poor* dates from forty years earlier.

24. (Antoine Henri) Becquerel

25. Washington DC

26. Emma (Lady) Hamilton. She was still Emma Hart when he met her, although prior to that, her birth name was Amy Lyon.

27. 1940s. 1948 and 1949 respectively – the 1950 prize was then won by *South Pacific*. You could call it a golden period.

28. Glass

29. The Tomb of the Unknown Warrior, in Westminster Abbey

30. The Four Ages of the World lasting respectively 4000, 3000, 2000 and 1000 years

31. Taras Bulba

32. Birdland. Named after Charlie Parker whose nickname was 'Bird'.

33. Medium. 'Mr Sludge The Medium' is the title.

34. Chestnut

35. The signing of the American Declaration of Independence by the thirteen colonies.

36. 26. Allegedly because 2/6 (two shillings and sixpence) was at one time a standard charge for a night's lodging. 26 is a common score in darts because the numbers 5 and 1 are either side of the 20 – so it's easy to hit 5, 20 and 1 with your three darts while aiming for the top.

37. Nepal

38. 'Journalist'

39. That the director wanted his real name removed from the credits – Alan Smithee is the accepted pseudonym in this eventuality.

40. Florence Nightingale. Florence and Parthenope were both born in Italy and named after the places of their birth – Parthenope being a place just outside Naples.

Quiz 34

1. Remains of *Homo habilis*, an early species of man whose name means 'handy man' because it's known to have used tools, were first discovered in the 1960s at Olduvai Gorge in Tanzania by which married couple of palaeontologists?

2. What is the longest river in Afghanistan, sharing its name with a province of that country?

3. Which well-known editor and publisher, whose twin brother was murdered by the IRA in 1975, had been the official timekeeper when Roger Bannister broke the four-minute mile in 1954?

4. According to W. S. Gilbert in the operetta *Princess Ida*, 'Man is Nature's sole...' what?

5. Which small appellation in the French Bordeaux wine region shares a name with a brand of car made by the General Motors Company?

6. If you are betrayed or cheated, you are said to have been 'sold down the river'. The phrase originated in reference to which river?

7. The biennial plant *Isatis tinctoria* was formerly cultivated as a source of which dye?

8. Which Peruvian city was the capital of the Inca Empire at the time of the Spanish conquest?

9. In Greek mythology, which favourite of Aphrodite became a hunter and died after being gored by a boar?

10. In the strict Inuit sense a canoe occupied by one man is known as a kayak. What, in that culture, is an umiak?

11. Antigua and Barbuda are part of an island state in the Caribbean. What are the literal meanings of the two words 'Antigua' and 'Barbuda'?

12. Which Hindu deity, often portrayed in paintings as having blue skin, is the eighth incarnation or avatar of Vishnu?

13. Alfred Hitchcock made three films based on stories by Daphne du Maurier – *Rebecca* being arguably the most famous. What are the other two?

14. What is the characteristic of a plant described as 'saprophyte'?

15. Which French chemist's law states that 'when any two gases react together, the volumes in which they do so are in a ratio of simple whole numbers'?

16. Which of the original Jackson Five is missing from this list: Jackie, Marlon, Michael, Tito – ?

17. Although he was born in Huddersfield in 1916, when he became a Peer the Labour Prime Minister Harold Wilson took what title, after what many would say is a somewhat more picturesque place in North Yorkshire?

18. Nigel Molesworth, the schoolboy malcontent created by Ronald Searle and Geoffrey Willans, attended which terrible prep school?

19. Holm of Grimbister, which has only one dwelling, and is cut off from the mainland at high tide, is part of which UK island group?

20. Princess Mary, daughter of Charles I, was the first holder of which official title?

Answers on page 236

21. Which British actor and author, born in 1910, once shared a house with Errol Flynn on Santa Monica beach in Los Angeles, which they named 'Cirrhosis by the Sea'?

22. Which Earldom, the site of a picturesque valley in Scotland, was bestowed on Prince William on the occasion of his marriage to Katherine Middleton on 29th April 2011?

23. The Seagram Building in New York and the Convention Hall in Chicago are among the major works of which German architect who died in 1969?

24. Which city, in what is now Turkey, is the setting for Shakespeare's *The Comedy of Errors*?

25. Which London club, the oldest of the St James's gentlemen's clubs, was founded by an Italian, whose real name is believed to have been Francesco Bianco?

26. Striding Edge and Swirral Edge are dramatic features negotiated by walkers climbing which English mountain?

27. What were the three forenames of the author J. R. R. Tolkien?

28. The Emperor Claudius's fourth wife, Agrippina the Younger, was also related to him in another way. How?

29. What famous feature of Lords Cricket Ground was presented in 1926 by the architect Sir Herbert Baker, who had also designed the W. G. Grace memorial gates for the same venue a few years earlier?

30. The 'babirusa', an animal native to parts of the Indonesian Archipelago, is most closely related to which domesticated farm animal?

31. Wagner's opera *Lohengrin* was first performed in 1850 and conducted by his future father-in-law. Who was he?

32. 'Drat! And double drat!' was the catch-phrase of which often-thwarted cartoon villain, in the Hanna-Barbera animated series *Wacky Races* and its spin-offs?

33. The Fourth Plinth in Trafalgar Square, now occupied by a regularly-changing series of works of art, was originally intended on its construction in 1841 to carry an equestrian statue, until the money to construct it failed to materialise. Who was to be the subject of the statue?

34. Which New Jersey-born documentary photographer, who worked for the body known as the Farm Security Administration during the 1930s, is credited with bringing the realities of the deprivation of the Depression era to a wider public?

35. In the original French-language versions of the Tintin stories by Hergé, what were the names of the almost-identical bowler-hatted characters known in English as Thomson & Thompson?

36. Which archipelago in the South Atlantic took its English name from a central channel or sound between the two main islands, in turn named by Captain John Strong, who landed on the islands in 1690?

37. Which is the only Swiss city to be classed as a World Heritage Site?

38. Flying fish, of which some 64 species have been identified, belong to which taxonomic family?

39. Which two colleges at Oxford and Cambridge, both with the same name, are named after a Scottish businessman and philanthropist, the Chairman of Great Universal Stores from 1946?

40. 'Digging', probably the most often-anthologised poem of Seamus Heaney, begins with the lines: 'Between my finger and my thumb / The squat pen rests...' What are the next four words?

Answers on page 236

Answers to Quiz 34

1. Louis and Mary Leakey
2. The Helmand/Helmund/Hilmand
3. Norris McWhirter. Joint editor of the *Guinness Book of Records* from 1955-75. He was also the announcer on the PA at that event.
4. '…mistake'
5. Cadillac
6. The Mississippi. That expression, dating from the mid-1800s, alludes to slaves being sold down the Mississippi River to work as labourers on cotton plantations.
7. Woad
8. Cuzco
9. Adonis
10. A canoe occupied by a woman
11. 'Ancient' and 'bearded', respectively. Antigua was named by Columbus after Santa Maria de la Antigua, 'St Mary the Ancient'.
12. Krishna. The name *Krishna* comes from a Sanskrit word meaning blue-skinned or dark blue.
13. *Jamaica Inn* and *The Birds*
14. It feeds on decaying organic matter. Generally, they have no chlorophyll, and most fungi fall into this category.
15. (Joseph Louis) Gay-Lussac
16. Jermaine
17. Baron Wilson of Rievaulx. After the ruined Cistercian abbey in Ryedale.
18. St Custard's. The series began with *Down With Skool* in 1953.
19. Orkney
20. Princess Royal
21. David Niven. He refers to it in his hugely successful memoir *The Moon's A Balloon* – although not every story in that book is, shall we say, entirely reliable.
22. Strathearn Robert Stewart, High Steward of Scotland, was the first Earl of Strathearn in 1357. He was also given the titles Duke of Cambridge and Baron Carrickfergus.
23. Mies Van Der Rohe

24. Ephesus

25. White's. Francesco Bianco became known as Francis White.

26. Helvellyn

27. John Ronald Reuel

28. She was his niece. Marrying one's niece was contrary to Roman law, so he changed the law.

29. The weathervane of Old Father Time

30. Pig. A bizarre-looking pig with males having curved tusks growing vertically up through its upper jaw and curving back towards the skull. The lower canine teeth also grow upwards and curve back to form a second set of tusks.

31. Franz Liszt

32. Dick Dastardly

33. King William IV

34. Dorothea Lange

35. Dupont & Dupond. Again there was a slight spelling variation.

36. The Falkland Islands/Islas Malvinas. The Spanish name, Islas Malvinas, is derived from the French name, Îles Malouines, named by Louis Antoine de Bougainville in 1764 after the first known settlers, mariners and fishermen from the Breton port of Saint-Malo in France.

37. Berne (the Old City is in the German part)

38. Exocoetidae

39. Baron/Sir Isaac Wolfson. He set up a foundation which helped establish both Wolfson Colleges.

40. ...'snug as a gun'

Quiz 35

1. Diego Maradona's infamous 'hand of God' goal against England was scored in which city?

2. Nevil and Shute were actually the forename and middle name of the author known for novels such as *A Town Like Alice*. His surname at birth was the name of a European country: which one?

3. Fenks, used as a manure and in the synthesis of prussian blue pigment, is the waste from which animal product?

4. Mahatma, the honorific title of Mohandas K. Gandhi, means what in Sanskrit?

5. Gaius Julius Caesar Germanicus, Roman Emperor from 37 to 41 AD, is better known by what name?

6. Which European politician was quoted in 1990 as saying of Margaret Thatcher that she had 'the eyes of Caligula, and the mouth of Marilyn Monroe'?

7. If the chemical elements are arranged in alphabetical order, which comes first?

8. What surname is shared by a Danish composer of six symphonies, and an actor whose roles include Frank Drebin in *Police Squad*?

9. Which rocky location off the south-west coast of England has had lighthouses constructed upon it designed by, in turn, Henry Winstanley, John Rudyard, John Smeaton and James Douglass?

10. Which animals are raced in the Sheikh Zayed International endurance race held at Hughenden in Queensland, Australia?

11. In which London borough was the Tabard Inn, where Chaucer's pilgrims set out from in the *Canterbury Tales*?

12. The so-called Saturn family of large US rockets was developed for the Apollo project by a team of scientists led by which aerospace engineer?

13. In Roman Britain, what was the *Classis Britannica*?

14. Batrachophobia is an irrational fear of what kind of animals?

15. The Northumberland National Park and Kielder Forest were given what official designation in December 2013, making them the largest so-designated area in Europe?

16. Mark Gatiss, Jeremy Dyson, Steve Pemberton and Reece Shearsmith were the writers and performers of which dark comedy series on British television in the 1990s?

17. 'The Mezzotint', 'The Stalls of Barchester Cathedral' and 'O Whistle and I'll Come to You, My Lad' are among the ghost stories of which Biblical authority and Provost of Eton College, who died in 1936?

18. In ancient Greece, what was a hoplite?

19. The British Labour Peer Baron Thomson, at the time the Secretary of State for Air, perished aboard which aircraft in 1930?

20. Which palace, the Paris residence of French kings since the 16th century, of which only the gardens remain today, was destroyed in the Commune of 1871?

Answers on page 242

21. What title is usually given to the poem by Robert Browning which begins: 'Oh, to be in England / Now that April's there'?

22. What was the Canadian airman Roy Brown's claim to fame in the First World War?

23. What name is given to a lift which consists of a chain of open compartments moving continuously in a loop, allowing passengers to get on and off as they wish?

24. Which is the only one of the five Boroughs of New York City that's on the mainland of the United States?

25. The name of which film character – created in 1982 – might be represented in Morse code by a single dot and a single dash?

26. 'All Human Life is There' was a slogan used to advertise which now-defunct national newspaper?

27. The coin known as the groat was minted in England from the 14th century until well into the 17th, and was worth how much in old money?

28. Which variety of garden plant, a member of the primrose family, is commonly known as 'sowbread'?

29. Which bestselling book of 1995 has the subtitle 'The True Story of a Lone Genius Who Solved the Greatest Scientific Problem of His Time'?

30. Possibly originating in Norse mythology, what is the correct name for the three-legged symbol that appears on the flag of the Isle of Man?

31. 1313 South Harbor Boulevard, Anaheim, California, is the postal address of what?

32. Which Italian-born queen became, in time, mother to three French kings, namely Francis II, Charles IX and Henry III?

33. What device for detecting subatomic particles and radiation was devised by C. T. R. Wilson and first constructed in 1911?

34. Which English novelist's father was a professional cricketer who took four wickets in four balls for Kent against Sussex in 1862?

35. Which American actor played the lead character Tony Soprano in the six seasons of the hit drama series *The Sopranos*?

36. An annual summer folk music festival has been held since 1976 at Cropredy in Oxfordshire, founded by which durable British folk band?

37. What's the name of the Japanese animation studio whose international successes have included the films *My Neighbour Totoro*, *Spirited Away* and *The Red Turtle*?

38. What term, meaning to stay or live in the countryside, is used for the dismissal of a student from university on a temporary basis as a punishment?

39. In which English county are the Neolithic flint mines known as Grime's Graves?

40. Whose death was greeted by Spike Milligan with the immortal words: 'Now I won't have to have him singing at my funeral'?

Answers on page 242

1. Mexico City on 22nd June 1986

2. Norway

3. Whale Blubber

4. 'Great Soul'/'Great-souled'

5. Caligula. His nickname means 'little boots'.

6. François Mitterand

7. Actinium

8. Nielsen – Carl and Leslie respectively

9. Eddystone Rocks in Devon. The first was destroyed by a storm, the second by fire, the third was unstable and all but the ground floor had to be pulled down.

10. Camels

11. Southwark

12. Wernher von Braun

13. The fleet which defended the English Channel

14. Amphibians. Specifically frogs, toads and newts.

15. Dark Sky Park/Dark Sky Area

16. *The League of Gentlemen*

17. M(ontague) R(hodes) James

18. A heavily-armed foot-soldier or infantryman

19. The R101 Airship which crashed in France a few hours into its maiden flight to Karachi

20. Les Tuileries

21. 'Home-Thoughts, From Abroad'

22. He shot down Baron von Richthofen. He dived down to aid a colleague in distress and, possibly aided by shooting from Australian troops on the ground, promptly despatched 'The Red Baron'.

23. Paternoster

24. The Bronx. Queens and Brooklyn are on Long Island; Manhattan and Staten Island are islands in their own right.

25. E.T. (The Extra-Terrestrial)

26. *News of the World*

27. Fourpence

28. Cyclamen

29. *Longitude* by Dava Sobel. The novel covers the background to John Harrison's invention of the Chronometer.

30. Triskelion

31. Disneyland (now Disneyland Park)

32. Catherine de Medici (Caterina Maria Romola di Lorenzo de Medici)

33. The Cloud Chamber

34. H. G. Wells. His father was Joseph Wells.

35. James Gandolfini

36. Fairport Convention

37. Studio Ghibli – the name *ghibli* taken from the Italian word for a hot desert wind, though the film company is pronounced with a soft g and the wind with a hard g.

38. Rusticate/Rustication

39. Norfolk, close to the border with Suffolk

40. Harry Secombe

Quiz 36

1. Who or what in the Arthurian legends was Dagonet, later Sir Dagonet?

2. In which decade was the last Mary Poppins story by P. L. Travers published?

3. Which high-ranking religious office in the Shi'ite sect of Islam means 'sign' or 'token of God'?

4. What alternative name, referring to its habit of flocking together in groups of twelve, is given to the Australian Grey Jumper or 'Lousy Jack' bird, *Struthidea cinerea*?

5. The film tune 'Song from *Moulin Rouge*', which became a no.1 hit in Britain and the US in 1953, was composed by which avant-garde French composer?

6. During the First World War, the Carlton Hotel in London employed a kitchen assistant who called himself Nguyen That Tanh. He would later become more famous under what name?

7. What do the following novels all have in common: *The Last Tycoon* by F. Scott Fitzgerald, *Sanditon* by Jane Austen and *The Weir of Hermiston* by Robert Louis Stevenson?

8. In which country is Batman Airport?

9. *The Man From Hell's River* was one of the first films to feature which Hollywood movie star discovered in Europe shortly after World War One by Lee Duncan, a US soldier?

10. Which Chilean poet, who won the 1971 Nobel Prize for Literature, took his pen name from a Czech poet?

11. An 'attercop' is an Old English word for what type of creature?

12. Which was the last ship in the British Navy in which sailors slept in hammocks?

13. Which battle, the bloodiest of the American Civil War, was fought on the 17th September 1862?

14. Which familiar sporting term is thought to have been first used to describe the achievement of H. H. Stephenson, when playing for the All-England cricket XI at Hyde Park in Sheffield in 1858?

15. Which name, long associated with exploration and adventure, did Amy Johnson give to the De Havilland Gipsy Moth in which she made her pioneering solo flight from Britain to Australia in May 1930?

16. 'Nut-Crack Night' is an alternative name for what?

17. The New York-born illustrator James Montgomery Flagg is best known for which piece of artwork, produced for the American Division of Pictorial Publicity under the chairmanship of Charles Dana Gibson?

18. The steamship *Stella* and HMS *Victory* are among the vessels to have foundered on which treacherous rocks off Alderney in the Channel Islands?

19. What name is given to the general neurological condition in which stimulation of one sensory or cognitive pathway leads to automatic, involuntary experiences in a second sensory or cognitive pathway, for example seeing numbers as colours?

20. George Stephenson's first successful steam locomotive, used for hauling coal at Killingworth Colliery on Tyneside, was named after which major figure of the Napoleonic Wars?

Answers on page 248

21. According to the title of a 1956 book by A. J. Liebling, which sport is *The Sweet Science*?

22. Which composer, born in 1858, was an activist in the UK's women's suffrage movement and wrote 'March of the Women', the song adopted as the suffrage anthem?

23. The formula $V = \pi r^2 h$ gives the volume of which three-dimensional shape?

24. 'Persons attempting to find a motive in this narrative will be prosecuted; persons attempting to find a moral in it will be banished; persons attempting to find a plot in it will be shot.' In which American novel of 1884 will you find this warning?

25. Which Dorset town has a harbour wall known as The Cobb, that featured prominently in the film *The French Lieutenant's Woman*?

26. The 1944 Education Act is often known by the name of the politician who was President of the Board of Education at the time. Who was he?

27. 'The Sentinel', a short story published in 1951, became the basis of a spectacular science-fiction film made twenty years later. Which film was that?

28. What name is given to the radiation theoretically emitted from just outside the event horizon of a black hole, first proposed in 1974?

29. In 2014, who became the first person ever to have won both the Turner Prize and an Oscar?

30. Halcyon is a poetic term for which bird?

31. NHK is the official public broadcaster of which country?

32. The VLT, situated on the mountain Cerro Paranal in Chile, has four 8.2 metre telescopes named Antu, Kueyen, Melipal, and Yepun, which are the names for the Sun, the Moon, the Southern Cross, and Venus in the language of the Mapuche people. What do the letters VLT stand for?

33. The name Yorick, most familiar as that of Hamlet's long-dead jester, is the Danish equivalent of which common boy's name in English?

34. How are the British television journalists Peter Snow and Jon Snow related?

35. Which London landmark gave its name to a now-disused underground station located just to the east of Tottenham Court Road on the Central line?

36. Which Superbowl-winning quarterback led the San Francisco 49ers in 1982, 1985, 1989 and 1990?

37. Three scientists shared the 1903 Nobel Prize for Physics. Marie and Pierre Curie were two of them. Who was the third?

38. The term for which salad dish of chopped meat, eggs and anchovies in vinegar and oil is also used to refer figuratively to any medley or multifarious mixture?

39. The stories of Armistead Maupin, published as *Tales of the City*, are about which city?

40. What do you fear if you suffer from Pogonophobia?

Answers on page 248

Answers to Quiz 36

1. The Fool or Jester of King Arthur

2. The 1980s, the final book being *Mary Poppins and the House Next Door*, published in 1988.

3. Ayatollah

4. The Apostlebird. It is native to Australia where it roams woodlands, eating insects and seeds at, or near, ground level.

5. Georges Auric. In Britain the chart-topping recording was by Mantovani, in the US by Percy Faith & his Orchestra.

6. Ho Chi Minh

7. They were all left unfinished at the time of their creators' death

8. Turkey. Serving the city of Batman which is in the south-east of that country

9. Rin Tin Tin

10. (Pablo) Neruda, original name (Neftalí Ricardo Reyes) Basoalto. After the poet and short-story writer Jan Neruda, known for his sardonic sketches in *Povídky malostranské* (1878, translated as *Tales of the Little Quarter*).

11. A spider. Sometimes abbreviated to 'cop', it's also the origin of the word 'cop-web' or 'cobweb'.

12. The Royal Yacht *Britannia*. This was prior to a major refit in 1970. It was considered a vast improvement when bunks replaced the hammocks, but there were still old salts who said they could never get used to a proper bed.

13. Antietam. Total casualties amounted to around 23,000.

14. Hat-trick

15. Jason. 'Jason' – in this case a contraction of the trademark of the family fish business run by her father.

16. Hallowe'en

17. (The poster of a finger-pointing) Uncle Sam. The slogan 'I want YOU for US Army' usually accompanied the image.

18. The Casquets

19. Synaesthesia. In its simplest form it is best described as a 'union of the senses' whereby two or more of the five senses that are normally experienced separately are involuntarily and automatically joined together.

20. (Marshal) Blücher

21. Boxing

22. Ethel Smyth

23. A cylinder

24. *The Adventures of Huckleberry Finn*

25. Lyme Regis

26. R. A. 'Rab' Butler/Lord Butler/Baron Butler of Saffron Walden

27. *2001: A Space Odyssey*. 'The Sentinel' was written by Arthur C. Clarke.

28. Hawking Radiation, after Professor Stephen Hawking

29. Steve McQueen – who won the 1999 Turner Prize, and the Oscar as Best Director for *Twelve Years A Slave* in 2014.

30. A kingfisher

31. Japan. *Nippon Hōsō Kyōkai*.

32. Very large telescope

33. George

34. They are cousins (with the same paternal grandparents)

35. British Museum

36. Joe Montana. Known as 'Joe Cool', 'Golden Joe', 'The Golden Great', 'Comeback Kid' and 'Comeback Joe'.

37. (Antoine) Henri Becquerel

38. Salmagundi

39. San Francisco

40. Beards

Quiz 37

1. When George Orwell left Eton, as Eric Blair, he became a policeman, in a place that inspired his first novel. Where was that?

2. In which European city did Yasser Arafat die in 2004?

3. Kevin Keegan was voted European Footballer of the Year twice, in 1978 and 1979, while playing for which club?

4. The name of which forerunner of the trombone came from that of a hook used to pull a person off a horse?

5. *Da xiong mao* and *Baixiong* are Chinese names for which large mammal?

6. How would you write the number 975 in Roman numerals?

7. The series of six long novels which Anthony Trollope published between 1864 and 1880, including *Phineas Finn*, *The Eustace Diamonds* and *The Prime Minister*, are known by what collective title?

8. The Battle of the Nile, fought off the Egyptian coast in 1798, is also known by what more geographically precise name?

9. What name is given to the garment worn by aviators and astronauts who are subject to high levels of acceleration force, designed to prevent black-outs and loss of consciousness?

10. Walt Disney was awarded a Special Oscar for his work on *Snow White and the Seven Dwarfs*. What physical form did the award take?

11. The British artist Roger Dean is best known for the fantasy landscapes he created for the covers of *Fragile, Tales from Topographic Oceans, Close to the Edge* and other albums recorded by which 'progressive' rock band?

12. According to the Book of Ecclesiastes, 'He that increaseth knowledge, increaseth...' what?

13. The phrase 'the Maunder Minimum' refers to the period of reduced activity between 1645 and 1715 of which astronomical phenomenon, after the British astronomer Edward Maunder who drew attention to it?

14. In which Italian city will you find the *Torre Pendente*?

15. In Newtonian physics, which Greek letter is used to denote the universal gravitational constant?

16. In the TV series first shown in 1997, who played Buffy the Vampire Slayer?

17. In French cuisine, a crêpe is a pancake. But what is a crépinette?

18. A plaque on a traffic island at the junction of Edgware Road and Bayswater Road in central London marks the site of which notorious place of execution?

19. The city of Carrara, in the region of northern Tuscany known as the Lunigiana, is most famous for the production of what?

20. The mining village of Bestwood in *Sons and Lovers*, and Beldover in *Women in Love*, are thinly-disguised depictions of D. H. Lawrence's native village, a few miles from Nottingham. What's it really called?

Answers on page 254

21. In which Shakespeare play is Joan of Arc a character?

22. Which 18th century, Swiss-born French revolutionary social philosopher, who is associated with the idea of the 'noble savage', did Isaiah Berlin describe as 'the first militant low-brow'?

23. *The Reason Why* by Cecil Woodham-Smith is an analysis of the background to which historical incident?

24. In 1993, mitochondrial DNA analysis of the blood of which member of the British Royal Family was used by scientists to confirm the identity of the remains of several members of Tsarina Alexandra of Russia's family, decades after their 1918 massacre by the Bolsheviks?

25. Which familiar political term was created in reaction to a re-drawing of the Massachusetts state senate election districts in 1812 under the then-governor?

26. What name is given to the science and philosophy of law?

27. What room number – that of the apartment where he and his band were living at the time – provided the title of the 1928 tune Glenn Miller co-wrote with Benny Goodman, which is thought to be Miller's earliest composition?

28. Adolf Hitler was known by the title of *der Führer*, Mussolini by *Il Duce*; what equivalent title was borne by General Franco?

29. Rising to just short of 20,000 feet, what is the highest peak in Canada?

30. Which four-letter word can mean both a young oyster, and a tiff or dispute?

31. Which silent film star, his acting career destroyed by scandal, went on to become a director under other names such as William Goodrich?

32. Can you name two of the three distinct and basic patterns recognisable, to a forensic scientist, on a fingerprint?

33. What name is given to the migration by Boers, away from British control in the Cape Colony, during the 1830s and 40s?

34. Which novelist created the London private investigator Cormoran Strike, a former military policeman who lost a leg on a tour of service in Afghanistan?

35. In 1599, which actor and comedian made a celebrated Morris dance from London to Norwich lasting 9 days?

36. Where specifically in the human body would you find the frontalis muscle?

37. Which aromatic resin, obtained from trees and sometimes used in the production of perfumes, has the alternative name 'olibanum'?

38. Experimenting on dogs at Oxford in the 1660s, the physician Richard Lower conducted the first properly documented instance in Britain of which medical procedure?

39. What was the name of the private press set up by the artist William Morris at Hammersmith in the 1890s, to reproduce the quality of detail and decoration characteristic of books from the early years of printing?

40. Which Canadian actor, whose movie credits include *M*A*S*H* and *Don't Look Now*, appeared in the music video for Kate Bush's hit song 'Cloudbusting' in 1985?

Answers on page 254

Answers to Quiz 37

1. Burma. The novel was *Burmese Days.*

2. Paris

3. Hamburg (SV)/Hamburger Sport-Verein. He played for several clubs including Liverpool and Hamburger SV. He went on to manage Newcastle United, Fulham and Manchester City, and England.

4. Sackbut. It was common from the 14th century and has been revived in early music performance. The sackbut has a narrow bell and its sound is dignified and mellow.

5. The Giant Panda. The two names mean 'giant bear-cat' and 'white bear' respectively.

6. CMLXXV

7. The Palliser Novels

8. (The Battle of) Aboukir Bay. Fought on 1st August 1798, between the British and French fleets in Abūr Qīr Bay, near the mouth of the Nile – one of Nelson's greatest victories and considered by some historians to be more significant than that at Trafalgar.

9. G-suit/Anti G-suit

10. 'One conventional statuette with seven miniatures', mounted on a stepped base

11. Yes

12. …Sorrow. Bad luck, *Brain of Britain* contestants.

13. Sunspots

14. Pisa (it's the Leaning Tower)

15. Gamma

16. Sarah Michelle Gellar

17. A small sausage

18. Tyburn (Tree)

19. Marble. Its quarries provided the marble for some of the most famous buildings of ancient Rome.

20. Eastwood

21. *Henry VI, Part 1*

22. Jean-Jacques Rousseau. The Berlin quote appeared in an *Observer* article, published on 9th November 1952.

23. The Charge of the Light Brigade during the Battle of Balaclava in the Crimean War in 1854

24. Prince Philip/The Duke of Edinburgh. Tsarina Alexandra, the three children buried with her, and Prince Philip's mitochondrial DNA were an exact match on 740 tested nucleotides. Prince Philip is the great nephew of Tsarina Alexandra, wife of Czar Nicholas II and Grand Duchess of Russia.

25. Gerrymander(ing). Gerrymander is the drawing of electoral boundaries so as to give an unfair advantage to a particular interest. Governor Elbridge Gerry of Massachusetts redrew them in his state and was left with an area shaped, according to a local newspaper cartoonist, like a salamander – and the contraction of the words Gerry and salamander gave rise to the term.

26. Jurisprudence

27. 'Room 1411'

28. (El) Caudillo

29. Mount Logan, in the Yukon; it's the highest point in Canada and the second highest in North America, after Denali (formerly Mount McKinley) in Alaska.

30. Spat

31. 'Fatty' Arbuckle. Born Roscoe Arbuckle in 1887. He was accused of manslaughter in 1921 following the death of model Virginia Rappe at a Hollywood party. He was later acquitted, but the Hearst press led a campaign against him.

32. Arch/loop/whorl

33. The Great Trek. Their trek led directly to Blood River (16th December 1838) where they massacred several thousand Zulu.

34. J. K. Rowling under the pen name of Robert Galbraith (either answer acceptable). Strike made his first appearance in the novel *The Cuckoo's Calling*.

35. William Kemp(e)

36. In the forehead. Extending from the forehead to the upper eyelid.

37. Frankincense

38. Blood transfusion

39. The Kelmscott Press

40. Donald Sutherland. Sutherland plays a scientist operating a machine for making rain fall from the sky; Kate Bush plays his son.

1. In the 1960s, what name was well known both as that of Eliza Doolittle's elocution instructor in the musical *My Fair Lady*, and of a British bullfighter in Spain?

2. The Dutch-born anatomist Eugene Dubois discovered the first known fossil of which early species of man, in the 1890s?

3. The daughter of Asclepius, who was the goddess of Health in Greek mythology?

4. Which cartoon character, created by Elzie Crisler Segar, first appeared in the comic strip *Thimble Theatre* in 1929, and was later portrayed in a 1980 live-action film by Robin Williams?

5. Which limestone formation is believed to be the northern promontory of what were known in the ancient world as the Pillars of Hercules?

6. What name, also that of an opera by Verdi, is given to the revolt against Charles I of Naples and Sicily which began with the riot that took place on Easter Monday 1282 in a church outside Palermo?

7. Who was the last US President to die in office of natural causes?

8. Sir Charles Isham, a 19th century horticulturalist, is thought to be the first person to introduce which controversial feature to British gardens?

9. What is the meaning of the name of the Irish political party Fianna Fail?

10. Who are the only parent and child to have won the BBC Sports Personality of the Year award on separate occasions?

11. Which English poet, who died in 1861, is commemorated with blue plaques at Beacon Hill in Torquay and at 50 Wimpole Street, London W1?

12. What is the name of the swivelling rod that is attached to a motorbike or cycle to support the vehicle in an upright position when stationary?

13. At around 4,500 kilometres long, the Trans-Sahara Highway begins in Algeria – and ends in which country?

14. Which British no.1 hit single of the 1970s is about a girl called Brenda Ann Spencer?

15. Which mountain range, extending for around 225 miles on both sides of the French-Swiss border, lends its name to the geological period that dates from around 200 to 144 million years ago?

16. Which recipe, created in 1953 and especially familiar as a sandwich filling, is usually credited to Constance Spry and Rosemary Hume?

17. Which conquered territory became Rome's first province in 241 BC?

18. The director of the 1939 film *The Wizard of Oz* was also the accredited director of *Gone With the Wind* the same year, for which he won an Academy Award. Who was he?

19. PET scanning is commonly used in medicine to detect the location of a tumour. What do the letters PET stand for?

20. A sculpture by Maggi Hambling entitled *Scallop*, bearing words from Benjamin Britten's opera *Peter Grimes*, stands on the beach at which British coastal town?

Answers on page 260

21. What relation was King Edward the Confessor to his successor Harold Godwinson?

22. Which fictional character – in a novel of 1759 – is born on the 5th November 1718 at his family home, his nose crushed by the forceps of Dr Slop during the course of his delivery?

23. Which word did Ambrose Bierce define in his *Devil's Dictionary* as 'a temporary insanity curable by marriage'?

24. Which historic event took place in the French town of Annonay on the 4th June 1783?

25. The main character in the film of Len Deighton's novel *The Ipcress File*, and its sequels, is called Harry Palmer. What was his name in the original novels?

26. Which German astronomer, who lived between 1758 and 1840, discovered the minor planets Pallas and Vesta and has a paradox named after him?

27. Which lake, located south-west of Budapest, is the largest lake in central Europe?

28. Who was the British Prime Minister during the years of the American Civil War?

29. Highclere Castle in Hampshire, which doubled as the fictional Downton Abbey in the globally successful TV series, was built to a design by which 19th century British architect?

30. What colour is the live wire in a standard UK three-pin electrical plug?

31. The poem which begins 'My heart leaps up when I behold / A rainbow in the sky' – which also includes the line 'The Child is father of the Man' – is by which poet?

32. What sort of animal is a 'Sergeant Baker'?

33. In which play by Christopher Marlowe, first performed in 1594, does the title character refer to Helen of Troy with the words, 'Was this the face that launch'd a thousand ships / And burnt the topless towers of Ilium?'

34. Which actress, who gained fame in a number of iconic British film, TV and radio comedies, was married to the actor John Le Mesurier between 1949 and 1965?

35. The title character of Puccini's opera *Turandot* is a bloodthirsty princess in which city?

36. Since 1916, the annual eating contest for what fast food item has been held at Nathan's Diner at Coney Island?

37. The Seven Years' War, as its name suggests, took place across a period of seven years, between Britain's declaration of war on France and the Treaty of Paris, which brought it to an end. Name any one of the eight calendar years during which it was being fought.

38. The wisent is another name for the European species of which grazing mammal?

39. In 1966, during a famous – or indeed infamous – televised interview with Japanese journalists during the Vietnam Conflict, how was the American prisoner-of-war Commander Jeremiah Denton able to indicate to the viewing audience that he had been tortured?

40. *Cave of the Heart*, *Errand into the Maze* and *Night Journey* are among the works of which American choreographer, who died in 1991?

Answers on page 260

Answers to Quiz 38

1. Henry Higgins. The character in the film of *My Fair Lady* (released in 1964) was played by Rex Harrison.

2. *Homo erectus*, also known as Java Man. Dubois named his discovery *Pithecanthropus erectus*.

3. Hygieia

4. Popeye. Popeye made his first public appearance on 17th January 1929 in Elzie Segar's then nine-year-old comic strip, *Thimble Theatre*, which originally revolved around Olive Oyl's family.

5. The Rock of Gibraltar

6. The Sicilian Vespers (*I Vespri Siciliani*)

7. F(ranklin) D(elano) Roosevelt, who died of a stroke in 1945.

8. Garden gnomes. He imported them from Nuremberg. According to legend the gnomes were shot with an air rifle by his daughters after Sir Charles' death.

9. Soldiers of Destiny

10. Princess Anne and Zara Phillips. In 1971 and 2006 respectively.

11. Elizabeth Barrett Browning (not her husband, Robert Browning)

12. A kickstand

13. Nigeria

14. 'I Don't Like Mondays' by the Boomtown Rats. She was the teenage who opened fire on children and teachers at an elementary school in San Diego in January 1979, sparking the idea for the song which was a hit a few months later.

15. The Jura Mountains. Their limestone was laid down during the Jurassic period.

16. Coronation chicken – the clue's in the date.

17. Sicily

18. Victor Fleming. In fact Fleming was only one of the directors who worked on *Gone With the Wind*, the other principal director being George Cukor.

19. Positron Emission Tomography. The process detects the emission of gamma rays after a radio-isotope is injected into the patient.

20. Aldeburgh in Suffolk. The inscription, cut in the metal of the sculpture on the frill of the shell, reads 'I hear those voices that will not be drowned'.

21. They were brothers-in-law. Edward married Edith, Harold's sister and Godwin, Earl of Wessex's daughter, on 23rd January 1045.

22. Tristram Shandy in the novel of that title by Laurence Sterne

23. Love

24. The Montgolfier Brothers' first (unmanned) balloon flight.

25. He didn't have one – the narrator in the books is anonymous

26. (Heinrich Wilhelm Matthias) Olbers. The paradox, stated in simple terms, asks why, if space is infinite, the night sky is dark.

27. Lake Balaton

28. Lord Palmerston. His second period in office lasted from 1859-65. He came close to taking Britain into the war – on the Confederate side.

29. Sir Charles Barry – who also designed London's Houses of Parliament.

30. Brown

31. William Wordsworth

32. A fish – a large brightly coloured fish of the genus *Latropiscis*, found in temperate waters of Australia.

33. *Doctor Faustus*. Faustus himself speaks the lines in response to a vision of Helen conjured up by Mephistopheles.

34. Hattie Jacques. Originally Josephine Edwina Jacques, she died in 1980.

35. Peking (Beijing)

36. Hot dogs. The first such hot dog eating contest was held in 1916, when the winner put away only 13 frankfurters. In 2013, Joey 'Jaws' Chestnut won by eating 69 (with buns) in 10 minutes.

37. Any year between, and including, 1756-1763. It was the last major conflict before the French Revolution to involve all the great powers of Europe.

38. Bison

39. By blinking. He blinked the word 'torture' in Morse Code.

40. Martha Graham

Quiz 39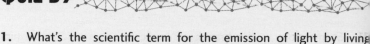

1. What's the scientific term for the emission of light by living organisms such as glow-worms and fireflies?

2. Which Danish philosopher observed that 'life can only be understood backwards; but it must be lived forwards'?

3. To which pioneering film-maker, an illusionist and designer whose fantasy films date from the first few years of the 20th century, did Martin Scorsese pay affectionate tribute in his 2011 film *Hugo*?

4. What's the principal spirit ingredient in a Mai Tai cocktail?

5. Which Spanish football club, for many years in the shadow of another club in the same city, has among its nicknames 'Los Colchoneros', or 'The Mattress Makers'?

6. Which murderer, who was hanged in Pentonville Prison in 1910, graduated from the Michigan School of Homeopathic Medicine in the 1880s?

7. Tubulidentata is the smallest extant order of mammals, comprising only one species, an insectivorous mammal native to Sub-Saharan Africa. What is it?

8. What proverbial phrase, roughly meaning 'You can't make progress unless both sides do what's required of them', is thought to originate from the title of a 1952 song by Al Hoffman and Dick Manning?

9. Number 263 Prinsengracht, in Amsterdam, is now a museum to the memory of whom?

10. Which scholar and churchman's *Ecclesiastical History of the English People*, dating from about the year 731, is regarded as one of the most important sources of information about the early history of Britain?

11. Stomatology is the branch of medicine concerned with which part of the body?

12. Now among the best-known British actors of their generation, Christopher Eccleston, Daniel Craig, Gina McKee and Mark Strong first came to prominence playing the four central characters in which BBC TV drama series of the 1990s?

13. What is the flavour of the cream or paste called frangipane, widely used in bakery products?

14. What is the name of the highest of the distinctive table-top mountains that rise from the forests of Venezuela's Canaima National Park, which are thought to have provided the inspiration for the primeval *Lost World* of Arthur Conan Doyle's novel?

15. Who killed the English knight Henry de Bohun in single combat in 1314, in the early stages of a major battle?

16. Which breed, or group of breeds, of short-legged dog originated in France and takes its name from a French term meaning 'rather low down'?

17. Belomancy is an ancient form of divination by means of which objects, marked in certain ways to indicate their supposed significance?

18. Which film director once said: 'Television has brought back murder into the home – where it belongs'?

19. In motor racing, you are said to have gained the Triple Crown if you have won the Indianapolis 500, the Le Mans 24-hour race, and the Monaco Grand Prix. Who is the only driver ever to have achieved this, completing the triple in 1972?

20. Who became the first Chairman of BOAC in 1939, but is better remembered for his work with another high-profile organisation in the years between the wars?

Answers on page 266

21. In physics, what is measured in newtons?

22. Which naval figure, born in Newcastle-upon-Tyne in 1748, is buried near Nelson's tomb in St Paul's Cathedral?

23. Which eccentric American performer and record producer created the 1970s R&B groups Parliament and Funkadelic?

24. In which Scottish town do the football team St Mirren play their home games?

25. What term is generally given to sound with a frequency above 20,000 Hertz?

26. According to legend, a one-legged man named 'Bumper' Harris was employed by London Transport at Earls Court Station to demonstrate to travellers the safety of an innovation introduced there in 1911. Which innovation?

27. Which well-travelled character from an 1873 novel is named after a French term for a master key?

28. Who was Roman emperor when Vesuvius erupted destroying the cities of Pompeii, Herculaneum and Stabiae?

29. Which rod-shaped, gram-negative bacteria, that causes food poisoning, was named after an American veterinary pathologist?

30. What surname is shared by the originator of a music teaching method developed in the mid 20th century, and an environmentalist and broadcaster sometimes described as 'the Canadian David Attenborough'?

31. What English name is most commonly used for house plants of the genus *Schlumbergera*, known for winter flowering and sold in huge numbers in late autumn?

32. Sunset Strip in Los Angeles is part of which longer thoroughfare?

33. Who was the architect of the Royal Crescent in Bath?

34. Which famous dog, originally known as 'Little Curly', is remembered today by a name that means 'Barker' in Russian?

35. Of whose funeral did the English diarist John Evelyn write: '[it was] the joyfullest funeral that I ever saw; for there was none that cried but dogs…'?

36. Which two literary figures met for the very first time in May 1763, in a bookshop belonging to Thomas Davies in Russell Street in London?

37. According to former British Prime Minister Harold Macmillan in 1981, 'there are three bodies no sensible man directly challenges'. Can you name one of those three organisations?

38. 'On an exceptionally hot evening in early July, a young man came out of the garret in which he lodged in S. Place, and walked slowly, as though in hesitation, towards K. Bridge' is a translation of the opening sentence of which great Russian novel?

39. The Shah Jehan Mosque, dating from 1889 and consequently the oldest in the UK, is in which town in Surrey?

40. Walker Smith Jr, born in Georgia on the 3rd May 1921, became a major sporting figure under which other name?

Answers on page 266

1. Bioluminescence

2. (Soren) Kierkegaard

3. Georges Meliès

4. Rum

5. Atlético Madrid

6. Dr (Hawley Harvey) Crippen

7. Aardvark

8. It takes two to tango

9. Anne Frank. It's in the house in whose secret annex she and her family hid between 1942 and 1944.

10. (The Venerable) Bede. He was a monk at the monastery of Jarrow, on the southern bank of the Tyne.

11. The mouth

12. *Our Friends in the North*

13. Almond

14. Mount Roraima. In local legend the mountain is believed to be a that remains of a once-mighty tree which produced all the fruits and vegetables in the world.

15. Robert The Bruce/Robert I at the Battle of Bannockburn

16. Basset (Hound). There are six recognised Basset breeds in France, of which the best known in the UK is the Basset Hound.

17. Arrows. Labels are attached to a given number of arrows, the archers shoot them and the advice on the label of the arrow that flies furthest is accepted.

18. Alfred Hitchcock

19. Graham Hill

20. Lord (John) Reith – who was, of course, General Manager and then Director General of the BBC, between 1922 and 1938.

21. Force

22. Admiral Cuthbert Collingwood (1st Baron Collingwood). He assumed command of the British fleet after Nelson's death at Trafalgar.

23. George Clinton

24. Paisley. The first church was built there in the 6th century by St Mirin.

25. Ultrasound

26. The escalator. Earls Court was the site of the first escalator installation in the UK. It's thought 'Bumper' was given the job after his leg was crushed in a construction accident while he was working for London Transport.

27. (Jean) Passepartout. Phileas Fogg's French valet in Jules Verne's novel *Around the World in Eighty Days*.

28. Titus

29. Salmonella, named after Daniel Elmer Salmon – and nothing whatsoever to do with fish!

30. Suzuki. Shin'ichi Suzuki and Dr David Suzuki, respectively. David Suzuki was named 'the greatest living Canadian' in a poll conducted in 2004.

31. Christmas cactus. The plant is known as Thanksgiving cactus in the USA.

32. Sunset Boulevard

33. John Wood (The Younger)

34. Laika, the first living creature to be shot into space and orbit the Earth, having been captured as a stray on the streets of Moscow. She didn't survive her pioneering trip.

35. Oliver Cromwell

36. James Boswell and Dr (Samuel) Johnson

37. The Roman Catholic Church/The Brigade of Guards/The National Union of Mineworkers

38. *Crime and Punishment* by Dostoevsky. The locations in question are in St Petersburg.

39. Woking

40. Sugar Ray Robinson

1. Which type of cloth is named after a west-central German state with its capital at Wiesbaden?

2. The actor Maurice Gosfield, who played Doberman in *Sgt Bilko* or *The Phil Silvers Show* as it was properly known, also featured in a cartoon series of a similar style, in which he provided the voice for a character called Benny The Ball. What was the name of that show?

3. What was the name of the German spiked helmet worn especially before and during the earlier part of the First World War?

4. What is the last letter of the Hebrew alphabet?

5. In the human body, what section of the small intestine lies between the duodenum and the ileum?

6. Which state of India, literally meaning 'Northern State', has the city of Lucknow as its capital?

7. What is the name of the island that separates the two largest waterfalls at Niagara?

8. Which number is referred to by Australian cricketers as a 'Dorothy'?

9. In 1885, nine-year-old Joseph Meister became the first person ever to be treated by a vaccine, administered by Louis Pasteur. Against which illness was he vaccinated?

10. The trilogy of books comprising *Palace Walk, Palace of Desire* and *Sugar Street* by Naguib Mahfouz is named collectively after which African capital city?

1. Martha 'Mamah' Borthwick Chaney was murdered in 1914, along with six others, at Taliesin – the Wisconsin home she had shared with her lover, an American architect. Who was he?

2. Chipolopolo, or the 'Copper Bullets', is the nickname of which African country's national football team?

3. What term for a specious line of reasoning in which contradictory arguments lead to the same conclusion, often unpleasant, comes from the tax collection policies of the Archbishop of Canterbury appointed by Henry VII in the latter years of the 15th century?

4. After nitrogen and oxygen, which noble gas is the most abundant element in the Earth's atmosphere – constituting almost one per cent of the total?

5. Haiti occupies the western portion of the Caribbean island of Hispaniola; which nation state occupies the eastern portion?

6. What would you do with a Munsell Tree?

7. The sweets known as Pomfret cakes, or Pontefract cakes, are made using the roots of which plant?

8. The play *The Two Noble Kinsmen*, attributed to William Shakespeare and John Fletcher, concerns the same characters as the story told by which of Chaucer's pilgrims in *The Canterbury Tales*?

9. Original editions of the 1973 album by Paul McCartney & Wings, *Red Rose Speedway*, included an embossed message in Braille on the sleeve reading WE LOVE Y(A) BABY. For which fellow musician was this tribute intended?

10. Which long distance footpath runs from Ivinghoe Beacon in Buckinghamshire to Overton Hill in Wiltshire?

Answers on page 272

21. Who is the malevolent fairy of the ballet *Sleeping Beauty*, whose evil curse is changed by the Lilac Fairy?

22. Which South Caribbean island off the Venezuelan coast lends its name to a liqueur flavoured with the dried peel of bitter orange known locally as Laraha?

23. Thought to have been born some time between 2 BC and AD 119, Lindow Man or Lindow II – the well-preserved corpse of the victim of a possible ritual killing – was discovered in 1984 in a peat bog in which English county?

24. A sulphate of which chemical element is most commonly added to garden soil in order to lower its pH level, sometimes to intensify the colour of blue hydrangea blooms?

25. The murder of Laura Palmer is the focus for the plot of the early episodes of which American TV series, first shown in 1990?

26. Vectis was the Roman name for which part of the British Isles?

27. Which word, originally used for a blancmange-like dessert of sweetened bran or oatmeal boiled into a jelly, is also used figuratively to mean empty flattery or humbug?

28. The ceiling of London's Banqueting House, a pictorial representation of the Apotheosis of James the First, was commissioned by King Charles I from which artist?

29. Whose law of elasticity is an approximation that states that the extension of a spring is in direct proportion with the load applied to it?

30. *A Pagan Place*, published in 1970, is a childhood memoir by which Irish writer, whose other books include *Girls In Their Married Bliss*?

31. Surgically, what is removed in an orchidectomy?

32. Which ruler introduced the form of trial known as Wager of Battle or Trial by Combat into England?

33. Mercaptans are an important feature of natural gas production. Can you say why?

34. What event is referred to in Russia as the 'Caribbean Crisis'?

35. Which collection of stories was first introduced into Europe in a French translation by Antoine Galland at the beginning of the 18th century?

36. Who was the first French driver to win the World Formula 1 Championship?

37. The polecat, the otter, the pine marten, the stoat, the badger and the weasel are the six species native to Britain of which mammal family?

38. The accolade of *Time* Magazine Man of the Year was inaugurated in January 1928, when the aviator Charles Lindbergh appeared on the famous front cover. But whom did the magazine name as the first Woman of the Year nine years later?

39. Also called fennel flower or devil-in-the-bush, by what poetic name is the flowering herb *Nigella damascena* most commonly known?

40. In June 1963 who became the first woman in space?

Answers on page 272

1. Hessian. After the state of Hesse or Hessen.

2. *Top Cat* – re-named *Boss Cat* for the UK audience as there was a brand of cat food called 'Top Cat' and the BBC was anxious to avoid promoting it

3. A Pickelhaube

4. Tau/Taw

5. Jejunum

6. Uttar Pradesh

7. Goat Island

8. Six. It's rhyming slang – after Dorothy Dix, the agony aunt.

9. Rabies

10. Cairo

11. Frank Lloyd Wright. Julian Carlton, an estate worker, set fire to the house Two of her children died with her.

12. Zambia

13. Morton's Fork. Those who were very rich were forced to contribute on the grounds that they could well afford it; those who lived without display were made to contribute on the grounds that their economies must mean they had savings.

14. Argon

15. The Dominican Republic

16. Describe, grade or classify colours

17. Liquorice, *Glycyrrhiza glabra* – Pomfret being a contraction of Pontefract

18. The Knight. The Knight's story of Palamon and Arcite was taken by Chaucer from the work of the Italian poet Boccaccio.

19. Stevie Wonder

20. The Ridgeway

21. Carabosse

22. Curaçao

23. Cheshire – at Lindow Moss, near Wilmslow

24. Aluminium

25. *Twin Peaks*

26. Isle of Wight

7. Flummery

8. (Sir) Peter Raul Rubens. He was paid three thousand pounds for his work, and knighted.

9. (Robert) Hooke

0. Edna O'Brien

1. Testicle(s). Usually for the removal of tumours.

2. William I/The Conqueror

3. They are added to provide smell – for reasons of safety, as natural gas, unlike coal gas is odourless.

4. The Cuban Missile Crisis. It's known as the 'October Crisis' in Cuba.

5. *The Arabian Nights* or *The Thousand and one Nights*

6. Alain Prost, World Champion in 1985, 1986, 1989, and 1993.

7. *Mustelidae.* The family includes the mink and the wolverine, neither of them, strictly speaking, native to the British Isles.

8. Mrs (Wallis) Simpson or, as she later became, The Duchess of Windsor.

9. Love-in-a-mist

0. (Valentina Vladimirovna) Tereshkova. She orbited for three days before returning successfully, in Vostok 6.

1. Which Shakespeare play features characters described in th
   dramatis personae as 'A Son that has killed his father' and 'A Fathe
   that has killed his son'?

2. *Science of Logic*, completed in 1816, is the work of which Germa
   philosopher?

3. Of which Cabinet Minister, one of Mrs Thatcher's most truste
   lieutenants, did John Junor write that he 'would not be two-face
   if there was a third one available'?

4. In psychology, which term – derived from the Latin for 'flight
   – is used to refer to an abnormal state of mind in which som
   emotional stress compels a sufferer to leave home, usually i
   a temporary state of amnesia, and sometimes assume a ne
   identity?

5. Leinster House in Dublin, seat of the Irish parliament, is said t
   have been the model for which famous building?

6. Which capital city would have hosted the 1916 Summer Olympi
   Games but for the First World War?

7. Which figure in English history was known by various unflatterin
   nicknames including 'Tumbledown Dick' and 'Queen Dick', an
   spent about twenty years in exile in continental Europe using th
   name John Clarke?

8. Which weekly literary magazine – first published in 1919 an
   especially popular between the wars – took its title from the pe
   name of Wilfred Whitten, its founding editor?

9. What term is widely used in art for the halo around the head o
   a sacred figure?

10. In 1714, which German physicist invented the first mercur
    thermometer?

11. Hisarlik in present-day Turkey is generally accepted by archaeologists to be the location of which important ancient city?

12. *Il Milione* (or *The Million*) was a contemporary title of a bestselling book of the 14th century, a record of the travels of which merchant and explorer?

13. A dzo is a hybrid of which two mammals?

14. The Druid in the *Asterix* books by Goscinny and Uderzo is known in the English translation as Getafix. What's his name in the original French version?

15. According to the Book of Proverbs, the price of a virtuous woman is – what?

16. The tragic heroine of Scott's *Bride of Lammermoor*; Miss Westenra, Dracula's first victim in England; and the protagonist and narrator of Charlotte Brontë's *Villette*, share which forename?

17. Biliary calculi, or cholelithiasis, is a medical condition more colloquially referred to by what name?

18. Fort Sumter, whose bombardment in April 1861 opened the American Civil War, is a site on an island that protected the harbour of which US city?

19. The actress Melanie Griffith is the daughter of which movie star noted especially for roles in Alfred Hitchcock films?

20. Which highly explosive mixture of mostly picric acid – once used by British troops in ordnance shells – is named after the village on Kent's Romney Marshes where it was first manufactured?

Answers on page 278

21. What is the fanciful name for the leathery egg case of the ray, skate or shark, frequently found washed up by the waves on the beach?

22. Which literary work, published in 1876, has the subtitle 'An Agony in Eight Fits'?

23. In 1702, which successful English General was appointed the first Duke of Marlborough?

24. In 1907, which American photographer took the iconic picture showing people on the decks of the steamer SS *Kaiser Wilhelm II* as it crossed the Atlantic, with the title 'The Steerage'?

25. By what name is crystalline sodium carbonate better known when used in the home?

26. In one of the most famous heckles in musical history, what name was hurled at Bob Dylan by a member of the audience at a concert in Manchester in May 1966, in protest at his use of electric instruments?

27. In the human body the canal of Wirsung connects the duodenum with which organ?

28. Which three allied leaders met at the Cairo Conference of November 1943?

29. Where, in 1834, did Sir Robert Peel issue a political manifesto credited as having laid down the principles upon which the modern British Conservative Party is based?

30. What name is given to a bridge which has a suspended platform in order to carry vehicles and passengers over water, examples of which have been in use at Newport, Runcorn-Widnes, and Middlesbrough?

31. Solidus, virgule and shilling are terms used to describe a punctuation mark now more commonly known by which name?

32. Poll taxes were imposed on the English people in 1377, 1379 and 1380; under which king?

33. What substance is responsible for variation in skin, eye and hair colour?

34. Once the tallest building in the world, before it was superseded by American skyscrapers, the Gothic *Münster* in which south-western German city has a steeple measuring some 161 metres or almost 530 feet?

35. Which American soul singer was the long-standing lead vocalist with the Four Tops, and also provided the voice of the plant in the 1986 Frank Oz film of *Little Shop of Horrors*?

36. What branch of theology deals with the 'last things' – death, judgement, heaven and hell, in short what might be called 'The Last Judgement'?

37. Which town's Rugby League team were at one time known as 'The Chemics' and are now known as the Vikings?

38. What term was coined by Ukrainian-American Nobel laureate Selman Waksman for the bacteria-killing chemicals derived from micro-organisms?

39. *The Belly of an Architect, A Zed and Two Noughts* and *The Pillow Book* are among the films of which idiosyncratic British director born in 1942?

40. Horace Lindrum, in 1952, was the first Australian winner of the World Championships of which sport?

Answers on page 278

Answers to Quiz 41

1. *Henry VI, Part 3*
2. (Georg Wilhelm Friedrich) Hegel
3. William Whitelaw
4. (Dissociative) Fugue (State). Biographer Andrew Norman believes Agatha Christie, who briefly went missing after the death of her mother and her husband's demand for a divorce in 1926, may have suffered a fugue state.
5. The White House
6. Berlin – which, of course, hosted them twenty years later, in very different circumstances.
7. Richard Cromwell – the son of Oliver Cromwell
8. *John O'London's Weekly*. Regular contributions included Winston Churchill, Rebecca West and Somerset Maugham.
9. Nimbus, also called an Aureole or Glory
10. Gabriel Fahrenheit
11. Troy
12. Marco Polo. Other names by which the book was commonly known were *The Description of the World* or *The Book of the Marvels of the World*. It's thought to have been dictated by Marco Polo, in prison, in the last few years of the 13th century.
13. Yak and cow
14. Panoramix
15. Far above rubies
16. Lucy. Respectively Lucy Ashton, Lucy Westenra and Lucy Snowe.
17. Gallstones
18. Charleston
19. Tippi Hedren. Best known for her work in *The Birds* and *Marnie*.
20. Lyddite. From the village of Lydd.
21. Mermaid's purse (accept sea purse)
22. *The Hunting of the Snark* by Lewis Carroll
23. John Churchill. One of England's greatest generals, who led British and allied armies to important victories over Louis XIV of France, notably at Blenheim (1704), Ramillies (1706), and Oudenaarde (1708).

24. Alfred Stieglitz

25. Washing soda

26. 'Judas'. Some fans felt betrayed by Dylan's apparent abandonment of his acoustic folk roots.

27. Pancreas

28. Churchill, Roosevelt and Chiang Kai-Shek

29. Tamworth. Known as the Tamworth Manifesto.

30. Transporter Bridge. The Runcorn-Widnes bridge was demolished in the 1960s.

31. (Forward) Slash

32. Richard II

33. Melanin

34. Ulm

35. Levi Stubbs

36. Eschatology

37. Widnes

38. Antibiotic(s). He was awarded the Nobel Prize in Physiology or Medicine in 1952 for his isolation of the antibiotic streptomycin.

39. Peter Greenaway

40. Snooker. For the next 58 years, he remained the only Australian to have won the World Championship.

1. In Norse mythology, Balder, the son of Odin, was killed by which plant?

2. The 1970 Top Ten hit 'Up the Ladder to the Roof' was significant in the career of The Supremes for what particular reason?

3. The Cambridge landmark the Bridge of Sighs, built across the River Cam in 1831, belongs to which college?

4. In computing, what does the acronym 'MIPS' stand for?

5. Ike's Pond and the Eisenhower Tree, both named after the 34th President of the United States, are notable features of which major American golf course?

6. Marie Laveau, who died in 1881, was a hairdresser with a salon in New Orleans. But what other, more sinister role did she play in the life of the city?

7. In 1876, Sir Henry Wickham brought seeds from the Amazon to Kew Gardens that subsequently were shipped to Sri Lanka and Malaysia to establish plantations producing which crop?

8. A progestogen is any of a group of steroid hormones that can maintain which condition in humans and other mammals?

9. In simple terms, if an object is described as 'Quaquaversal', in which direction does it point?

10. Samphire, also known as glasswort, pickleweed, marsh or rock samphire among other names, has a name in French that associates it with which saint?

11. Which Hebridean island has three distinctively-shaped rocky mountains rising from its western side, known as The Paps?

12. Who was the father of Henry IV of England?

13. Although the first of the official *Carry On* series of movies was *Carry On Sergeant* in 1958, a year earlier a British comedy film with a nautical theme had appeared with the words 'Carry On' in the title, featuring David Tomlinson, Ronald Shiner and Joan Sims. What was it called?

14. Following the break-up of the USSR, which city in Belarus was designated as the administrative centre of the alliance of twelve former Soviet republics known as the Commonwealth of Independent States?

15. Captain Bill Turner was the last captain of which vessel?

16. Which Latin term is used to refer to that form of logical fallacy when an argument is attacked or rebutted essentially on the grounds of some perceived personal flaw or circumstance of its proponent?

17. Which fishing village in eastern Germany was the location for German rocket development under Wernher von Braun during World War II?

18. The works of which Victorian artist, confined for much of his life to asylums, include *The Fairy Feller's Master-stroke*?

19. The pair of giant sculptures by Andy Scott at Falkirk in Scotland, *The Kelpies*, were inspired by water spirits in Scottish folklore reputed to haunt rivers and lakes – and taking the form of which creature?

20. Which grey-white metal, discovered in 1803 by the English chemist Smithson Tennant, is the densest naturally occurring element?

21. Which snooker player, one of two brothers who dominated the game from 1927 until 1956, won the World Billiards Championship in 1980 and 1981 in his late 60s?

Answers on page 284

22. In co-ordinate geometry, which concept is conventionally represented by the algebraic equation $y = mx + c$?

23. Which present-day African capital city was named Fort Salisbury by the British, after the Prime Minister who was in office when it was founded?

24. Which practice – sometimes used in alternative medicine to induce analgaesia – was given its modern name by the British physician and surgeon, James Braid, in the mid-19th century?

25. Known variously as the 'Little Magician' and the 'Sly Fox', among other nicknames, who was the first US President to be born a citizen of the United States?

26. Which Greek god granted Midas his wish that everything he touched would turn to gold?

27. In the sixth Harry Potter novel and film, *Harry Potter and the Half-Blood Prince*, when Dumbledore and Harry call at the home of the former Hogwarts Potions master Horace Slughorn, they find him trying to hide by disguising himself as what?

28. Used as a pigment, vermilion is a bright red sulphide of which element?

29. A huge plaster monument on the site of the Bastille in Paris, which stood for more than thirty years in the early 19th century and plays a role in Victor Hugo's *Les Misérables*, was in the shape of what animal?

30. Who said in 1945: 'The war has developed not necessarily to Japan's advantage'?

31. For what is the biennial Laura Ingalls Wilder Award given in the USA?

32. What name is given to the cheaper spectator benches at an American sports stadium, a name derived from the fact their occupants often sit uncovered and in the sunshine?

33. The Fosse Way and Ermine Street are Roman roads that were built to run northwards from the South of England to meet at which city?

34. What was the name of the US space station launched into Earth orbit in May 1973?

35. Prominent in Gothic buildings of the Middle Ages, the curved angle formed by the intersection of two vaults or arches is usually known by which architectural term?

36. Edith Head, who died in 1981, holds the record as the woman who has won the most Oscars, with a total of eight – in which category were her successes?

37. Which dog breed, originating in Germany, shares its name with the German name for a moustache, more accurately a walrus moustache?

38. In the verse by Rudyard Kipling in the *Just So Stories*, 'I keep six honest serving-men, / They taught me all I knew'. Can you name them?

39. Which general and politician was in charge of Poland during the 1981 crisis involving the trade union Solidarity, placing the country under martial law, outlawing Solidarity, and ordering the arrest of its leaders?

40. Which of the Beatles was the youngest?

Answers on page 284

1. Mistletoe

2. It was their first hit without Diana Ross. She had left the group only a few days before the song was recorded, and the lead vocal was taken by Jean Terrell.

3. St John's College. It crosses the Cam between Third Court and New Court.

4. Million Instructions per Second

5. Augusta (National)

6. She was a voodoo priestess

7. Rubber

8. Pregnancy

9. Every direction/Everywhere

10. St Peter. It's known as *l'herbe de St Pierre* or St Peter's herb.

11. Jura

12. John of Gaunt

13. *Carry on Admiral*. Released in the United States as *The Ship Was Loaded*.

14. Minsk

15. Lusitania. It sank in around 20 minutes, with the loss of over a thousand lives.

16. (*Argumentum*) *Ad Hominem*

17. Peenemünde

18. (Richard) Dadd

19. A (water) horse

20. Osmium

21. Fred Davis – NOT Joe Davis. Fred was one of only two players ever to win the world title in both snooker and billiards. The other, Joe, his older brother by 12 years, was snooker champion from 1927 until he retired in 1946.

22. A straight line

23. Harare, Zimbabwe

24. Hypnotism

25. Martin Van Buren

26. Dionysus. Roman name Bacchus

27. An armchair. The character is played in the film by Jim Broadbent.

28. Mercury

29. An elephant

30. Emperor Hirohito. In his surrender speech.

31. Children's writing

32. Bleachers. The *Dickson Baseball Dictionary* states that the open seating area was called the 'bleaching boards' as early as 1877. Dickson lists as a secondary definition the fans sitting in them.

33. Lincoln. The Fosse Way ran from Axminster to Lincoln. Ermine Street ran from the City of London through Stoke Newington and Enfield to York, via Lincoln.

34. Skylab

35. Groin

36. Costume design. She had a total of 35 nominations.

37. Schnauzer. The Giant Schnauzer was bred to herd sheep and cattle; the smaller standard and miniature varieties of the breed were both used as rat-catchers.

38. '(Their names are) What and Why and When / and How and Where and Who.'

39. General (Wojciech) Jaruzelski

40. George Harrison was born in February 1943, eight months after the next youngest Beatle, Paul McCartney.

1. With which orchestra is the conductor Eugene Ormandy most closely associated, having been its music director for more than forty years?

2. Where on the anatomy of a whale would you find its 'flukes'?

3. Which Roman emperor, the last of the Flavian emperors, succeeded his brother Titus in 81 AD and was assassinated in 96 AD?

4. What is the popular name of the C_{60} molecule discovered by Sir Harry Kroto and named after the inventor of geodesic domes, which this allotrope of carbon resembles?

5. A leper from Bethany mentioned in the gospels of Matthew and Mark; the Cyrenian ordered to carry Christ's cross; and a Samarian magician called Magus, are all biblical figures sharing which forename?

6. What type of performance venue was probably first built by British-born actor William Chapman, and later celebrated in a musical by Jerome Kern?

7. In which British city is Queen Margaret University?

8. Which artist's canvases of American urban life include *Automat*, painted in 1927, and *Nighthawks*, dating from 1942?

9. The words 'defend the children of the poor and punish the wrongdoer' are carved on the exterior of which London building?

10. According to the Book of Genesis, how old was Noah when the Flood came on the Earth?

11. Which feminist and writer, born in London in 1759, wrote the book *Thoughts on the Education of Daughters*?

12. 'Bing Boys', derived from the name of their commanding officer Lord Julian Byng of Vimy, was a nickname given during World War I to troops from which country?

13. Which animated series created by Stephen Hillenburg focuses on characters who work at a fast-food restaurant in the submarine town of Bikini Bottom?

14. The great curassow, the male of which is black and white and can grow up to one metre in length, is found in South and Central America. What kind of creature is a great curassow?

15. '*Bas bleu*' is the French equivalent of which English term for an intellectual woman?

16. The Barbados Blackbelly, the Blackhead Persian and the Brazilian Somali are among the breeds of which animal?

17. Named after Gordon Dobson, an Oxford researcher, Dobson units are the standard way of expressing the proportion in the atmosphere of which polluting chemical?

18. Which American writer in 1970 coined the term 'Radical Chic', describing the tendency at that time for members of well-off high society to mingle with socialists and revolutionaries?

19. The 18th century actor Robert Baddeley made a bequest so that cake and wine could be enjoyed every Twelfth Night by the cast members performing at which London theatre?

20. *Simila similibus curentur* is an axiom espoused by the German physician Samuel Hahnemann, regarded as the founder of which form of alternative medicine?

Answers on page 290

21. The stately home – one of the grandest in England – created for the Earl of Carlisle in 1699 is still owned by his descendants, and still known by the family name. Which stately home is it?

22. Based on an Ernest Hemingway novel, which Howard Hawks wartime romance was the first film in which Humphrey Bogart and Lauren Bacall appeared together?

23. The Tsukahara, named after the Japanese competitor who introduced it in 1970, is a technique used in which gymnastics discipline?

24. At the base of a group of stars known as the 'Sickle', Regulus is the brightest star in which zodiac constellation of the northern hemisphere?

25. Dahomey was the name until 1975 of which West African country, whose capital is Porto-Novo?

26. What word is used in psychology or psychoanalysis to describe the unconscious transformation of an instinctive urge into something more socially acceptable?

27. What term is used by those of the Mormon faith to describe non-Mormons?

28. Why is unwanted e-mail known as 'spam'?

29. Of which star of MGM musicals was it once said, 'Wet, she was a star'?

30. 'Small mass' is the literal meaning of which common scientific term?

31. With music by Stephen Sondheim, and book by Hugh Wheeler, in which country is the show *A Little Night Music* set?

32. What was signified in Ancient Rome when the gates of the archway of the god Janus were left open?

33. What is the nautical term for a temporary mast to replace one that has been broken on a voyage?

34. Which highly flammable and explosive gas, C_2H_2, is produced by the reaction of water and calcium carbide?

35. Which Scottish poet, author of the novel *The Private Memoirs and Confessions of a Justified Sinner*, was known as the Ettrick Shepherd?

36. Appearing in the sky in the constellation of Taurus, the gas and dust remains of the supernova whose explosion was probably witnessed by Chinese astronomers in 1054 are now known by which name?

37. Of which fellow writer – in a letter sent to John Murray in April 1821 – did Byron write, 'I think he took the wrong line as a poet – and was spoilt by Cockneyfying and Suburbing'?

38. With an area measuring approximately 3,200 square kilometres, which Swedish island is the largest in the Baltic Sea?

39. The Companies Court, the Patent Court and the Bankruptcy Court form part of which division of the High Court of Justice?

40. The albums of which British rock group, led by guitarist Robert Fripp, include *Larks' Tongues in Aspic* and *Starless and Bible Black*?

Answers on page 290

Answers to Quiz 43

1. The Philadelphia Orchestra
2. The tail (fin)
3. Domitian. Full name: Titus Flavius Domitianus.
4. Buckminsterfullerene
5. Simon
6. A showboat
7. Edinburgh
8. Edward Hopper
9. The Old Bailey/Central Criminal Court
10. Six hundred years old
11. Mary Wollstonecraft (accept Mary Godwin). The mother of Mary Shelley.
12. Canada
13. *SpongeBob SquarePants*
14. A (game) bird
15. Bluestocking
16. Sheep
17. Ozone (sometimes known as Tri-Oxygen)
18. Tom Wolfe
19. Theatre Royal, Drury Lane. The custom of the 'Baddeley Cake' is still observed.
20. Homeopathy. The words mean 'let like be cured with like'.
21. Castle Howard – built by Vanbrugh and Hawksmoor for Charles Howard, the 3rd Earl.
22. *To Have and Have Not*. It was Bacall's film debut.
23. The vault
24. Leo
25. Benin
26. Sublimation
27. Gentiles

28. It's named after the processed meat product. Often thought to be some sort of acronym, in fact spam e-mail really is named after the tinned meat, and probably directly inspired by the Monty Python 'Spam' song, because it's unwanted and inescapable.

29. Esther Williams. Star of such aquatic musicals as *Neptune's Daughter* and *Million Dollar Mermaid*.

30. Molecule. From the Latin diminutive of *moles*, meaning mass.

31. Sweden. Although the title of the musical is the English translation of the German name for Mozart's Serenade no.13 for strings in G major – the theme music for *Brain of Britain*! – the story is based on Ingmar Bergman's 1955 film *Smiles of a Summer Night*.

32. Rome was at war

33. Jury (-rigged)

34. Acetylene

35. James Hogg

36. The Crab Nebula

37. John Keats

38. Gotland. The main productions on the island are agriculture and quarrying.

39. Chancery Division

40. King Crimson

1. Of which jazz musician's death in 1967 did the poet and critic Philip Larkin write: 'I can't conceal that it leaves in jazz a vast, blessed silence'?

2. Phlebotomy, and venesection, are scientific names for which, now largely obsolete, medical practice?

3. The world's smallest mammal, found in Thailand, with individuals typically weighing only 2 grams, is a species of what kind of creature?

4. In which EU member state is the town of Schengen, where the Schengen Agreement on border controls was signed in 1985?

5. Because of his submission to William the Conqueror in 1066, rather than being replaced by the invaders, Saint Wulfstan was allowed to remain as bishop of which city?

6. The 'ampullae of Lorenzini', named after the Italian anatomist who studied them, are minute structures in the snouts of which creatures, enabling them to detect electrical signals?

7. In Sir Walter Scott's novel *The Heart of Midlothian*, what is the Heart of Midlothian?

8. The wife of which former Prime Minister, knighted in 2005, is a Dame Commander of the British Empire in her own right, honoured in 1999 for her charity work?

9. In mathematics, what is the reciprocal of 2?

10. In which English county is the Neolithic burial mound known as Hetty Pegler's Tump?

11. Oscar Wilde wrote that 'All women become like their mothers. That is their tragedy. No man does. That's his.' In a play by which writer will you find the following parody: 'All women dress like their mothers, that is their tragedy. No man ever does. That is his'?

12. In the *Tom and Jerry* cartoons, Tom the cat only got the name by which we know him today in the second cartoon, 'Midnight Snack'. What name did he have in the first, 'Puss Gets the Boot'?

13. Which comet, which was widely sighted from Earth around Christmas 1973 but is now not due to return for another 75,000 years, is named after the Czech astronomer who discovered it?

14. William Pratt was the real name of which star of horror films, born in London in 1887?

15. Which 1932 novel by Erskine Caldwell, which became a long running Broadway play, tells the story of Georgia sharecroppers during the Great Depression?

16. Although it was not patented or commercially successful during his lifetime, the inventor William Lee pioneered which hand-powered textile machine in Nottinghamshire in the late 16th century?

17. Which record did the Hollywood actress Greer Garson set at the Academy Award ceremony in 1942?

18. Which German scientist was awarded the very first Nobel Prize for Physics in 1901, according to the citation for the 'discovery of the remarkable rays subsequently named after him'?

19. What's the most common English name for the bird with the taxonomic name *Crex crex*, also known as the land rail?

20. By a strange coincidence, two former US presidents died on 4th July 1826 – the 50th anniversary of the signing of the Declaration of Independence. Can you name either of them?

Answers on page 296

21. The Trio section of Sir Edward Elgar's *Pomp and Circumstance March No.1* is best known by what title, from the words set to it by A. C. Benson?

22. What type of weather would you be afraid of if you suffered from chionophobia?

23. One of the most illuminating biographies of Sir Winston Churchill is considered to be *Winston Churchill: The Struggle for Survival* by Lord Moran. What position did Lord Moran hold for much of Churchill's life?

24. The William Herschel Telescope, named after the German-born British astronomer, is located on which islands?

25. A game involving sending a ball through an iron hoop with a mallet, popular in the 17th century, gave its name to which London street?

26. What would you be most likely to find inside a Stevenson screen?

27. Konrad Kujau, the manager of a Stuttgart cleaning company and small-time forger of luncheon vouchers, was responsible for which prominent 20th century hoax?

28. Which composer's name was used as an acronym during the 19th century to show support for the King of Sardinia, the man who was to become king of Italy?

29. *Shir ha-Shirim* is the Hebrew name for which book of the Old Testament?

30. By European law, only cheeses aged in the natural Combalou caves of southern France are allowed to bear which famous name?

31. What is the name of the racetrack in Louisville where the Kentucky Derby and Kentucky Oaks are run?

32. Which chemical element gets its name from the Greek words for 'acid producer'?

33. In which month of 1066 did the Battle of Hastings take place?

34. The Apostle Thomas is also known as 'Didymos'. What does this mean?

35. A 'pilliwinks' was the deceptively innocent name for a medieval instrument of torture that crushed, or put pressure on, which part of the body?

36. Symbolic of the dawn of hope, a rising sun is incorporated into the national flag of which African country, which became independent of British rule in July 1964?

37. The diarist Samuel Pepys died during the reign of which British monarch?

38. Baltra, Genovesa and Bartolomé Island are among the 21 islands of which Pacific archipelago, administered by Ecuador?

39. Bloomsday, celebrated each year in Dublin, is named after the central character in *Ulysses* by James Joyce. It takes place on the date on which the novel is set. What date is that?

40. Which asteroid, the second most massive in the solar system, is the only one that routinely appears bright enough from Earth to be seen with the naked eye?

Answers on page 296

Answers to Quiz 44

1. John Coltrane

2. Blood-letting

3. A bat. The bumblebee bat, *Craseonycteris thonglongyai*, also known as Kitti's Hog-nosed bat.

4. Luxembourg

5. Worcester

6. Sharks

7. The Edinburgh Tolbooth – the city's prison. Its site is now marked by a heart-shaped memorial in the pavement of the Royal Mile.

8. (Dame) Norma Major

9. $\frac{1}{2}$ – the reciprocal being 1 divided by the given number

10. Gloucestershire

11. Alan Bennett, in *Forty Years On*. The original quotation is from *The Importance of Being Earnest*.

12. Jasper

13. Kohoutek after Luboš Kohoutek

14. Boris Karloff

15. *Tobacco Road*. It was dramatized by Jack Kirkland in 1933.

16. The stocking frame

17. The longest Oscar acceptance speech. She spoke for five and a half minutes while accepting the award for her role in *Mrs Miniver*. Acceptance speeches at the Oscar ceremony are now restricted to 45 seconds.

18. Wilhelm Röntgen

19. Corncrake

20. Thomas Jefferson or John Adams

21. 'Land of Hope and Glory'

22. Snow

23. His doctor. During and after the Second World War.

24. Canary Islands. On La Palma.

25. Pall Mall, from the Italian name *pallamaglio*. The street got its name from the long straight alley on which the game was played.

26. Meteorological instruments. It's the white box frequently seen at weather stations, invented in the 1870s by Thomas Stevenson, a Scottish lighthouse engineer.

27. (The forging of) the Hitler Diaries

28. (Giuseppe) Verdi. The slogan *Viva Verdi* stood for *Viva Vittorio Emanuele Re D'Italia*.

29. The Song of Solomon/Song of Songs

30. Roquefort

31. Churchill Downs

32. Oxygen

33. October – the 14th to be precise

34. Twin

35. The fingers and/or thumbs. 'Thumbkins' was another word for the same device.

36. Malawi

37. Queen Anne. Although his diary ends in 1669, Pepys lived until 1703, the year after Anne took the throne.

38. Galápagos

39. 16th June

40. Vesta

Quiz 45

1. Which English king raised the land based tax, the 'Danegeld', in 991?

2. In which US city will you find the Mob Museum, the Neon Museum and the Atomic Testing Museum?

3. The town of Coober Pedy in central South Australia produces over half the world's supply of which semiprecious stone?

4. Under what name does the future wife of the broadcasting administrator Harold Wycliffe Jackson appear in a celebrated poem of 1941?

5. The River Leven carries water southwards to the Clyde estuary from which Scottish loch?

6. A character called Alice, played by Milla Jovovich, is the central figure in which science-fiction film franchise, originally based on a Japanese video game?

7. Which pioneer of telegraphy, news reporting and news agencies was born Israel Beer Josaphat in Kassel, Germany in 1816?

8. Three British Labour Prime Ministers, Harold Wilson, Ramsay MacDonald and Gordon Brown, were all given the same first name, which they all chose not to use. What name is that?

9. Pitchblende is the chief ore of which metallic element?

10. How many balls of almond paste usually feature on a Simnel cake, traditionally eaten on Mothering Sunday or at Easter?

11. Which figure in Russian history is the subject of the Polish writer Isaac Deutscher's biographical trilogy comprising *The Prophet Armed*, *The Prophet Unarmed*, and *The Prophet Outcast*, published between 1954 and 1963?

12. Which British writer and journalist, extremely well known for a series of children's novels, married Leon Trotsky's secretary after they had met while he was in Russia covering the revolutions of 1917?

13. In which sport could you play a Stableford competition?

14. The rivers Wye and Severn have their sources on the eastern slopes of which peak of the Cambrian Mountains?

15. Saint-Saëns' Third Symphony is sometimes nicknamed the 'What?' Symphony because of its prominent part for a particular instrument?

16. Eugenol, used in perfumes, antiseptics and analgaesics, is an essential oil derived principally from which intensely aromatic spice, which gives it its alternative name?

17. Mount Ossa is the name of the highest peak on which island in the southern hemisphere?

18. The flat, rectangular, hand-held tool used by a plasterer to hold his mortar as he works, is usually known by the name of what type of bird?

19. With which inventor did Elisha Gray fight a protracted legal battle, beginning in the 1870s, having filed a patent for the same device at the same time?

20. In geography, what is an arête?

Answers on page 302

21. Which heraldic device links the flags of Wales, Bhutan and Malta?

22. What nickname was given to men conscripted to work in the mines rather than to serve in the armed forces at the end of the Second World War?

23. How many 'Brandenburg Concertos' did J. S. Bach compose?

24. Which infectious and potentially fatal disease, characterised by extreme and painful cramps, results from the effect on the nervous system of a toxin produced by bacteria of the genus Clostridium?

25. The church of St George the Martyr, in Borough High Street in London, contains a stained glass window commemorating the title character from which of Charles Dickens' novels?

26. The last recorded individual of a particular species of large bird was shot in a turnip field in Cornwall in 1843, and it became extinct in Britain after that date – but is now the subject of a re-introduction programme using birds from the steppes of southern Russia. Which bird is this?

27. In the BBC TV comedy series *The Good Life*, Good was the surname of the lead characters Tom and Barbara. What was the surname of Margo and Jerry who lived next door?

28. Lying at an altitude of 1,518 feet, the village of Flash claims to be the highest village in England. In which of the National Parks would you find it?

29. The Curragh, the home of the Irish Derby, is in which county of the Republic of Ireland?

30. Olga da Polga, Monsieur Pamplemousse and Paddington Bear are among the characters created by which British children's author?

31. In 1837, which Russian poet died of his wounds after a duel with his brother-in-law Baron George d'Anthès, whom he suspected of having an affair with his wife Natalya Goncharova?

32. What would a 17th century sailor have done with galligaskins?

33. In the UK in the 1960s radio frequencies were commonly given in metres. When the BBC launched Radio 1 in 1967, what much-publicised medium wave frequency did it use?

34. Which Caribbean island, the southernmost of the Windward group, has St George's as its capital?

35. What is the literal meaning of the name of the Jewish festival Rosh Hashanah?

36. Which organisation, formed following the publication of a Peter Benenson article in 1961, won the Nobel Peace Prize in 1977?

37. The margay, native to some parts of Central and South America, belongs to which family of mammals?

38. Who was the first footballer to be voted BBC Sports Personality of the Year?

39. Founded in 1994, the website 'Jerry and David's Guide to the World Wide Web' was given which new name later in the same year?

40. Which hard, lustrous, greyish-white metal is, alphabetically, the last chemical element of the periodic table?

Answers on page 302

1. Ethelred II ('The Unready'). The Anglo-Saxon nickname *unræd* really means 'badly-advised' rather than 'unready' in the way we'd understand it today.

2. Las Vegas

3. Opal

4. Miss Joan Hunter-Dunn in the poem 'A Subaltern's Love Song' by John Betjeman: it was Mrs Jackson's real maiden name.

5. Loch Lomond

6. *Resident Evil*

7. (Paul Julius) Reuter. Founder of one of the first news agencies, which still bears his name.

8. James

9. Uranium

10. Eleven – representing the eleven faithful apostles.

11. Leon Trotsky

12. Arthur Ransome. Evgenia Petrovna Shelepina became his second wife in 1924.

13. Golf. Named after its inventor, Dr Frank Stableford. Each player or side plays against the par of each hole and receives points according to how he scores in relation to par.

14. Plynlimon/Pumlumon (Fawr)

15. Organ

16. Cloves. Eugenol is otherwise known as oil of cloves.

17. Tasmania

18. A hawk

19. Alexander Graham Bell

20. A thin ridge of rock formed by glacial erosion on both sides, leaving a sharp edge or crest between valleys; the term is actually the French word for an edge or ridge.

21. A dragon. Wales has the Red Dragon of Cadwaladr, King of Gwynedd; Bhutan the Thunder Dragon from that country's mythology; and Malta's flag has a representation of the George Cross in the canton, bearing a depiction of George and the Dragon.

22. Bevin Boys. Named after Ernest Bevin, wartime Minister of Labour and National Service.

23. Six. They were instrumental pieces presented to the Margrave of Brandenburg-Schwedt in 1721.

24. Tetanus, also known as lockjaw. The bacterium, *Clostridium tetani*, is naturally present in the soil.

25. *Little Dorrit*. The church is close to where the Marshalsea Prison, an important setting in the novel, used to stand.

26. The Great Bustard

27. Leadbetter

28. The Peak District. It's in Staffordshire.

29. Kildare

30. Michael Bond

31. (Alexander Sergeyevich) Pushkin

32. Wear them – they were breeches

33. 247 metres

34. Grenada

35. 'Beginning of the year'/'Head of the year'

36. Amnesty International

37. *Felidae* or the Cat Family. A species of the genus Leopardus, it's also called the long-tailed spotted cat.

38. Bobby Moore in 1966

39. Yahoo! David and Jerry being its founders, David Filo and Jerry Yang, then both post-graduate electrical engineering students at California's Stanford University.

40. Zirconium. It just beats zinc.

TOUGH

Not for the faint-hearted: we think these last five are just a little bit more challenging. See what you think.

1. What was the name of the Swiss educationalist whose teaching method was first propounded in a work of 1801 entitled *How Gertrude Teaches Her Children*?

2. Can you name either of West Germany's goal-scorers in the football World Cup Final of 1974, in which they defeated Holland 2-1?

3. The paddymelon is most commonly found in coastal areas of Australasia: what is a paddymelon?

4. Which pair of lovers are the subject of the only known work by the Greek writer Longus, which was later turned into a ballet with music by Ravel?

5. The works of which writer, who committed hara-kiri in 1970 and whose story was told in a cult film of 1985, include *The Temples of the Golden Pavilion* and *Confessions of a Mask*?

6. 'By office boys, for office boys' was the dismissive verdict of Lord Salisbury on which national newspaper, at the time of its foundation in 1896?

7. The region of southern France known as the Languedoc derives its name from a particular feature of the language spoken there in the Middle Ages. What feature is that?

8. Corradino d'Ascanio, chief engineer of the Italian company Piaggio, designed which iconic form of transport first sold in 1946?

9. The Celsius temperature scale is named after the 18th century Swedish scientist who invented it, Anders Celsius. But the scale used today differs from Celsius's original in one important respect. How?

10. The small daughter of Beale and Ida Farange is the eponymous protagonist of which novel by Henry James?

1. Which was the first of the Labours of Hercules?

2. Dating from around 1170, the Jew's House, near the bottom of Steep Hill, is thought to be one of the oldest houses still in use anywhere in Britain. In which English cathedral city will you find it?

3. According to Greek mythology, which people of fabled virtue and prosperity were said to live 'beyond the North wind'?

4. *You Only Live Twice* is a James Bond film, with a screenplay by Roald Dahl, originally released in 1967. Thirty years earlier, which great director – an Austrian who fled Nazism to work in Hollywood – made a film called *You Only Live Once*?

5. The name of which Argentine city was used as a codeword for the invasion of the Falkland Islands in 1982?

6. Which US President was born on exactly the same date as Charles Darwin?

7. If a written sentence has what is termed an 'Addisonian termination', how does it end?

8. Which American-born painter, a protegée of Degas, worked in Paris and exhibited at the Impressionist shows of 1879, 1880 and 1881, and is known particularly for her studies of mothers and children?

9. Heather McKay played hockey for Australia as a schoolgirl, but later took up the sport for which she would win the British Open in sixteen successive years, and the world championship in 1976 and 1979. Which sport was that?

20. Which character in a Charles Dickens novel often used the saying 'When found, make a note of'?

Answers on page 310

21. *Etudes sur le vin*, in 1866, and *Etudes sur le vinaigre*, in 1868, are, as their titles suggest, major studies of wine and vinegar respectively – by which French scientist?

22. If you saw the abbreviation *V. S.* on a piece of music, probably written in pencil by a previous performer of the piece, what would it be telling you to do?

23. Which pianist and conductor, the founder of a great British orchestra, was the inventor of a mechanical device to help pianists turn the pages of sheet music quickly without having to lift their hands from the keys?

24. Why is Lake Malawi also known as 'Calendar Lake'?

25. Although the ancestral home was in Nottinghamshire, the poet George Gordon was the Sixth Baron Byron of which town in Lancashire?

26. What name is given to the instrument – devised in 1849 by a French engineer – used for measuring pressure, and often fitted to cylinders of compressed gas used in industry and in hospitals?

27. In the classically-based medieval theory of bodily humours, yellow bile came to be identified with choler; with which disposition was black bile associated?

28. *The Tale of Peter Rabbit* was the first of Beatrix Potter's children's stories to be published, in 1902. Her publisher Frederick Warne issued her next two books both at once, in 1903. Can you name either of them?

29. In which state of the USA did the notorious Scopes 'monkey trial' of 1925, in which the teaching of evolution in schools was contested, take place?

30. 'Welcome Stranger' was the name given by John Deason and Richard Oates to the object they discovered near Ballarat in Australia in 1869 – what was it?

31. The Indian film industry is often referred to as 'Bollywood', because of its traditional base in Bombay, now of course renamed Mumbai. But which country's film industry is colloquially known as 'Nollywood'?

32. The psychologist and physician William Sheldon classified the human body into three distinct body shapes: Endomorph, typically fleshy and rounded; Ectomorph, meaning someone of lean build; and which other, the type that can easily put on muscle and lose weight relatively quickly?

33. In order of Civic precedence, which is the first of the City of London livery companies?

34. In the classic TV comedy series *Dad's Army*, what job was held by Timothy Farthing?

35. *Heath's Keepsake* of 1833 is generally accepted as the first book to include which now common feature?

36. Of which piece of English classical music did George Bernard Shaw write, "I sat up and said 'Whew!' I knew we had got it at last."

37. Which moon of Neptune orbits in the opposite direction to its parent planet's rotation, and has one of the coldest surfaces of any object in the solar system?

38. What was Bing Crosby's real first name?

39. The presence of small amounts of which metal gives an emerald its distinctive green colour?

40. 'Best Friend of Charleston', completed in 1831, was the first example of what to be built in the USA?

Answers on page 310

Answers to Quiz 46

1. J. H. Pestalozzi

2. Paul Breitner or Gerd Muller

3. A small species of wallaby

4. Daphnis and Chloe

5. Yukio Mishima

6. *The Daily Mail*

7. The word for 'yes' was 'Oc'. The word *Languedoc* was often used in opposition to *Langue d'oil*, which meant the northern part of France where the word for 'yes' was *oil* (it later became *oui*).

8. The Vespa motor scooter

9. Celsius's scale ran downwards not upwards – with freezing point at 100 degrees, and boiling point at zero.

10. *What Maisie Knew*

11. Killing the Nemean Lion

12. Lincoln

13. The Hyperboreans

14. Fritz Lang

15. Rosario

16. Abraham Lincoln – on 12th February 1809

17. With a preposition. Said by some to be a cardinal sin of English grammar but Winston Churchill is often quoted as mocking this pedantry when he said, 'Ending a sentence with a preposition is something up with which I will not put'.

18. Mary Cassatt

19. Squash

20. Captain Cuttle in *Dombey and Son*. Cuttle's saying is surely a motto for quiz players – and quiz setters!

21. Louis Pasteur

22. Turn the page quickly *(Volti Subito)*

23. Sir Charles Hallé – founder of the Halle Orchestra. His device was operated with the feet.

24. Because it's 365 miles long and 52 miles wide

25. Rochdale

26. The Bourdon Gauge – after Eugene Bourdon, 1808-84.

27. Melancholy

28. *The Tale of Squirrel Nutkin* and *The Tailor of Gloucester*

29. Tennessee – in the small town of Dayton

30. A gold nugget – the largest alluvial gold nugget ever found, measuring 61 cm by 31 cm.

31. Nigeria's

32. Mesomorph

33. Mercers (The Mercers' Company)

34. The Vicar of Walmington-on-Sea – played by Frank Williams

35. A (dust) jacket

36. Elgar's *Enigma Variations*

37. Triton. The largest moon of Neptune, its surface of frozen nitrogen and methane is thought to be the coldest place anywhere in the solar system, at minus 235 degrees Celsius.

38. Harry – he was Harry Lillis Crosby

39. Chromium

40. Locomotive

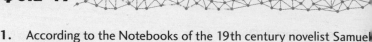

1. According to the Notebooks of the 19th century novelist Samuel Butler, 'life is one long process of getting...' what?

2. The church at Kirkbean, on the Solway Firth, contains a memorial font presented by the US Navy – because the man regarded as the founder of that Navy, a hero of the American War of Independence, was born nearby. What was his name?

3. In which city could you visit the establishment known as 'Ye Olde Trip To Jerusalem', reputed to be England's oldest pub?

4. What is the main distinguishing feature of a piece of writing known as a lipogram?

5. We're familiar with the term 'long wave' in connection with radio frequencies – but what wavelength must a radio wave exceed in order to be called a 'long wave'?

6. Who was the last British monarch not to succeed either a parent or a sibling?

7. The catchphrase 'Very interesting, but stupid' was a feature of which American television comedy series which ran from 1968 to 1973?

8. According to Alvin Toffler in his book *The Culture Consumers*, the law that 'the wider any culture is spread, the thinner it must become' is known as the Law of... what?

9. Where in the human body would you find Glisson's capsule?

10. Henderson's Model, the Roy Model and the Roper-Logan-Tierney Model are recommended frameworks or programmes intended to assist members of which profession in their practice?

1. Prior to Barack Obama, three other US Presidents have been awarded the Nobel Peace Prize, either during or after their term of office. Can you name two of them?

2. In the sequence of year names in the Chinese calendar, which animal follows the snake and precedes the sheep?

3. The spiny Eurasian shrub *Ribes grossulaia* produces which edible fruit?

4. In which town, then in Kent, but now in the London Borough of Bromley, did the French Emperor Napoleon III die in 1873?

5. Which Scottish-born scientist, who lived from 1892 to 1973, was knighted in 1942 for his role in the development and introduction of Radar?

6. What's the name of the valley dividing the Mount of Olives from the Temple Mount in Jerusalem, which was crossed by Jesus when retiring with his disciples after the Last Supper?

7. Stephen Frank, a frontiersman killed in a native Indian skirmish at a river ford in 1780, lends his name to the capital of which US state?

8. Who is the New Zealand-born screenwriter and director who won an Academy Award for *The Piano* in 1994, and co-created the TV drama serial *Top of the Lake*?

9. In 1942, which comedian and musician was the first-ever guest on BBC Radio's *Desert Island Discs?*

20. The name of the rock band The Doors was inspired by a 1954 book of philosophy by which British writer?

Answers on page 316

21. Sisyphus, who was punished in the underworld by being forced perpetually to push a rock to the top of a hill, was, in life, the first king of which Greek city?

22. Morketiden is a Nordic term referring to what period of the year?

23. The autobiography *Without Stopping*, by a 20th century American writer and composer who had spent much of his life in North Africa, was scathingly nicknamed *Without Telling* by William S. Burroughs because of the amount of personal revelation it withheld. Who was its author?

24. Blepharitis is a medical term describing inflammation of which specific part of the body?

25. James Stuart, one of the key architects of the so-called Greek Revival in Britain in the 18th century, was popularly known by a nickname reflecting this trend in his designs. What was it?

26. *It Wasn't All Velvet* was the title of the 1988 autobiography of which American singer, nicknamed 'The Velvet Fog'?

27. Which British traveller and archaeologist was dubbed 'The Uncrowned Queen of Iraq' because of her influence in the creation of that country following the First World War?

28. Which novelist, when working as a film critic in the 1930s, was sued for libel for his review of a film starring Shirley Temple?

29. In Dante's *Inferno*, the Devil is depicted as having three faces, and in each of his jaws chews three figures from history: Brutus, Cassius – and which figure from the Bible?

30. The name of which abbey, near Dumfries in Scotland, commemorates the love of its foundress Lady Dervorguilla of Galloway for her husband John Balliol?

31. Since 1908 the emergency Morse Code signal has been S.O.S. (dot-dot-dot, dash-dash-dash, dot-dot-dot). Which three-letter signal was used before 1908?

32. Writing in the *New Scientist* in 1964, what did the American behavioural psychologist B. F. Skinner define as 'what survives when what has been learned has been forgotten'?

33. What's the proper term for a female octopus?

34. Passed as a response to the Jacobite risings, the 1715 Riot Act laid down a specific minimum number of people that could be considered to constitute a riot. How many people is that?

35. 'I had the upper part of her body in my hands, and I did kiss her mouth.' Thus did Samuel Pepys describe his encounter at Westminster Abbey with the embalmed body of which English queen?

36. Rotating on its axis once every 9.84 Earth hours, which planet of the solar system has the shortest day?

37. Irishman Willie John McBride, captain of the most successful Lions rugby union team, which toured South Africa in 1974, actually isn't 'Willie John', although his first name is William. What is his actual middle name?

38. Workers in which industry used to be susceptible to the condition known as 'phossy jaw', a disfiguring illness involving the onset of gangrene in the face?

39. What's the two-word name used by geographers for the debris and rubble deposited at the end snout of a melting glacier, usually marking the furthest point of its advance?

40. Which African capital city takes its name from the Arabic for an elephant's trunk?

Answers on page 316

1. '…tired.'

2. John Paul Jones

3. Nottingham

4. It deliberately avoids using one particular letter of the alphabe throughout its length – or words to this effect.

5. 1,000 metres (one kilometre)

6. Queen Victoria. She succeeded her uncle, William IV.

7. *Rowan and Martin's Laugh-in.* It was uttered by Arte Johnson, in the guise of a German soldier.

8. Raspberry Jam

9. The liver. It's the layer of connective tissue that completely surround the liver and its associated blood vessels and bile ducts.

10. Nursing – after the American nursing theorists Virginia Henderson and Sister Callista Roy, and Nancy Roper, Winifred Logan, and Alison Tierney all British.

11. Jimmy Carter (2002), Woodrow Wilson (1919), Theodore Roosevel (1906)

12. Horse

13. Gooseberries

14. Chislehurst

15. (Sir Robert Alexander) Watson-Watt

16. The Kidron Valley

17. Kentucky. Frankfort is a corruption of Frank's ford. The ford was on the Kentucky River.

18. Jane Campion

19. Vic Oliver – originally Victor Oliver von Samek. Born in Vienna, he was at the time Winston Churchill's son-in-law, having married Sarah Churchill.

20. Aldous Huxley – it was *The Doors of Perception*, and it describes his experiences under the influence of mescaline.

21. Corinth

22. Deepest winter/the months of darkness – roughly November to January when the sun never rises above the horizon. 'Morketiden' means 'murky times'.

23. Paul Bowles

24. The eyelid – which is also known as the blepharon

25. 'Athenian'

26. Mel Tormé

27. Gertrude Bell

28. Graham Greene. The film was John Ford's *Wee Willie Winkie*, set in India and based on a Rudyard Kipling story. The libel action by 20th Century Fox against Greene was successful.

29. Judas Iscariot

30. Sweetheart Abbey

31. C.Q.D. It goes: dash-dot-dash-dot; dash-dash-dot-dash; dash-dot-dot. Altogether more cumbersome!

32. Education

33. A hen

34. Twelve

35. Catherine de Valois. The wife of Henry V, she had died over 200 years before their 'meeting'.

36. Jupiter

37. James

38. Matchmakers. The disease is properly called phosphorus necrosis, and was caused by the absence of any protection from the effects of phosphorus used in the manufacture.

39. Terminal moraine. 'Moraine' on its own would do.

40. Khartoum

Quiz 48

1. The massive twenty-novel sequence by Emile Zola set during the French Second Empire, which includes such works as *Nana*, *La Bête Humaine* and *Germinal*, is often known collectively by the names of the two families whose story it traces. What are those names?

2. What was the name of the British cleric, a reader of Geology at Oxford University from 1818, who identified the fossil bones of a prehistoric reptile that he called Megalosaurus, the first dinosaur to be given a scientific name?

3. In the periodic table, which hard, brittle, pinkish-white metal has at 83, the highest atomic number of all the stable elements?

4. The contraction 'Interpol' actually only utilises two of the four words in the organization's name in English: what is the full four-word name?

5. Which powerful poison is extracted from the seeds of the castor oil plant?

6. When signing a letter in place of someone else, it is common to place the abbreviation *pp* before one's signature. What do the letters *pp* stand for?

7. Although derived from different sources, which term for an argument is the same as that for a short heavy arrow shot from a crossbow or arbalest?

8. Two pop groups, both with their origins in Sheffield, released hit albums with the title *Hysteria*, within three years of one another in the 1980s. Which two?

9. The word 'Eureka', which Archimedes reputedly exclaimed on lighting upon a hydrostatic method of assessing the amount of alloy in the crown of the king of Syracuse, was adopted as the motto of which US state?

10. Named after the 5th Marquess of Salisbury, the Salisbury doctrine or convention relates to what policy regarding the House of Lords?

11. Which controversial novel of 1928 opens with the line: 'Ours is essentially a tragic age, so we refuse to take it tragically'?

12. Which of the wives of Henry VIII died last, surviving until 1557?

13. The children's novels *Dick Willoughby* and *The Otterbury Incident* are the work of which British poet laureate?

14. Taking its oxygen directly from the air, which part of the body uniquely has no blood supply?

15. An exhibition of reclining nudes, judged obscene by Parisian police officials and shut down in 1917, was the work of which Italian painter?

16. Which film of 1950 completes the director John Ford's so-called 'Cavalry' trilogy of westerns, the first two being *Fort Apache* in 1946 and *She Wore A Yellow Ribbon* in 1949?

17. The Neandertal, the German valley in which skeletal remains discovered in 1856 proved to be those of a palaeolithic hominid, is crossed by which river?

18. Which colonial soft coral, with the scientific name *Alcyonium digitatum*, gets its popular name from its fleshy pink appearance?

19. Terry, who starred as Toto in the film *The Wizard of Oz*, was what breed of dog?

20. Computers routinely use USB connections and devices. What do the letters USB stand for?

21. The line 'Play up! play up! and play the game,' comes from a poem called 'Vitaï lampada', by which Victorian poet?

Answers on page 322

22. The novelist William Golding; the 19th century world heavyweight boxing champion Bob Fitzsimmons; and the chemist and inventor Sir Humphry Davy were all born in which English county?

23. Which British artist was a founding father of the Pop Art movement and became famous for canvases incorporating collage, such as *My Marilyn* and *Just What Is It That Makes Today's Homes So Different, So Appealing*?

24. Scrofula, which affects the lymph glands, especially in the neck, and was once known as the 'King's Evil', is a form of which chronic infectious disease?

25. What name is given to that region of the atmosphere in contact with the Earth's surface and which contains almost all of the clouds?

26. A salt lake in Western Australia called Dumbleyung became the centre of some attention on New Year's Eve in 1964 – for what particular reason?

27. Which city in the former East Germany was known as Karl-Marx-Stadt from 1953 to 1990?

28. Which British physical chemist, who pioneered research into atomic disintegration, also coined the term 'isotope'?

29. The annual rise in stream levels in cold climates brought about by melting snow is known by what name?

30. The Venetian Renaissance painter Giorgio da Castelfranco is better known by which one-word name?

31. Flight Lieutenant Kirsty Moore achieved a notable 'first' in 2009, by becoming the first female recruit to which well-known outfit in the British armed forces?

32. Which famous sporting venue stands on the site of a failed venture to build a London rival to the Eiffel Tower?

33. Can you name the two ships in which Captain Robert Scott sailed to the Antarctic for his expeditions there, the first taking place between 1901 and 1904, and the second, fatal, one from 1910 to 1912?

34. What term did the French theorist, actor and director Antonin Artaud coin, to refer to his idea that theatre should communicate to its audiences at a visceral level 'like a plague', rather than through words?

35. 'Cockaigne', the name of an imaginary country of luxury and idleness, was sometimes given to which real city, in a play on words on the nickname of its inhabitants?

36. When Lord Salisbury left office as British Prime Minister in 1902, he was succeeded by his nephew. Who was that?

37. Which wild plant, also called keck, that grows abundantly and spectacularly in British hedgerows in spring, has the Latin name *Anthriscus sylvestris*?

38. In the Bible, who was the husband of Ruth, and became the great grandfather of King David?

39. Which writer's skit on Shakespeare's *Hamlet*, entitled *Rosencrantz and Guildenstern*, was given its first professional production in 1892?

40. Claiming to be the chief of an Abyssinian tribe, under what name did racing tipster Peter Mackay become better known on British racecourses in the inter-war years?

Answers on page 322

Answers to Quiz 48

1. Rougon-Macquart

2. William Buckland

3. Bismuth. All the elements from atomic number 84 upwards are radioactive.

4. International Criminal Police Organisation. Founded in 1923.

5. Ricin

6. Per procurationem. Meaning 'through the agency of'.

7. Quarrel. The name of the crossbow bolt is ultimately from the late Latin *quadrus*, meaning square (its head was usually squared off), and that of the argument is from *querella* in the same language, which is a complaint.

8. The Human League and Def Leppard

9. California. There is a city called Eureka on the 'Redwood Coast' north of San Francisco.

10. Peers do not impede legislation that has been foreshadowed in a government's manifesto

11. *Lady Chatterley's Lover* by D. H. Lawrence

12. Anne of Cleves. Catherine Parr, Henry's sixth and last wife, died in 1548.

13. C(ecil) Day Lewis. Pseudonym, Nicholas Blake.

14. The cornea. The oxygen is diffused throughout the cornea from the pre-corneal tear film.

15. Amedeo Modigliani

16. *Rio Grande*

17. The Düssel

18. Dead Men's Fingers

19. Cairn Terrier

20. Universal Serial Bus

21. Sir Henry Newbolt. The poem's title refers to the 'torch of tradition' which generations are supposed to hand on, like runners in a relay.

22. Cornwall

23. Richard Hamilton

24. Tuberculosis

25. Troposphere

26. Donald Campbell broke the world water speed record there

27. Chemnitz

28. Frederick Soddy

29. Freshet

30. Giorgione

31. The Red Arrows aeronautic display team

32. Wembley Stadium – the tower became known as 'Watkin's Folly' after the scheme's promoter, Sir Edward Watkin. It only ever reached 200 feet in height, out of a planned 1,150 feet, and it was demolished in 1907. The engineer was Sir Benjamin Baker, one of whose more successful ventures was the Forth Rail Bridge.

33. Discovery and Terra Nova (must have both)

34. Theatre of Cruelty

35. London. As in 'Cockneys'/'Cockaigne-ees'. Cockaigne is mentioned in a number of tales by the Brothers Grimm, and may derive from the German for a cake, Kuchen.

36. Arthur Balfour

37. Cow parsley

38. Boaz

39. W. S. Gilbert. It tells how Claudius as a young man had written a five-act tragedy which was laughed off the stage, all reference to it thereafter being forbidden by him on pain of death. Unconscious that it is by his uncle, Hamlet has it performed at court and is banished to England, leaving Ophelia in the arms of Rosencrantz.

40. Ras Prince Monolulu – whose famous catchphrase was 'I Gotta Horse!' He was actually born on St Croix in the Caribbean. He had made his fortune, and also his reputation as a tipster, in 1920 when he backed the horse Spion Kop to win the Derby at rather long odds.

1. At 1,053 feet or 321 metres, The Vaalserberg is the highest point in which European country?

2. In 1907 Rudyard Kipling became the first Englishman to be awarded the Nobel Prize for Literature. It was twenty-five years before another Englishman won the same award. Who was he?

3. The Second World War song 'Praise the Lord and Pass the Ammunition' was by which American songwriter, who went on to major success with Broadway musicals?

4. In the Walt Disney film of *Snow White and the Seven Dwarfs*, the wicked stepmother visits Snow White in disguise and gives her a poisoned apple. But in the Grimm Brothers' telling of the story, she makes two previous visits in which she attempts to kill her, unsuccessfully, using other objects. Can you name one of those other objects?

5. The tsomgomby or kilopilopitsofy, which is said to resemble a hornless cow, and the tratratratra, described as a lemur the size of a gorilla, are mythical beasts claimed to inhabit which African country?

6. During the reign of which English king did the Addled Parliament sit, so called because they never passed a single act?

7. According to the Oxford English Dictionary, which decade saw the first recorded use of the word 'hip', in the modern sense of being 'well-informed, knowledgeable and aware'?

8. Which other novelist did William Faulkner describe as 'the nicest old lady I ever met'?

9. The French actress Simone Signoret won an Oscar for her performance as Alice Aisgill, the mistress of the main character, in which very British film released in 1959?

10. Which Greek philosopher, who lived between about 460 and 370 BC, earned the epithet the 'Laughing Philosopher', because of his supposed inability to restrain his mirth at the prospect of human life?

11. The Bishop of Urgel and the President of France act as joint Heads of State of which European principality?

12. The first US satellite to go into orbit, launched in January 1958, enabled the discovery of the Van Allen radiation belt around the Earth. What was the satellite called?

13. Although they're thought of as coming from very different generations, the writers George Orwell and George Bernard Shaw both died in the same year. Which?

14. Tyre, Sidon and Byblos were the main cities of which ancient people?

15. Malcolm Morley became the first winner of what, in November 1984?

16. A blivet is an optical illusion or undecipherable paradox that takes which form?

17. The test cricket match between Zimbabwe and New Zealand in November 2011 was the first Test match in which the captains of both teams had the same surname. Which common English surname was that?

18. 'She's a big lass and a bonny lass, and she likes her beer' is how which character is described, in a traditional folk song from the north east of England?

19. Which law of physics is expressed in the equation $F = ma$?

20. In the 1933 film *She Done Him Wrong*, who was the actor to whom Mae West said, 'Why don't you come up sometime, and see me'?

Answers on page 328

21. In the 2012 James Bond film *Skyfall*, what is 'Skyfall'?

22. The 1942 report on Social Insurance and Allied Services, popularly known as the Beveridge Report, famously identified five 'Giants' that needed to be defeated. One was 'Want'; can you name two of the other four, exactly as they were named in the report?

23. If you suffered from Siderodromophobia, what would you fear?

24. Like his elder brother John, the American politician Bobby Kennedy had the middle initial F. In his case, what did it stand for?

25. What's the name of the naturally occurring alloy of gold and silver, which in its refined form contains between 55 and 80 per cent gold, that was first used to make coins as long ago as the 7th century BC?

26. Which three Greek letters make up the name of an achievement-based honour society across a number of American universities, that originated at William and Mary College in Virginia in 1776?

27. What's the name of the shallow lake in South Australia, first sighted by settlers in 1840, which is normally a salt marsh and fills completely only twice a century, on average?

28. Golden sombrero, platinum sombrero and titanium sombrero are (rather unflattering) terms in which sport?

29. Originally only issued to army recruits, but later available to civilians, which useful device was invented in the 1890s by Karl Eisner?

30. The term 'splatter movie' is said to have been coined by which film director, who first used it to describe his own film *Dawn of the Dead*?

31. In 1925 the German scientists Walter Noddack, Otto Berg and Ida Tacke detected which new element in platinum ore and columbite?

32. Which French composer set out on a journey from Italy to Paris in 1831, intent upon the murder of his fiancée Camille Moke, after learning that she had abandoned him for a wealthy piano manufacturer?

33. Which biologist and geneticist, born in Oxford in 1892, wrote the futuristic utopian work *Daedalus*, introducing his vision of ectogenesis that raised the prospect of 'test-tube babies'?

34. Which part of the brain stem, occupying its lower half, contains within it centres for the regulation of the heart, respiration, salivation and swallowing?

35. According to Charles Dickens, in *The Old Curiosity Shop*, 'If there were no bad people there would be no good...' what?

36. In the late 1800s, the Canadian railway engineer Sir Sandford Fleming put forward a proposal that gave rise to which enduring international convention?

37. Camp David, the US Presidential retreat, is located in which state of the USA?

38. Zip codes are the US equivalent of postcodes. What do the letters ZIP stand for?

39. In 1959 which British city became the first to adopt a postcode system?

40. The seeds of the native deciduous Asian tree *Nux vomica* are the major natural source of which highly poisonous alkaloid, used in some places as a pesticide?

Answers on page 328

1. The Netherlands. It's probably a surprise to you to find there is a point even that high.

2. John Galsworthy – in 1932

3. Frank Loesser. Previously he'd been known as a lyricist: this was one of the first songs for which he wrote the melody too.

4. Laces or stays, which she pulls so tight that Snow White falls into a faint; and a poisoned comb.

5. Madagascar. Which almost certainly does contain many species still unknown to science.

6. James I

7. The 1900s (i.e. the first decade of the 20th century). The first use recorded by the OED is by writer G. V. Hobart in 1904, but there are many examples from that decade, some with the spelling 'hep'.

8. Henry James (!)

9. *Room at the Top* – based on the John Braine novel. The main character was played by Laurence Harvey.

10. Democritus of Abdera

11. Andorra

12. Explorer I

13. 1950. The difference is that Shaw was 94 when he died, Orwell just 46.

14. Phoenicians

15. The Turner Prize

16. An impossible fork (with three apparent cylindrical prongs at one end but only two rectangular prongs joining the handle at the other). Also known as an 'Impossible Trident'.

17. Taylor. Brendan for Zimbabwe and Ross for New Zealand.

18. 'Cushy Butterfield'

19. Newton's Second Law of Motion. Force = mass x acceleration.

20. Cary Grant. Note the correct form of the quotation!

21. The childhood home of James Bond – in the Scottish Highlands

22. Illness, Ignorance, Disease, Squalor

23. Trains or railways. From Greek *sideros*, iron + *dromos*, running.

24. Francis

25. Electrum. Electrum is also an ancient name for amber, which could generate static electricity, and thus gave rise to our word 'electricity'.

26. Phi Beta Kappa

27. Lake Eyre. It's official name is now Kati Thanda-Lake Eyre, incorporating the native Australian name for it. It's the lowest point in the Australian continent, lying 12 metres below sea level, and the chances are that with the changing climate it will be dry for even more of the time.

28. Baseball, where they denote striking out four, five and six times respectively

29. The Swiss Army knife

30. George A. Romero

31. Rhenium – one of the rarest of all elements in the Earth's crust, it's named after the river Rhine, though the world's most productive deposits of rhenium are in Chile.

32. (Louis-)Hector Berlioz

33. J. B. S. (Jack) Haldane

34. The medulla oblongata

35. Lawyers

36. He proposed that the globe be divided into 24 time zones

37. Maryland

38. Zone Improvement Plan

39. Norwich. Norwich was chosen as it already had eight automatic mail sorting machines. Postal areas (1850s) and districts (1934) were the forerunners of the postcode system.

40. Strychnine

Quiz 50

1. Where will you find the Mohorovicic Discontinuity?

2. According to Rupert Brooke's poem 'The Soldier', 'there's some corner of a foreign field that is for ever England'. After his own untimely death in 1915, Brooke was himself buried in a 'foreign field', in which country?

3. Which term is used to describe the split in the Church of Scotland when, in 1843, its Evangelical wing formed the Free Church of Scotland?

4. When Leonidas led his three hundred Spartans to their deaths at the Battle of Thermopylae in 480 BC, he was accompanied by four hundred soldiers from Thebes, and seven hundred from which other Greek city?

5. The novel *Futility*, written by Morgan Robertson and published in 1898, described an event that was to make it seem tragically prophetic a few years later. What was its subject matter?

6. What's the name of the large triangular bone at the base of the spine which connects at the top with the last lumbar vertebra, and at the bottom with the coccyx?

7. The author of the book *10 Rillington Place*, an account of the Christie murders published in 1961, has been credited with having played a major role in the abolition of capital punishment. Who was he?

8. If you suffer from trichotillomania, what are you compelled irrationally to do?

9. In 1954, Elvis Presley released his first single, a cover of a song made popular by the blues singer Arthur 'Big Boy' Crudup. What was its title?

10. In the ancient process known as 'encaustic' painting, by which the Egyptians, Greeks and Romans made paintings on walls, what substance was mixed with the coloured pigments in order to 'fix' the design?

11. What species was Ota Benga, the star exhibit of the Bronx Zoo in the summer of 1906?

12. The Bactrian Camel is named after a region in which country?

13. Which organisation began life as a body called the Office of Strategic Services?

14. John Dryden's play *All For Love, or The World Well Lost,* deals with the romance between the same two historical figures as which play by Shakespeare?

15. One of the first setbacks for Edward Heath's newly elected Conservative government in 1970 was the death, a month after the election, of the Chancellor of the Exchequer. Who was he?

16. Can you name the Austro-Hungarian officer who gained notoriety just before the First World War, by betraying military secrets to the Russians? A film about his life, starring Klaus Maria Brandauer, was released in the mid-1980s.

17. One of George Orwell's most celebrated essays was entitled 'Inside the Whale'. Which writer produced a scathing attack on the depiction of India in British literature, in a 1984 essay called 'Outside the Whale'?

18. Which term, alluding to a well-known fairytale, do some astronomers use to describe the zone of space around a star where temperatures and conditions are neither too hot nor too cold for water, and possibly for life?

19. Part of a series of 2010 stamps commemorating the art of the album cover, the painting *A Basket of Roses* by French artist Henri Fantin-Latour was included, as it had been used on the cover of a 1983 record by which group?

20. In a compound in which town in Pakistan was Osama bin Laden discovered and shot dead in May 2011?

Answers on page 334

21. Which historical figure is thought by many to have become sole king of his people following the murder of his brother and co-ruler Bleda, around 445 AD?

22. Which word, in common use, is taken from the Greek for 'Circle of animals'?

23. The acronym O.V.N.I., common to French, Spanish, Portuguese and Italian, is the equivalent of which three-letter abbreviation in English?

24. If you were practising catoptromancy, which everyday object would you be using to predict the future?

25. Deriving from the Latin for 'lightning', what name is given to the tubes of glassy mineral matter formed in sand or soil by lightning strikes?

26. A tyrannosaur, as everyone knows, was a dinosaur. But what is a tyrannulet?

27. Throughout his political career, Enoch Powell only held one cabinet post. What was it?

28. Pedology is the science of what?

29. Many British athletic clubs derive at least part of their name from which form of cross country racing that became popular in English public schools from the 18th century?

30. When she was made a life peer in 1992, Mrs Thatcher became Baroness Thatcher of where?

31. In the traditional game table skittles, what name is used for the ball or disc or 'lump' cast at the pins – a name sometimes also given to the plastic tokens won for a correct answer in the game of *Trivial Pursuit*?

32. What is a Scotch argus?

33. Which acclaimed Scandinavian film of 1967 is about an affair between a married Swedish army lieutenant and a tightrope-walker?

34. Which English writer once telegraphed to his wife: 'Am in Market Harborough. Where ought I to be?'

35. Considered a prophet in Islam, how is the 'patiently enduring' Ayyub, who appears in the Qur'an, known in the equivalent eponymous book of the Bible?

36. Being sweeter and less prone to crystallisation, the mixture of fructose and glucose obtained by splitting sucrose into those two components is given what name?

37. London was frequently referred to in the 19th century as 'The Great Wen'. What is a wen?

38. The German-born theologian Thomas à Kempis; the reformer Martin Luther; and the Austrian botanist and geneticist Gregor Mendel all belonged to which monastic order?

39. Which character in Shakespeare speaks the lines that begin: 'The barge she sat in, like a burnished throne / Burned on the water. The poop was beaten gold / Purple the sails, and so perfumed that / The winds were love-sick with them'?

40. In what way did Rosemary Watson achieve a notable 'first' on British radio in 1957?

Answers on page 334

1. Within the Earth (between the crust and the mantle)
2. Greece
3. The Disruption
4. Thespiae (Thespians)
5. It anticipated the sinking of the Titanic – the plot is centred on a liner spookily called the Titan, of almost exactly the same dimensions as its real-life equivalent (and with the same tragic shortage of lifeboats), which collides with an iceberg and sinks.
6. The sacrum
7. Ludovic Kennedy
8. Pull out your own hair
9. 'That's all right (mama)'. On the Sun record label.
10. (Molten) Beeswax
11. Human – incredibly he was an Mbuti pygmy from what was then the Belgian Congo.
12. Afghanistan. From the ancient country of Bactria located between the Hindu Kush mountains and the Oxus River, now part of the district of Balkh in northern Afghanistan.
13. The CIA/Central Intelligence Agency. When the OSS was disbanded in 1945, the X-2 and SI divisions formed the nucleus of what was to become the CIA in 1947.
14. *Antony and Cleopatra*
15. Iain Macleod
16. Colonel (Alfred) Redl
17. Salman Rushdie
18. The Goldilocks Zone
19. New Order. The record in question was their album *Power, Corruption and Lies*.
20. Abbottabad. It was named after its founder, the British Major James Abbott, in 1853.
21. Attila (The Hun)
22. Zodiac

23. U.F.O. *objet volant non-identifié, objeto volador no identificado, objecto voador não identificado* and *oggetto volante non identificato* respectively

24. A mirror

25. Fulgurites

26. A bird – specifically a type of South American flycatcher

27. Minister for Health

28. Soils. Not feet!

29. Hare and Hounds. By being called 'Harriers'. A harrier was a member of the Hare and Hounds team.

30. Kesteven, the ancient subdivision of the county of Lincolnshire that includes her birthplace, Grantham.

31. Cheese

32. A species of butterfly. Brown, with an orange chain of eye-spots near the wing-margins.

33. *Elvira Madigan.* The film was notable for its prominent use of Mozart's Piano Concerto no.21.

34. G. K. Chesterton

35. Job. Job's story in Islam is very similar to the Hebrew Bible story but, in Islam, the emphasis is paid to Job remaining steadfast to God and there is no mention of lengthy discussions with friends.

36. Invert/Inverted sugar. Inverted sugar is therefore valued by bakers, who refer to the syrup as trimoline or invert syrup.

37. A wart or tumour. Lump, cyst, or similar. OED has it 'a lump or protuberance on the body, a knot, bunch, wart'.

38. Augustinians

39. Enobarbus. In *Antony and Cleopatra.*

40. She was the first female winner of the *Brain of Britain* title

APPENDIX

The strange story of "John P. Wynn"

Hans Priwin was born in Magdeburg in 1906, and educated, according to his own information, at the Gruenewald High School, Berlin, and at both Aachen Technical University (1925-28) and Berlin University (1928-29). Though some of his job descriptions have an inflated look, his claim was that during the Aachen years, he'd been "Foreign News Commentator and Special Correspondent" with the *Politisches Tageblatt* newspaper. Aachen was still occupied by the Allies at the time, in the long aftermath of the Great War.

Priwin made his first contact with the BBC in 1928, as a correspondent and columnist of the BBC's foreign journal *World Radio*. This connection seems to have lasted until 1935. His command of English must already have been impressive. Also in 1928, the British periodical *Wireless World* published a capsule review of Priwin's little German-language manual *Kurzwellen-Verkehr* ("Short-wave communication"), published in Berlin: "a handbook for amateur transmitters, including the Morse Code, use of abbreviations and list of German amateur transmitters". Within a couple of years, still in Berlin, he had his own weekly newsletter for the industry, *Radiopress*, and also contributed to the magazine *Die Sendung* ("Transmission") as a roving reporter, visiting radio stations all over Germany. But Hans Priwin's interest in the hardware of the trade inevitably intertwined with more urgent political matters, making his role in German public life a hazardous one. As a German Jew with access to broadcasting outlets, he was undoubtedly being watched.

A crisis in his progress was reached on 1st April 1933, when he gave a transatlantic talk to the American radio audience, via the National Broadcasting Company networks, speaking in English about the status of Jews under the emerging Nazi regime. The broadcast was not heard by listeners in Germany, because Priwin's right to appear on home radio, and in German newspapers, had recently been withdrawn. What he said to his American listeners we know, since the *New York Times* reprinted the entire text. It reads strangely, but then Priwin was caught between saving his career (and quite possibly his life), and giving the distant audience some idea of the anxiety of the moment. All the signs point to the probability that he was heavily leaned on by those supervising his address. After all, it was transmitted from the Reichs-Rundfunk-Gesellschaft in Berlin, a confederation of regional companies notorious, from 1933 to 1945, for disseminating Nazi misinformation. There are some passages which flatly state the opposite of the truth, and in a governmental style:

> The German Jews are pictured as the victims of a deliberate, despicable incitation to pogroms. It is even foolishly asserted that the national Revolution in Germany was the work of a group whose only aim was to massacre the Jews....

> Anyone who knows the Germans -- and many of you who hear my voice do know them -- must know that such atrocity reports, which sound as if they came from the Middle Ages, are despicably false, are a groundless misrepresentation of the facts. We have had a revolution in Germany, a revolution so bloodless and so quiet as has not been seen in centuries...

> The government is doing all in its power to assure this. It has decreed punishments for individual acts; it has in Cologne, for example, expelled storm troop-men from the party because they were apprehended while doing unauthorised things...

> The Berlin Jews have no intention of keeping off the streets. Nobody will molest them because of their religion. The injury caused abroad by the atrocity reports recoils with double force on the German Jews. The boycott measure abroad against German products were [sic] answered with a boycott against the Jews in Germany.

That last detail had to be mentioned; because in fact, Priwin's broadcast -- if it was indeed his voice speaking -- was made on the very Saturday, All Fools' Day 1933, when a 24-hour national boycott of all Jewish businesses had been organised by the odious Julius

Streicher. The whole piece reads for all the world like a government press release masquerading as a quietistic German-Jewish point of a view, and arriving at a highly Trumpist conclusion.

We [i.e. German Jews] are at one with the government in the desire that German shall again become great. Our fatherland must be saved from distress and dissension.

It seems clear Priwin was pressurised or blackmailed into uttering these thoughts, which more or less inaugurated a whole tradition of mendacious propaganda issuing from the Reichs-Rundfunk-Gesellschaft, until its abrupt closure at the end of the war. His task complete, Priwin remained at large, but his prospects of employment were now minimal, which explains why, in the following days, he more than once arranged to meet James Grover McDonald, the Berlin-based High Commissioner for Refugees Coming from Germany. The Commission was affiliated with, but not financially supported by, the League of Nations. We know their meetings took place because McDonald stated as much, naming Priwin, in his published diary for 1933. "His tale is just one more," the Commissioner confided sadly to the journal.

And yet that contact proved vital to Priwin's future freedom. Within the year, he'd departed for Geneva, where he worked as Editor and Director of the Agence Generale de Presse, a news agency attached to the League of Nations itself. Priwin also pursued a post-graduate university course in Geneva, and seconded himself to a satellite office maintained by the same agency in Copenhagen, where he acquired fluent Danish. Meanwhile, James G. McDonald, whose efforts to help refugee Jews in Germany had no doubt included sponsorship of Priwin, had become disillusioned with the lack of American finance and international support for his crusade. In the last days of 1935, he resigned.

But by then, Priwin (the original surname of the Berlin-born André Previn, incidentally) had made another move, and was to be found living in Belsize Park, North London. The speed of his engagement with British culture, and especially broadcasting, was remarkable. By the following year, he'd produced a BBC radio drama character, Inspector Hornleigh, who appeared in dozens of short episodes. In due course, they grew into a novel, a stage play and three feature films from Twentieth Century-Fox, featuring the dour Gordon Harker as Hornleigh and the much sprightlier Alastair Sim as the Sergeant assisting him. Priwin's taste for creating puzzling questions was already on show. He opened up the crime-detection process – made it "interactive", as we'd say today – by planting a giveaway clue in the dialogue, and inviting the listener to spot it. Simultaneously, and still billed as Hans W. Priwin, he was supplying a weekly "radio problem" spot to the hit comedy show *Band Waggon*. The item might well have been called "What Do You Know?" Instead, Priwin called it "What Do You Think?"

Had Priwin been content to remain an "Outside Contributor" at the BBC, his life might have remained quite placid. But such an arrangement would have suited neither his bank manager (a Mr Gribble of the Westminster Bank, Haverstock Hill) nor his ambitions. So, on 10th October 1938, he joined the staff of the BBC as a part-time German Announcer/Translator, in the Overseas Department. And from that moment, his career became ever more complicated. Anyone simultaneously acting as a staff member and creating freelance material for other departments of the Corporation is bound to encounter problems of demarcation, and disputes over payment. But Hans Priwin was also a German passport holder, and destined to be a Registered Alien, along with his wife, Marga (née Kronheim), and a daughter.

He was working, therefore, at two jobs -- one creative and diverse, the other concentratedly news-based and political -- and all under circumstances causing inbuilt strains. Not surprisingly, his personal file at the BBC opens with a strenuous sick-note from his doctor: "Mr Hans W. Priwin, whom I examined this afternoon, is in a state of physical exhaustion, which has been brought on through overwork and lack of relaxation." His heart and nervous system required complete rest, the doctor said, "for at least four weeks". That was granted, and Priwin retired to his favourite haunt of the time, a hotel in Brockenhurst in the New Forest ("the place is full of old ladies and still older colonels"). But not long after his return to duty, Priwin was asking for a slice of statutory leave, causing one of the BBC bureau chiefs, V. Duckworth Barker, to exclaim in a memo, "I ask with Ambrose Bierce, 'Can such things be?'" (In case a future *Brain* contestant needs to know, *Can Such Things Be?* was the title of a collection of Bierce's stories.)

In spite of all, Priwin was engaged full-time in April 1939. A Confidential Report on him had been prepared, and had pronounced him "efficient and practical; rather universal curiosity", which was a sign of careers to come. However, "His tendency towards over-assertiveness would doubtless be corrected by an effective supervisor" was also a portent. A further report warned against placing him in a position of authority in the German team, "for we think that this may make for disharmony and undermine the authority of the Sub-Editors (Translation) who are about to be appointed". Doubts about Priwin's manner tended to be reinforced by the confusions caused by his travels. In July 1939, he rang up from Avignon in France, anxious to know whether he should return to England at once. "In the event of a crisis", Priwin had said, his German passport would not be much use to him, so could he have a "To whom it may concern" letter to show to French officials? The BBC obligingly sent one.

War duly broke out; and a week into the conflict, while Priwin himself had reached home, his young daughter was now stranded in Aberystwyth, after a holiday. The school she attended in Hampstead had meanwhile been evacuated to Tintagel. Her father applied both to BBC and the Aliens Department at Scotland Yard for a car and driver to be supplied, but the law-enforcement authorities decreed that "it was absolutely impossible for any alien to be granted car facilities", while the Corporation classified the plan as "too expensive and unfair". Priwin was reportedly "very bitter about the whole thing", pointing out that the Priwins had been "responsible for the translation of the R.A.F. leaflets into German" and were enemies of the Nazi regime. In the end, it seems to have been Mrs Marga Priwin who made the necessary journey to release their child from Welsh captivity.

Hans Priwin's chief grievance at this time, however, concerned his citizenship status. Having completed the necessary four years' residence, he expected to be naturalised, but the Home Office was reluctant in wartime to endorse the process. Priwin hoped the BBC could help, but didn't help his case by making farcical travel requests. On 10th May 1940, he asked, in a departmental note, "I wonder if you can tell me whether there is a possibility of me taking my holidays in France." That 10th May happened to be the day on which German troops advanced into neutral Holland, and the fall of France was complete within a month. From upstairs came the natural reply, "There is no possibility whatever of his obtaining an exit permit to France on his present status." The vigilant V. Duckworth Barker added an inky note: "I should hardly advise a holiday in France just now with a German passport."

But Priwin couldn't keep quiet, and eventually it was the end of him as a BBC staff figure. His capacity for self-dramatisation had led him, very early in the war, to write an article called "Tell The Germans", intended for publication in the *Daily Herald*, the national newspaper. In it, he described the activities of the BBC German service in which he was working, with special reference to himself. No names were given, but "a man who had formerly been in the employ of the German Broadcasting System and was thus familiar with the microphone and certain special requirements for broadcasting news bulletins" was clearly Priwin himself. The tone is informative, but immodesty breaks through: "There is no dictionary in the world which can keep pace with the invention of new words which crop up every day... the extended general knowledge which this sort of work requires can be found only among a few outstanding persons... "

The author of this screed did at least have the sense to show it to his BBC taskmasters before giving it over to the presses, but the adjudication of their spokesman (A. E. Barker) was understandable: "I am absolutely clear in my own mind that the publication of an article on the German service by a member of the German staff is undesirable and should not be permitted." And there that particular matter rested. But on 13th June 1940 – three days after Priwin's request for a French holiday – he was obliged to inform the BBC's European Language Service that: "The *Evening Standard* published a story about me in today's lunch edition to the effect that I have applied for nationalisation, that I am registered as a 'friendly alien', and that I am doing war work which I am not at liberty to divulge." After the appearance of the item, further telephone calls had been received from the *Standard*, and from the well-known *Daily Telegraph* correspondent, L. Marsland Gander.

What kind of indiscretion or self-advertisement had led to this revelation is not recorded, but it was certainly not welcomed at Scotland Yard. Within a week, the Assistant General Establishment Officer of the BBC was writing:

Dear Mr Priwin,

I am writing to give you formal notice of the termination of your engagement with us as German Announcer/Translator... with effect from 17th June 1940.

The cause outside either our or your control which prevented the further performance of your engagement is the withdrawal by the Aliens War Service Department of their permission for you to work in the BBC.

Clause 10 of Priwin's contract stipulated no compensation in such an eventuality, "but in your case an ex gratia payment of one month's salary from 17th June 1940 shall be made". And then, more poignantly:

You handed me on Monday your Police Registration Certificate, your BBC pass and badge, and I am acknowledging hereby receipt of these articles. Will you please let us have your gas mask as soon as possible? I am making arrangements for your books to be returned to you.

I am taking this opportunity of thanking you on behalf of the Corporation for the work you have done for us.

344

There followed a painful search for work, during which Priwin tried in vain to extract a "testimonial" from the BBC. There was, they said, a Corporation rule "against the issue of open testimonials", but they undertook to provide details of his BBC work. A certain amount of discussion persisted at Broadcasting House about Priwin's departure, mixing guilt with personal distaste. The Controller, Overseas Services, J. Beresford Clark, was typical in his reaction: "I find it difficult to know what to say. Priwin did not appear to me at any time to have an attractive personality but I feel a sense of social obligation in the circumstances not to stand in his way of earning a living." Clark added a strong P.S. to this message: "Prima facie I still think it is monstrous that he was deprived of the opportunity of working for us and yet is still left to fend for himself."

In the event, Priwin joined Kemsley Newspapers, in his own words "mainly analysing foreign news broadcasts, and preparing and editing daily digests of monitored material for information and publication". Since he was applying for a monitoring post when he wrote that summary, he may have exaggerated those aspects on his output. On another occasion, he testified: "For the past five years I have been Senior News Coordinator and Analyser with the *Daily Graphic* and Kemsley Newspapers." Evidently, though, in some combination of these roles he was effective. The most remarkable evidence of that, preserved for some reason in the BBC files, is a letter from Ian Fleming to Christopher Chancellor, the head of Reuters. After his years in Naval Intelligence, Fleming, who had not yet begun to write the James Bond books, arrived as Foreign Manager at Kemsley House in 1945, and so had roughly two years to observe Priwin at work. Fleming himself had no place for Priwin once Kemsley's "radio station" had closed down, but wrote:

It seems to me, however, that Reuters might be interested in this exceptional man, less in connection with his radio experience than for his interpretative writing on foreign affairs. He has excellent contacts in many countries and was responsible for very many of the paragraphs which appeared daily in the *Daily Graphic*'s 'Inside Information' series during the war.

But Priwin did not go to Reuters: as his files show, he was determined to re-enter the BBC. And the BBC was equally determined to exclude him. One of his various applications brought him into contact with the German Service Director, Hugh Carleton Greene, later famous as an unusually influential Director-General of the entire BBC. A colleague from those earlier years described Greene as "a beast -- but a just beast", though beastliness does tend to drown justice in the following adjudication from July 1945:

I saw Priwin on Friday afternoon. My general impression was that he is an able man but an extremely unpleasant one. I do not think we should consider taking him back on the staff. We have had some experience in the past of this type of German who is apt to delight in making the life of people around him difficult and in bullying the weaker brethren. Such people, however able, are usually more trouble than they are worth.

Guilty though it is of some huffy, end-of-war stereotyping, Greene's view, it must be said, was corroborated by others in the hierarchy. Two years later, when Priwin was still trying other points of entry, the Director of the European News Department, Donald Edwards, recorded his own post-interview reactions:

He is a man of obvious ability and initiative ... but I must say his unpleasant personality terrified me. I think he would be very uncontrollable and would be continually bullying to get into something better than ordinary sub-editing. I afterwards noted in reports "difficult to get on with personally" and "an upsetting influence on the rest of the staff". In the circumstances, I do not recommend his engagement in the News Department.

It may be that his years of exile from the Corporation had embittered Priwin. In yet another application, he remarked:

Let me add that ever since I had to leave the Corporation seven years ago on grounds which have been recently described to me as 'a panicky measure without any foundation', it has been my wish to return the Broadcasting House as soon as conditions would permit.

Conditions never did permit the kind of return he had in mind. But of course, the newly naturalised John P. Wynn was not barred from the BBC's central premises, once he had resumed his role as an "Outside Contributor". Among his new scriptwriting ventures was a bunch of documentaries for the German Service (on the Hudson Bay Company, Lloyd's, Rhodesia, Radar and the House of Lords) and a drama series called *Gordon Grantley K.C.*, which among other things gave the young Kenneth Williams his first work in broadcasting. But of course Wynn's most famous achievement was yet to come. And as this book shows, it still continues.

ACKNOWLEDGEMENTS

At roughly the half-way point in any *Brain of Britain* contest, the contestants combine to answer listeners' questions designed to "Beat The Brains". On the face of it, that's the only moment when *Brain* becomes a team game. But behind the scenes, things are entirely different. The team headed by the producer, Paul Bajoria, invariably includes his Assistant Producer, Stephen Garner, who, in between producing duties of his own, acts as my scorer, paper-shuffler, issuer of alerts ("Last Round!") and manager of the complex cue-light system. Steve also leads the audience in applause and generally communicates with the multitude while my head is in the list of questions -- more about those below, from Paul himself. Back at the office, we all owe the fact that we have scripts to read from, and contestants on hand to wrestle with them, to the organising talents of the invaluable Lizzie Foster. And all of us are grateful, season by season, for the support and encouragement of two senior editorial figures at BBC Salford, Nicola Swords and Ian Bent.

In the compilation of the programme's history, and the story of John P. Wynn, its inventor, I relied – as I knew I'd be able to – on my favourite BBC resource, the corporation's Written Archive at Caversham. Apart from being the last outpost of the calm and gentility once widespread in the BBC, the Archive is full of surprises, always generously unveiled by Jeff Walden, the veteran Archives Researcher and presiding spirit. If files need to be called in from distant and semi-forgotten sub-archives far from Caversham – as happened with Wynn's personal records – Jeff will not only locate them but arrange vetting and "clearance". He also answered some extra-obscure questions I lobbed at him, leaving me, as always, tremendously grateful to him and his staff.

Particular thanks also go to Richard Edis, long-time producer of *Brain of Britain*, with whom I worked on other projects (*Radio Roots*, etc.) in the old Light Entertainment Department, and through whom I got to know both the late Ian Gillies and today's quiz-king, Kevin Ashman. Their memory for the detail of contests long past was impressive enough, but Richard's is prodigious, leading me to believe that if ever he'd been a quizzer, he would have prospered. He gave me my first work on *Brain* as the deputy to the absent Robert Robinson. I never ran into Bob in the context of the quiz, though oddly enough I was a TV panellist on *Call My Bluff* under his chairmanship.

And of course, it's a great pleasure to thank the ultimate team captain, the *Brain of Britain* programme producer, Paul Bajoria. Paul has *Counterpoint* and the immemorial *Round Britain Quiz* under his wing as well, but retains, I think, a special affection for *Brain*, which certainly showed through in the preparation of this book. Paul and I chose the questions cooperatively from the programme archive of scripts past, but it was Paul who arranged them in their groups of 40, with an ascending order of difficulty in mind. That the questions exist at all is also Paul's doing, since he appoints the ever-changing panel of setters, and collects their contributions from them, year by year.

In that connection, Paul says this: "The ingenuity of the *Brain of Britain* question-setters never fails to impress. This book includes the substantial contributions of Chris Ansell, Saira Dunnakey, Stephen Follows, David Kenrick, Stewart McCartney, Elissa Mattinson and Danny Roth. Research and verification – no less important, to ensure we are as factually watertight as is feasible – has been mainly the work of Lizzie Foster and Angela Sherwin, who have also kept hundreds of contestants (and the producer) in order over the years, and worked many other miracles of cheerful organisation. Stephen Garner has fulfilled most of the above roles, in addition to ensuring, in his inimitable way, that the audiences at *Brain of Britain* recordings never get bored." I would add that Paul's introductory address to the audience at every recording is a highlight of the occasion, done with a combination of charm and thoroughness that is typical of the man.

As for outside sources, the internet is not teeming with information about John P. Wynn, but several websites proved useful. The very lively Bear Alley blogspot offers a good deal of biographical detail; a photograph of Wynn, Engelmann and Joan Clark in broadcasting action; and the full text of the 1933 Priwin broadcast to America. The Andy Walmsley blogspot ("Random Radio Jottings") includes a good *Brain* feature, to be found in its archive at 25th March 2014. Dotted elsewhere about the net are a comprehensive illustrated survey of quiz books through several decades (http://londinius.webs.com/tvquiztieinbooks. htm) and a thesis-style history of early quizzes (http://mcs.sagepub. com/cgi/content/abstract/29/1/53). For German speakers, there is a Radio Museum site which contains one of Priwin's accounts of a visit to a regional broadcasting station, in this case Breslau, reprinted from a 1931 edition of *Die Sendung*. The regrettably fiddly address is http:// www.radiomusaeum.org/kir/index.php?cat=12_Sender&page=22_ Schlesische-nbsp~Funkstunde.

It's customary to close this section of any arduously-compiled book with thanks to one's nearest and dearest, and I do – but in this case, the acknowledgement must go beyond family pieties. I am guilty of trying out *Brain of Britain* questions with cruel regularity on my captive audience at home, and it's especially interesting to see what peculiar things three teenage boys of today combine to know. And how many once-familiar things we still have to teach them.

Russell Davies

If you want to compare today's questions with those of the past, the previous *Brain* quizbooks are:

What Do You Know? 1000 General Knowledge Questions and Answers: Based on the BBC Programme of the Same Name by John P. Wynn, G. Bell & Sons Ltd, 1955. (Strangely, the Internet Archive carries the full text of this book: https://archive.org/details/in.ernet.dli.2015.201290.)

Brain of Britain: A Quiz Book from the BBC Radio Programme by John P. Wynn, BBC, 1972

Brain of Britain: A family quiz book based on the ever-popular radio series by Ian Gillies, Robson Books, 1986.